THE FAITH HEALERS

JAMES RANDI

THE FAITH HEALERS

Foreword by CARL SAGAN

PROMETHEUS BOOKS
Buffalo, New York

90 89 88 87   4 3 2 1

This book was typeset by the author using WordPerfect software, AT&T PC6300 computer, and the Hewlett-Packard LaserJet printer.

Library of Congress Cataloging-in-Publication Data

Randi, James.
    The faith-healers.

    1. Spiritual healing—Controversial literature.
2. Healers—Controversial literature. I. Title.
BT732.5.R36   1987   615.8′52   87-17241
ISBN 0-87975-369-2

There was a small boy on crutches. I do not know his name, and I suspect I never will. But I will never forget his face, his smile, his sorrow. He is one of the millions robbed of hope and dignity by charlatans discussed in this book. Wherever and whoever he is, I apologize to him for not having been able to protect him from such an experience. I humbly dedicate this book to him and to the many others who have suffered because the rest of us began caring too late.

Contents

Foreword
by Carl Sagan

Hippocrates of Cos is the father of medicine. He is still remembered 2,500 years later by the Hippocratic Oath (a modified version of which is still commonly taken by medical students upon their graduation). But he is chiefly celebrated because of his efforts to bring medicine out of the pall of superstition and into the light of science. (A similar emergence of medical science from mysticism occurred a few centuries later in China under the tutelage of Bian Que.) In the diagnosis of disease, Hippocrates helped lay the foundations of the scientific method—urging careful observation, honest evaluation, and a willingness to admit the limitations of the physician's knowledge. In a typical passage he wrote: "Men think epilepsy divine, merely because they do not understand it. But if they called everything divine which they do not understand, why, there would be no end of divine things." As knowledge of medicine has improved since the fourth century B.C., there is more and more that we understand and less and less that has to be attributed to divine intervention—either in the causes or in the treatment of disease. Childbirth and infant mortality have decreased, lifetimes have lengthened, and medicine has improved the quality of life for many people on Earth.

But science imposes, in exchange for its manifold gifts, a certain onerous burden. We are enjoined also to consider *ourselves* scientifically, to surmount as best we can our own hopes and wishes and beliefs, to view ourselves as we really are. We know that in looking deep within ourselves, we may challenge notions that give us great comfort in the face of the many terrors of the world. In a life short and uncertain, in a time when—precisely because of the success of medicine—people die mainly from medically incurable disease, it seems heartless to deprive them of the consolation of superstition when science cannot cure their anguish. But we cannot have science in bits and pieces, applying it where we feel safe and ignoring it where we feel threatened. That way lies hypocrisy, self-deception, and a dangerously constrained future.

Few rise to this challenge as fearlessly as James Randi, accurately self-described as an angry man. Randi is angry not so much about the survival into our day of antediluvian mysticism and superstition, but about how this mysticism and superstition work to defraud, to humiliate, and sometimes even to kill. Randi is a conjuror who has done much to expose spoon-benders, remote viewers, "telepaths," and others who, perhaps through insufficient self-knowledge, have bilked the public with claims at the boundaries of science. He has received wide recognition among scientists and is a recent recipient of the MacArthur Foundation (so-called "genius") Prize Fellowship.

In this book, which can properly be described as a tirade, Randi turns his attention to faith-healers. He has done more than anyone else in recent times to expose pretension and fraud in this lucrative business. He sifts refuse, reports gossip, listens in on the stream of "miraculous" information coming to the faith-healer—not by inspiration from God, but by radio from the preacher's wife backstage; he challenges the reluctant clergymen to provide any serious evidence for the validity of their claims; he invites local and federal governments to enforce the laws against fraud and medical malpractice; he chastises the news media for their studied avoidance of the issue. He shows concern for the sick who are being bilked and remorse that, even after they've been taken to the cleaners, they will not acknowledge that they've been bilked. It's simply too painful to admit.

He asks, with devastating effectiveness, the simplest common-sense questions: Do we have any independent medical knowledge that the person whose "blindness" has been cured was in fact sightless before going to the faith-healer? Was the individual who dramatically stands up from her wheelchair and walks after being "blessed" really confined to a wheelchair before the "service"? Only because we so want to believe in such cures do we accept such shoddy evidence—experiments without controls.

Randi is rambling, anecdotal, crotchety, and ecumenically offensive. He raises questions that many of us would prefer not to consider. But I think it is important that we pay attention. It is not only a matter of rooting out bunko and cruelty directed to those least able to defend themselves and most in need of our compassion, people with little other hope. It is also a timely reminder that mass rallies and television and mail-order technology permit other kinds of lies to be injected into the body politic, to take advantage of the frustrated, the unwary, and the defenseless in a society with political illnesses that are being treated ineffectively if at all. We may disagree with Randi on specific points, but we ignore him at our peril.

Acknowledgments

I wish to thank the following persons for their help in gathering data for this book. They did so without any promise of fame or fortune because they believed in truth.

David Alexander is a valued colleague and fellow investigator. Richard Brenneman and Shawn Carlson are faith-healer-watchers deluxe. Jason Kafcas, and Brian Schwartz provided valuable legwork in Detroit in pursuit of Peter Popoff.

Scot Morris is a buddy who came through many times when needed. Ronn Nadeau, Steven Schafersman, Gae Kovalick, and Andrew Skolnick are tireless workers who care very much, and Chuck and Paula Saje are two of my valued friends who helped snare W. V. Grant in Fort Lauderdale.

As for the conjurors who generously gave of their time, Willy Rodriguez is a clever devil who dared much for me, and Steve Shaw is the mental wonder who solved the Popoff gimmick. Bob Steiner is a busy skeptic and valued friend who brought his considerable magical talents to the work.

Joe Barnhart is a scholar who suggested valuable additions and ideas for this book. Martin Gardner, as always, has offered me perpetual support and encouragement in all these endeavors.

Walter Heckert volunteered as my German translator. Stan Krippner was generous with suggestions, and Paul Kurtz, as always, nagged me gently and continued to support me as a friend when it got tough. Gerry Larue knew much of what I only suspected about various scalawags and shared that knowledge with me. Gary Posner and Wally Sampson, both M.D.s, gave much of their time and expertise to help me with medical advice and information.

The Bay Area Skeptics, the Houston Society to Oppose Pseudoscience, the Rationalist Association of St. Louis, the Southern California Skeptics and other, similar organizations formed a powerful group of allies who performed dedicated fieldwork and follow-ups on cases and events across the United States and Canada.

Those in the media who gave of their talents include: Eli Brecher, of the *Louisville Courier-Journal*; John Dart, of the *Los Angeles Times*; Gene Emery, of the *Providence Journal;* Leon Jaroff, former senior editor of *Time*; the staff of the *Tulsa Tribune*; Camilla Warrick, of the *Cincinnati Enquirer*; and Al White, of WWOR-TV.

The financial support of the MacArthur Foundation enabled me to travel to gather first-hand information.

Juan Carlos Alvarado helped by reading and criticizing the manuscript, and the Fort Lauderdale Public Library provided research assistance. Bill Williamson and Gary Clarke helped me with needed data and shared valuable information with me.

Johnny Carson allowed me to make my findings public and showed once more his continuing concern about misuse of the media.

Special thanks are due to Alec Jason. His electronic wizardry popped the Popoff bubble. Without his technical assistance, we could not have been nearly so effective.

Most especially, we all wish to thank Don Henvick. He is the one person above all others whose enthusiasm, dedication, and tireless efforts made much of this investigation—and this book— possible.

I must not forget that when my quest became known, many ordinary folks wrote and called me to share their experiences at the hands of faith-healers. They were a rich source of leads and information, and encouraged me to tell this story.

And very special thanks are due to David Peña, who endured the long hours, the late visitors, and the endless interviews needed to produce this manuscript and tried to ignore the clutter of stacks of paper, notebooks, videotapes, and clippings, with very few serious complaints. He also designed the jacket of this book.

Introduction

I am a professional conjurer and I have followed the minor muse of Magic for more than four decades. As a conjuror, I possess a narrow but rather strong expertise: I know what fakery looks like. As a result, I have been consulted by a wide variety of people who have needed to know the truth about matters that appear to be occult, supernatural, or paranormal, and I have lectured in most parts of the world on my investigations of these subjects. In the process, I have been subjected to considerable abuse from certain elements of the media, of my own profession, and of the public. Several years ago, an imaginative blackmail campaign was launched against me by a once-prominent "psychic" and a very minor scientist who fancied himself a parapsychologist. On the other side of that picture, I have won the recognition of prominent persons and organizations in the world of science, and I have been supported by friends who never wavered in their enthusiasm.

My entrance into the investigation of faith-healing began long ago. For more than four decades I have been looking into claims made by psychics, water dowsers, astrologers, and every sort of flimflam artist imaginable. In fact, I established an offer in 1964 which applies to all such claims. The rules are simple, and the document that I send to all potential claimants can be found in Appendix I of this book.

While investigating paranormal claims, I had put all religious claims on a back burner to await my possible attention at a much later date. The recent intense interest in faith-healing, largely brought about by the announced possible candidacy of faith-healer

Pat Robertson for the presidency of the United States, captured my interest. Upon beginning my investigation, I quickly became aware of the very sordid, sad, and frightening nature of the entire business, and realized that my knowledge of conjuring techniques could be put to good use in the quest, since faith-healers were using quite recognizable magicians' methods—both technical and psychological—to accomplish their performances. This book can cover only the first stages of what will surely be a difficult and never-ending endeavor. Regardless of the book's effect on the trade, faith-healers will always be with us. The small but irreducible fraction of humanity that will believe anything, no matter how ridiculous, will continue to support the fakery and the fakers well into future generations.

It is impossible to give any sort of an estimate of how much money is extracted yearly from the victims of faith-healers. In these pages, I will try to outline the financial excesses of several of the leading figures in the field, who bring in fortunes that can only begin to suggest the vast sums generated by the entire industry. The political influence, the attempt to control public morality, and the human suffering that are part of the faith-healing business are factors that are even more difficult to assess.

Until I began receiving the cooperation of some of the workers who were either still inside the operations or had recently left them, I had little notion of just how large the faith-healing business was and how much misery it produced. The data I have gathered in the form of computer printouts, photocopies of letters and documents—and some originals—along with the more than 200 videotapes directly relating to this investigation, now occupy eleven file drawers in my office, and only representative samples have been included in this book.

Under the auspices of the Committee for the Scientific Examination of Religion (CSER) and the Committee for the Scientific Investigation of Claims of the Paranormal (CSICOP) I was able to travel from city to city, following various stars of the faith-healing business and recording their activities. After I began to be recognized by the performers, I wore various disguises for a while, then delegated such colleagues as Don Henvick, Alec Jason, David Alexander, and Robert Steiner to replace me at the encounters. These gentlemen—and many, many other volunteers—all performed faithfully and well beyond what I might have expected of them, and we became the first investigators to effectively expose the faith-healing racket as practiced in the United States and Canada.

In 1986, when the MacArthur Foundation awarded a fellowship to me and thus enormously increased my flexibility and my reach, I was able to reimburse my colleagues for the rather large amounts of cash they had spent in pursuing our quarry. They had gladly given of their time and their money without expectation of reward or repayment, and since the MacArthur grant provided funds for me to continue the investigation, I found that such use of the money was appropriate. For their dedication and perseverance I cannot thank my colleagues enough, and I hope that my readers will join me in recognizing that they made this book possible.

I was personally further honored when the Academy of Magical Arts, in Los Angeles, gave me a special award in 1987, after many years during which I had borne serious criticism from my peers in the magical profession. Following that, I had the distinction of becoming the only person to receive the Blackstone Cup for the second time from the International Platform Association as outstanding speaker in my category. All of this recognition must be shared with those who so willingly stood by me during this very trying investigation.

After all that CSER and CSICOP have done to develop the truth about the faith-healing industry, one galling fact remains: Law enforcement agencies have failed to act upon these findings by prosecuting the guilty. I am infuriated by that fact. My colleagues and I have telephoned and written to numerous agencies and individuals who should have an active interest in these matters, but it appears they don't. We have met in person with a few of them who made appropriate clucking noises at the evidence we presented, but we never heard from them again. The buck was passed in some cases, but nothing was ever done.

This, then, is my challenge: I am not asking for action to be taken against charlatans. I am *demanding* it. As a taxpayer and citizen, I have a right under the U.S. Constitution to demand such action. I will not stand by and watch politicians ducking under their own wings and the tailfeathers of others to avoid their responsibilities to the public. I ask readers of this book who support me in my rage to write letters to their representatives in Congress demanding immediate action. I will not suggest how such letters should be worded, but readers will find in these pages quite sufficient ammunition to supply their needs.

This book is written by an angry man. It is a cry of outrage against a wrong that needs to be righted. People are being robbed of their money, their health, and their emotional stability. The little boy on crutches to whom I dedicate this book, and the countless thousands of others who have suffered as he has, deserve your attention and your help. Those who have hoaxed them deserve the full impact of the law, which can only be brought to bear if *you* demand it.

There are some aspects of the faith-healing business to which I will give very little attention in this book. First, Christian Science—which has nothing whatsoever to do with science—receives scant mention simply because others have handled the subject in great depth. Second, outright quackery in medicine is brought into discussion only when needed to illustrate a point, and I may not presume to write upon such matters with authority. Again, others have written on it well and thoroughly. Third, if I develop information on the activities of certain persons that does not deal directly with the subject of faith-healing, it is because I felt it necessary to show these aspects of their personalities which bear upon their qualities as human beings.

The matter of just what is meant by "faith" merits some attention here. H. L. Mencken said:

> Faith may be defined briefly as an illogical
> belief in the occurrence of the improbable.

The *International Webster New Encyclopedic Dictionary* gives the meaning of the word *faith* as "confidence or trust in a person or thing; . . . belief not substantiated by proof; spiritual acceptance of truth or realities not certified by reason; . . . belief in the doctrines or teachings of a religion." These three definitions should satisfy most persons. But philosopher Paul Kurtz, in his book *The Transcendental Temptation*, defines three distinctly different *kinds* of faith, derived from the amount (or total lack) of evidence drawn upon to support it.

Kurtz defines the first kind as "intransigent faith." By this is meant faith that will not be affected by any sort of contrary evidence, no matter how strong. My own experience with some few persons who persist in believing in certain paranormal claims that have been conclusively proven false enables me to label their faith as Type I. A would-be parapsychologist in Wisconsin was one of those completely taken in by my Project Alpha, an experiment which sent two young student conjurers into a laboratory in St. Louis posing as psychics. They convinced the researchers there that they had "psychic" powers, as evidenced by the researchers' communications with other scientists and by their lab reports and records. The intent of the Project Alpha experiment was to show that the researchers would have sufficient faith in their abilities to detect trickery and in the assumptions of their trade that they would not exercise either common sense or careful scrutiny in performing their tests. When the hoax was finally revealed, with full explanations from the two participants on exactly how they had performed their tricks, the Wisconsin amateur still insisted that they were genuine. He provides us with a perfect example of Type I faith.

Gerry Straub, who spent two and a half years as evangelist/healer Pat Robertson's television producer and wrote *Salvation for Sale*, to describe his experiences there, gave his opinion:

> I am convinced that if Pat Robertson or any other of television's faith-healers were proven to be pranksters and frauds, the vast majority of their staff and viewers would not drop their belief in the ministers' healing power or weaken their faith in God.

Those people would be exhibiting Type I faith.

Type II faith was called by philosopher William James "the will to believe." As defined by Professor Kurtz it is "willful belief . . . where there is insufficient or no evidence either way to make a rational choice." It really involves making a decision to believe, even though the reasons for doing so are not compelling. However, there may be reasons for believing that have nothing to do with the logic of the matter; it may be more comforting, more socially advantageous, or simply easier to choose to believe. One who goes along with a political party only because that party has *always* been the family party exhibits Type II faith. Were I to investigate claimed faith-healings for 60 years and fail to uncover one that meets the bare needs of rational acceptance, Type II believers would still choose to believe—even though they themselves had not been able to produce a single healing—just because I had not *disproved* the matter.

Last, Type III faith is described as "hypotheses based upon evidence." Here, there is evidence, but not enough evidence or evidence of good enough quality to support total belief. As I step off a curb to cross with a traffic light that has just turned green, I may safely assume that the light will stay green long enough for me to reach the other side. That assumption is based upon my long experience with traffic lights and the knowledge of the general intent of those who designed, manufactured, installed, and maintain the device. I have exhibited Type III faith. Science creates a hypothesis based upon observations, then sets out to examine the validity of that hypothesis. After enough observations have been gathered and the idea has been tested thoroughly with positive results, the hypothesis becomes a theory. The beauty of that theory is that *it is subject to revision and/or retraction upon the presentation of contrary evidence.* Thus scientists can be said to exhibit Type III faith.

Is all "confidence or trust" then based upon faith? No. I myself have *absolute* confidence and trust in the simple statement that "4 objects added to 6 objects results in 10 objects." I can test this statement by, for example, mixing 4 apples in a bag with 6 nails and counting the resulting total. If the total is *not* 10, since I have great confidence in the truth of this statement, I must examine my counting procedure for accuracy and the bag for holes, among other possibilities.

For faith to have any value, it must be based on evidence. Faith without evidence may be well invested; it is just as likely not to be. Type I faith is almost surely wasted. Type II faith, particularly concerning a highly unlikely premise, is equally suspect. Type III faith may be safely relied upon, subject to contrary evidence.

As for *faith in supernatural healing* (faith-healing), most victims use Type I or Type II faith. They will either not read books like this or shut their minds to the evidence produced for consideration. Those who are somewhat skeptical, and use Type III faith, may find this book valuable.

So much for "faith." Next we need to discuss "healing." Well on in this book, I will outline the expectations and the reach of medical science. But my reader should first be made aware of how easily it may appear to the incautious observer that healing has occurred as the result of some mysterious methodology. Often, the quack operator cannot fail to produce the illusion of healing.

Emil J. Freireich, M.D., who works with the Department of Developmental Therapeutics at the University of Texas Cancer Center at Houston, has presented us with a remarkable observation concerning all manner of quack procedures. I will attempt here to condense his idea into a few paragraphs. First, Dr. Freireich warns of three major harmful effects of the use of quack methods:

(1) Interference with regular treatment of the patient.
(2) Financial loss to the patient.
(3) Diversion of vital, expensive community resources.

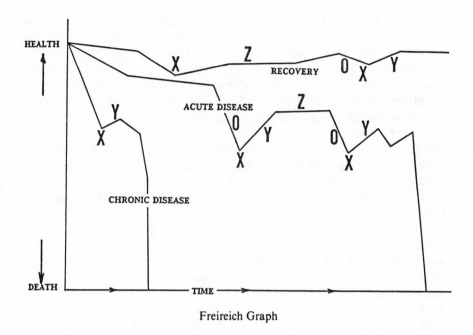

Freireich Graph

Next, he outlines what he calls the Freireich Experimental Plan (FEP),

> which assures that any remedy, whether it be a drug or a psychological treatment, a mystical therapy or a physical treatment, will always prove to be effective for virtually every patient with any serious disease.

There are two essential requirements for this plan to be effective. Some form of treatment, *any* kind of treatment, must be applied, whether it has any effect or not, and it must be totally harmless to either a well or sick person. (This is usually offered as one of the inherent virtues of the quackery, contrasted to an M.D.'s intention of surgery, powerful medication, or other dramatic therapy.)

Every disease has a natural variability; it has "ups and downs." Attacking the system of a human being, the illness goes through stages of increase and retreat. This is illustrated by Dr. Freireich in his diagram. It shows the progress of two eventually terminal diseases, one acute and the other chronic. I have added a third line representing the progress of a disease from which the patient eventually recovers. The intersection of this line with the "death" point is somewhere off to the right, depending upon the history (age, habits, etc.) of the patient. We assume that the quack method (as required by the FEP) has no effect on the condition in this discussion, and we will show that such ineffectiveness does not in any way disprove the quack claim.

Most patients seek unorthodox help when it appears that regular care is not serving them properly or it has not met their expectations. The quack operator benefits greatly from this situation. Since the quack method enters the graph at points like those marked "X," there are four different courses that can then follow.

The condition can improve, as shown at point "Y." If so, the quack method appears to have been effective. (The faith-healers would say that God has intervened and has cured the ailment. Hallelujah!) If the disease stays the same, as at point "Z," quack opinion holds that the method was applied just in time and needs to be continued because it has stabilized the ailment. (Faith-healers declare that God has applied divine intercession, pending further proof of faith from the afflicted.) Should the disease worsen (point "O"), the quack complains that his help was sought too late, but treatment should be redoubled in order to save the patient. (The faith-healer says that God works in mysterious ways, and that God's will must be done.) Finally, if death is the next phase of the disease, the quack again says that help was sought too late. (The faith-healer again invokes the mysterious nature of God.)

In any case, *the quack method is never proved wrong!* Any and all possible results can be accommodated into the quack theory, and in no case is the quack method shown to be without value, especially since it is not in itself harmful anyway. Similarly, the faith-healer cannot lose, and for the same reasons.

The Freireich idea continues to prove itself in cases where the condition either stays the same or worsens, the process reverting once again to point "X" and repeating itself until either recovery or death results. In summary, Dr. Freireich has shown that a method of useless treatment that is without harmful effects (some vitamin megadoses, manipulation, irradiation with colored lights, administration of sugar pills, chanting of magical phrases, striking upon the forehead, wearing a copper bracelet) will appear to be effective in the treatment of disease with virtually every patient, despite the fact that the quack method has no actual effect on the progress of the disease.

I must note here that faith-healer Oral Roberts, in his book *God Still Heals Today*, unknowingly brings the Freireich observations into account. He says:

> During the [faith-]healing process, there may be pain, or slight relapses, or even what may appear to be a reoccurrence of the problem.

Roberts goes on to explain that this reversal means nothing, and that those who experience it must remain convinced of their healing and await further improvement. This is in exact congruence with what Dr. Freireich has said. The formula works, the healer seems effective, and the victim is deceived.

I have made use of several excellent references, most notably *Faith Healing*, by U.K. clinical psychologist Louis Rose, and *Oral Roberts*, by historian David Harrell. Unlike those authors, I must admit that my approach has been much more of a personal one, and I do not hesitate to express personal feelings about the matters I discuss in these pages. One editor who examined an early version of the manuscript criticized (quite properly) my failure to disassociate myself from the material, but since I make no pretensions to being an accomplished writer, I believe I can indulge myself in breaking a few rules. The result is perhaps not great literature, but it is a genuine expression of an individual who has come upon a situation that cries out for attention.

As you read these pages, it may seem to you that you have been whisked back to the Dark Ages. But the beliefs outlined and the practices described here actually exist in the twentieth century. They are believed in by millions of civilized people whose brothers and sisters have traveled to the moon, walked on the bottom of the ocean, created gardens where deserts once were, extracted wondrous substances from nature, and wrested secrets from our universe that make all of our lives richer every day. The believers have little interest in that world. They are frightened and unsure about it. They are moths eagerly fluttering about a bright flame in what they perceive as a dangerous, dark forest, and they are often gladly consumed by that flame. To read this book is to take a step through time into an age when superstition reigned, and what we will discover is frightening and dangerous for us all.

1
The Origins of Faith-Healing

Sickness is one of the basic problems of mankind. Thus, there has always existed, in most religions, a tradition of miraculous cures brought about by the touch of prominent individuals, contact with a sacred relic, amulet, or place, anointing with sanctified oil or water, or any other medium presented by chance or intent to the ailing. Buddhism, hundreds of tribal sects, and scores of cults have advertised healing as an attraction. As with all magic, this is an attempt by man to control nature by means of spells, incantations, or rituals. Its effectiveness has been a matter of discussion for centuries; only now is the power of suggestion beginning to be understood.

The Christian notion that certain people can heal the afflicted by means of special gifts granted them is derived from the New Testament (I Corinthians 12), in which this power is defined. Besides the Gift of Healing, among the other nine "Gifts of the Spirit" that are described are the Gift of Knowledge and Speaking in Tongues. All three have been used by faith-healers to establish their traditions.

A Plethora of Religious Flotsam

Though all the Protestant denominations have historically condemned the veneration of holy objects (relics) and their use in healing, the Catholic church—until recently—preferred to depend entirely upon the magical qualities attributed to the possessions or actual physical parts of various saints and biblical characters for healing. The Vatican not only permitted but encouraged this practice, which entered history in the third century. Catholic churches and private collections still overflow with hundreds of thousands of items. Included are pieces of the True Cross (enough to build a few log cabins), bones of the children slain by King Herod, the toenails and bones of St. Peter, the bones of the Three Wise Kings and of St. Stephen (as well as his *complete* corpse, *including* another complete skeleton!), jars of the Virgin Mary's milk, the bones and several entire heads and pieces thereof that were allegedly once atop John the Baptist, 16 foreskins of Christ, Mary Magdalene's entire skeleton (with two right feet), scraps of bread and fish left over from feeding the 5,000, a crust of bread from the Last Supper, and a hair from Christ's beard—not to mention a few shrouds, including the one at Turin.

One avid German collector claimed to have more than 17,000 of these objects, which inspired Pope Leo X to calculate that the man had saved himself exactly 694,779,550½ days in purgatory by such pious devotion to his hobby. But his efforts were outdone by the Schlosskirche at Halle, West Germany, which boasted 21,483 relics in its vaults.

The Royal Touch

Part of the tradition of divine healing through the touch of special persons is validated from scriptural references to such healings by Christ and the disciples and in direct instruction from Christ to his disciples in Matthew 10:8:

> Heal the sick, raise the dead, cleanse the lepers, cast out devils.

Never loath to adopt a good public relations idea, European royalty decided that because they claimed to rule by divine right they could also claim to have the divine ability to heal. As early as 1307, people in need of healing were visiting Philip the Fair, king of France, for his holy touch. Soon the English kings were "touching" for scrofula, a tubercular inflammation of the lymph nodes often confused with similar afflictions of the face and eyes. Thus originated the "Royal Touch," which was said to be effective against this condition, and the disease became known in those days as "The King's Evil."

Charles II of England "touching" for scrofula.

The presence and involvement of kings doubtless had an effect upon people with psychosomatic and quite imaginary ailments, and subjects eagerly provided affidavits to the monarchs in support of strong belief in this sort of healing.

Paracelsus (more properly, Theophrastus Bombastus von Hohenheim, 1490-1541) was a savant who was probably born somewhat sooner than he might have wished, considering the rapid advances in genuine scientific thinking that occurred soon after his demise. Along with descriptions of magical procedures that he took as having some value, he made observations which indicated his grasp

Paracelsus, who sought medicine in magic.

of both human nature and correct, methodical thinking. Though he was inescapably subject to the superstitions of his day and the necessity of catering to popular prejudices—including a tendency to immolate those who doubted scriptural declarations—he was frequently able to rise above those burdens, as when he discoursed on medical matters and public attitudes. In his fourth book on diseases, *A Paramiric Treatise*, he closed with these words:

> You have seen how natural bodies, *through their own natural forces*, cause many things

[believed to be] miraculous among the common
people. Many have interpreted these effects as
the work of saints; others have ascribed them
to the Devil; one has called them sorcery,
others witchcraft, and all have entertained
superstitious beliefs and paganism. I have shown
what to think of all that.

Reformer Martin Luther, among others in the sixteenth century, took credit for spontaneous, miraculous cures while Paracelsus and other savants were attempting—with highly varying
degrees of success—to bring out of the superstition of magic what
we know today as the science of medicine. The Mormons and
Episcopalians established a history of faith cures as part of their
theologies, and Mary Baker Eddy founded her Christian Science
church solely on the borrowed notions that pain is an illusion and
that bacteria are the result rather than the cause of diseases.

In the 1600s, one practitioner known as "The Stroker" was
astounding England with his performances. A remarkable English
author, Charles MacKay, who in 1841 wrote his classic, *Extraordinary Popular Delusions and the Madness of Crowds*, observed
in that book that

> Mr. Valentine Greatraks . . . practised *upon
> himself* and others a deception . . . that God
> had given him the power of curing the king's
> evil. . . . In the course of time he extended his
> powers to the curing of epilepsy, ulcers, aches,
> and lameness. . . . crowds which thronged
> around him were so great, that the neighboring
> towns were not able to accommodate them.
> (Italics added.)

I am grateful that MacKay recognized that Greatraks deceived
both his patients *and* himself. As with fortune-tellers, healers
often begin to believe in their own powers because their subjects
tend to give them only positive feedback. Thus they can excuse
and forget their many failures, and their legends grow.

Greatraks made a huge impression on the public, and accumulated a fortune in the process. In this respect, he helped to
establish the precedent for modern healers. And, in several other
important respects, he mirrored the modern healers, as evidenced
in an account written by a contemporary in 1665:

A rumour of the prophet's coming soon spread all over the town, and the hotel . . . was crowded by sick persons, who came full of confidence in their speedy cure. [Greatraks] made them wait a considerable time for him, but came at last, in the middle of their impatience, with a grave and simple countenance, that shewed no signs of his being a cheat. [The host] prepared to question him strictly, hoping to discourse with him on matters that he had

Valentine Greatraks, the "Stroker."

> heard of. . . . But he was not able to do so,
> much to his regret, for the crowd became so
> great, and cripples and others pressed around so
> impatiently to be first cured, that the servants
> were obliged to use threats, and even force,
> before they could establish order among them.
> . . . The prophet affirmed that all diseases were
> caused by evil spirits. Every infirmity was with
> him a case of diabolical possession. . . . He
> boasted of being much better acquainted with
> the intrigues of demons than he was with the
> affairs of men. . . . Catholics and Protestants
> visited him from every part, all believing that
> power from heaven was in his hands. . . . So
> great was the confidence in him, that the blind
> fancied they saw the light which they could not
> see—the deaf imagined that they heard—the lame
> that they walked straight, and the paralytic
> that they had recovered the use of their limbs.

If the reader has actually witnessed a modern faith-healer in action with crowds of worshipers around and about, that scenario will be familiar. Four major observations made by that witness more than three centuries ago apply to today's situation:

(1) The healer made his audience wait for him, thus enhancing his importance and increasing anticipation.

(2) Skeptics were unable, because of the choreography of the event, to question the healer before the show.

(3) Illnesses were attributed to evil spirits (demons, devils) rather than to living habits, infections, or other real causes.

(4) The sick imagined that they were cured, when actually they were not.

London again became a center for faith-healing in the 1870s. It was very popular and widely practiced then, and the idea continues to attract huge numbers of followers in England.

Structures and shrines, such as the tombs of Saint Francis of Assisi and others, are said to have caused miracle cures for those who visited them. The tomb of Catherine of Siena, a literate woman who was never granted her most ardent desire, "the red rose of martyrdom," has been credited with bringing about countless healings, though no such cures were attributed to her in her lifetime.

St. Catherine of Siena, and early healing saint.

The Most Famous Christian Shrine

It is the town of Lourdes, France, that has attained the strongest
international reputation for miracles of healing. This acclaim is
the result of a commercial venture that began with a story about
Bernadette Soubirous, an ignorant peasant girl who said she had a
visitation there from "the lady" in 1858. A shrine was established
in 1876 to which some five million visitors a year now flock,
occupying 400 hotels built for them. The public relations people
who sell Lourdes as a business claim that there are about 30,000
healings a year, but church authorities deny that figure, caution-
ing that only about 100 claims have been properly documented
since the founding of the shrine, and the church has as of this
date accepted only 64 as miracles, from the millions of cures
claimed over the years.

Whether these were simply remissions of various kinds, or
perhaps recoveries brought about by orthodox medical attention,
we cannot know. In several cases, we have no evidence that the
ailments were even real. In the absence of proof that the attendance of the afflicted at the shrine was the one element responsible for the termination of the ailment, common sense, as well as

the simple principle of parsimony, would require us to doubt the miraculous nature of these events.

Bathing in the mineral springs of Lourdes and drinking of the spring water have been confused with the healing stories. The church has never made any claim that the spring water from the Lourdes grotto is curative in any way, yet every year the souvenir shops sell thousands of gallons to the faithful in tiny vials, as amulets. Those who attend Lourdes in person have consumed millions of gallons more. It is amazing that more worshipers have not contracted diseases from that practice. Europeans are prone to accept the medicinal value of almost any natural spring water— especially if it smells bad. They cannot resist drinking from and washing in the Lourdes spring.

Regarding the claims of healings at Lourdes, the CBS-TV program "60 Minutes" said in 1986 of the famous shrine:

> There are stories of the crippled who suddenly could walk, the blind who suddenly could see, the incurable cancers that were cured. But most of these remain undocumented stories, part of the mythology that gives other pilgrims hope.

"60 Minutes" was appalled by the commercial aspects of the operation. Commenting on the endless theatrical and carefully choreographed candle-lit processions and the heartless exploitation of the faithful by the souvenir salesmen, the TV program told viewers:

> The sanctuary of Lourdes, with its many basilicas and shrines, is like a multicomplex theater that gives a dozen religious performances a day, and the church stage-manages them all with care. This is the Lourdes that they would like you to see, but just outside the gates of the sanctuary, a different Lourdes was unhappy at being seen at all, at least on camera.

The CBS cameramen were blocked and pushed by the entrepreneurs and prevented from filming the garish displays of holy water, religious statues, gimcracks, and cheaply printed booklets that are peddled at this holy site. The merchants apparently were not willing to allow the outside world to see them as they actually were; that might destroy the Hollywood image they so eagerly trade on. But concealed cameras managed to show television viewers that the whole Lourdes operation is an exercise in bad taste and opportunism. In the words of the "60 Minutes" script, Lourdes is "curios rather than cures."

Virgins Galore

In Patrick Marnham's book *Lourdes*, there is a description of the commercial grossness of the area. He provides a vivid description of the infamous "souvenir alley," the shame of the town:

> . . . These shops are not selling little dolls in national costume, or scarves painted with the regional arms, or cheap jewellery; they are selling "objects of piety." [As one gets closer] the strings of beads turn into rosaries, thousands and thousands of rosaries of every size, colour and price. The mannequins turn into Virgins; baby virgins, haggard virgins, flashing virgins—("Our Mama with the lights on," as one Brazilian pilgrim put it). There are virgins in a snow storm, virgins in a television set, little cutie-doll bug-eyed half-witted virgins praying on velveteen mats; virgins in make-up, virgins in modern dress and the world-renowned hollow, plastic virgins whose crowns unscrew to turn into bottle stoppers. There are Virgins in Grottos, and there are virgins in grottos mounted on varnished Dutch clogs, an international two-horrors-in-one.

The Afflicted Visionary

Most who uncritically accept the miracles of Lourdes are unaware of what occurred to young Bernadette Soubirous, the originator of the grotto story. She herself never made any claim that the vision she said she had seen there promised cures at the shrine. In fact, she called the vision the local French equivalent of "the lady" and the identification of the figure with Mary was made by others. Bernadette was asked by an English visitor about certain miracles that had been reported during her last visit to the shrine. She replied, "There's no truth in all that." Asked about cures at the shrine, she answered, "I have been told that there have been

miracles, but . . . I have not seen them." Bernadette was herself
chronically ill, and she chose to visit hot springs in another town
to treat her ailments. She was taken into a convent and died
slowly and painfully in 1879, at age 35, of tuberculosis, asthma,
and several complications. Her father, crippled and partially blind,
died still afflicted.

Lourdes is only the most famous of 15 similar shrines that
were already located in that area of France and were all visited
regularly by the ailing before the Bernadette story was told. The
tradition of healing grottos was well established by the time
Bernadette came up with her vision, and the town merchants of
Lourdes were already selling souvenirs and holy water long before
the inevitable shrine was built. They were aware of the commercial possibilities presented to them and they were prepared and
eager for prosperity.

There Is a Baby in the Bath Water

Alexis Carrel, a French physician who dropped then re-embraced
his Catholic faith, wrote a book which has been taken to be
highly supportive of medical miracles. *The Voyage to Lourdes* tells
of a Dr. Lerrac (obviously "Carrel" reversed) who visits Lourdes
and discovers miracles there. The manuscript was found among
Carrel's papers after his death, and it has been taken to be a dis-
guised account of his own 1902 visit to that shrine, though there
is no reason to believe it is such an account. Libraries place it in
category "230"—Religious Nonfiction.

Statements by the character Lerrac are quoted in several
other books that support belief in the Lourdes miracles, fortified
by the fact that author Carrel was a Nobel laureate in medicine.
The baby in the bath water here is in a very perceptive statement
Carrel made early in this century, before the relationship between
mind and health was at all understood by medical science:

> [These events] prove the reality of certain
> links, as yet unknown, between psychological
> and organic processes. They prove the objective
> value of the spiritual activity which has been
> almost totally ignored by doctors, teachers and
> sociologists. They open up a new world for us.

For expressing this opinion, Dr. Carrel was severely repriman-
ded by his medical colleagues, who had yet to accept such an idea.

They had long known about what is called "bedside manner," but they had failed to recognize the more far-reaching effects of tender loving care. The danger of this fascinating baby in this very murky bath water is that it can grow up to be a monster.

The Problems of Examining Claims

Examining most claims can be an involved process, a fact not obvious to many who have never had to carry out such an operation. We need rules and standards that are based upon various qualities of the claims, which can vary in three important ways:

(1) complexity of the phenomenon
(2) size of the data base available
(3) strength and validity of the evidence.

Let us treat each of these in turn. Concerning the complexity of the phenomenon we are examining: If we are testing the simple claim that 6 plus 4 always equals 10, we can demand that it *always* prove true. Any exception to this single requirement would, in this case, inarguably prove a miracle. However, this is obviously a claim of a very low order of complexity. Moving up the scale all the way to the phenomenon of a medical recovery, we begin to deal with an entirely different sort of entity. Medical recoveries are exceedingly complex matters, still imperfectly understood. A certain small percentage of "inexplicable" recoveries must be expected, and medical scientists are faced with them from time to time. These are referred to as "spontaneous remissions," and are found—in various proportions—in many diseases.

That brings us to the second quality of a claim, the amount of data available for examination. The larger the data base, the better the chance of a good investigation and the greater the strength of the conclusions that may be arrived at. But selecting a small number of "inexplicable" examples of any data base and proving a miracle by them is not an acceptable process. More important, going back to point No. 1, the higher the order of complexity of the examples examined in any investigation, the less valid is the process of "data selecting." In medical recoveries, again, the order of complexity is very high, and therefore the data base must be suitably large and not "selected."

Third, the integrity of any investigation depends upon the qualifications of the witnesses. At the very least, they should be both unbiased and expert. In claims of medical miracles, the "recovered" people themselves are often the poorest witnesses simply because they have ample reason to want to believe they are healed, and they usually cannot judge their own conditions. Just "feeling better" may have nothing to do with recovery. Relief of symptoms is not a cure of the disease.

In spite of all these caveats, I have been willing to accept just *one* case of a miracle cure so that I might say in this book that at least on one occasion a miracle has occurred. In order to be included here, that cure would have to have these qualities:

(1) The disease must be not normally self-terminating.

(2) The recovery must be complete.

(3) The recovery must take place in the absence of any medical treatment that might normally be expected to affect the disease.

(4) There must be adequate medical opinion that the disease was present before the application of whatever means were used to bring about the miracle.

(5) There must be adequate medical opinion that the disease is not present after the application of whatever means were used to bring about the miracle.

I do not have the medical expertise to judge the claimed cures at Lourdes. And, because I am mainly concerned in this book with the examination of faith-healers rather than healing, I will refer readers to extensive studies already done on the Lourdes phenomena, which are listed in the bibliography. Also, I have found it more productive to investigate ongoing events, because the individuals and the claims are accessible and can be reduced to easily understood packets of data that a reader can examine and consider without extended expertise. There are two relatively recent claims that can be examined—with difficulty—and I will discuss them briefly here.

A Remarkable Case from Lourdes

The one very singular healing reported from Lourdes is that of a 22-year-old Italian named Vittorio Micheli. Extensive documentation of his apparently miraculous recovery is found in a book by Patrick Marnham, *Lourdes: A Modern Pilgrimage*, published in 1981.

Briefly, Micheli entered a military hospital on April 16, 1962, suffering from a large mass on his buttock that immobilized him. He had been in pain for a month. His left leg appeared shortened, and his general condition was bad. Doctors prescribed the drug ACTH and vitamins B-1 and B-12. He was X-rayed on May 22, and the results suggested a malignant tumor. He continued to worsen. A week later, a biopsy was carried out, and a sarcoma type of tumor was diagnosed.

The patient's condition grew worse. On July 18, another X-ray revealed that severe deterioration of the hip area had occurred. The bone structure there had virtually disappeared, eaten away by cancer. X-ray photographs reproduced in several magazine articles indicate the absence of parts of the pelvis, the iliac (hip) bone, and the muscle surrounding it. Reports clearly state that Micheli received no medical treatment, such as chemical or radiation therapy. Further X-rays revealed even worse damage to the bone structure, and on August 1 he was transferred to another hospital for cobalt (radiation) treatment. Apparently he never received it. All this time the patient was immobilized in a plaster cast.

On May 24, 1963, Micheli decided to visit Lourdes as a last resort; his condition was worsening rapidly. He bathed in the water, and immediately experienced the usual sensations reported by those who claim such healings. He felt a sudden warmth and a ravenous appetite and said he felt that he was healed. Within a month of his return, it was reported that he felt much better, his pain had subsided, and his cast was removed some time after. Summing up, the Lourdes medical bureau said:

> A remarkable reconstruction of the iliac bone and cotyloid cavity has taken place. The stereotypes [X-rays] made in 1964, 1965, 1968, 1969 confirm categorically and without doubt that an unforeseen and even overwhelming bone reconstruction has taken place of a type unknown in the annals of world medicine. We ourselves . . . have never encountered a single spontaneous bone reconstruction of such a nature.

The limb that had once been essentially useless to Micheli now functions, 24 years after his first visit to Lourdes, though he walks with a pronounced limp due to a severely shortened leg. He wears a special shoe to accommodate that defect.

On May 26, 1976, the case of Vittorio Micheli was officially recognized as miracle No. 63 at the shrine of Lourdes.

The Search for Evidence on Micheli

The complete medical dossier on the Vittorio Micheli case has been published. A few contrary opinions appeared there, including opinions that Micheli's original diagnoses had been made without adequate data, and that he had actually received at least some orthodox medical therapy (chemical) during his hospitalization. In order to submit all available evidence to my medical colleagues, I needed good copies of the X-ray photographs. I contacted the religious magazine that had published the X-rays. It had ceased publication. I wrote Lourdes and several friends in France, asking for a source from which I might obtain the photographs. I was not successful. Finally, I submitted all available material—including poor photocopies of the radiographs—to my colleague Dr. Gary Posner for examination and evaluation. Posner agreed to discuss this data with another physician who specializes in such diagnoses.

It developed that there were major irregularities in the accounts of Micheli's treatment. First, it is "inconceivable," in Posner's opinion, that this patient had to wait 36 days before an X-ray was taken. The prescribed vitamins could certainly not have been of benefit to his condition, and a mass of the nature described would be immediately suspected of being cancerous. Furthermore, it was *43 days* before the hospital performed a biopsy! There are hints in the medical reports that drugs and radiation may have been administered. One very effective medication, in particular, is mentioned.

Various writers have described this case, and one statement stands out. It is said that just before Vittorio Micheli went to Lourdes he was "given only a few days to live." When he was taken for the cobalt treatment, accounts say that then, too, he was told he had only a few days left. This estimate shows up twice in the medical reports, and is obviously wrong both times. Micheli lived on in the military hospital in great discomfort for another ten months before he went to Lourdes. It is difficult to accept the physicians' testimony that in those ten months *he received no medical treatment of any kind other than pain killers, tranquilizers, and vitamins.* What equally puzzles my medically informed colleagues is the bizarre treatment that Micheli received initially. An X-ray examination and a biopsy should have been done *within a day or two after the patient entered the hospital.*

Did a miracle take place? We have the living patient available to us for examination. Prominent French medical journals have carried convincing accounts of the case that offer strong support of the "inexplicable" aspects of the evidence. Malignant primary bone tumors make up only .5 percent of all malignancies; therefore, spontaneous remissions of these tumors must be extremely rare. However, there are about a dozen recorded cases of just such remissions, and Micheli's appears to be one of them. Could it be that some element was present in Micheli's system that has not been encountered often enough before to have been recorded? That seems unlikely, but it is not impossible.

Somewhere, the original X-rays probably exist. The medical board at Lourdes has not responded to requests to see them. Experts I have consulted want very much to consult those X-rays, particularly to determine if Micheli's hip bone was "completely regenerated" as the reports claim. That would call for not only the bone structure to be replaced, but also the complex ball-and-socket formation with its lubricants. If that did take place, it would be the very first time such a regeneration has been recorded, and as a layman I am astonished that this event did not make a major news item, in both the popular and the academic press.

But there is a very important aspect to this "regeneration" claim: *If such a "complete" regeneration took place, that fact could only have been determined by exploratory surgery.* X-rays cannot differentiate between a genuine regeneration and what is known as a "pseudoarthrosis," in which the bone structure is naturally replaced by a more primitive arrangement that looks similar in an X-ray photo and also allows adequate articulation of the joint. Such a regrowth is not at all unheard of. But the medical records at Lourdes do not record any surgical procedure being done to validate Micheli's "complete regeneration."

A search of medical literature reveals that similar recoveries have occurred. The following summary description, quoted directly, word-for-word from a medical journal, *Acta Orthopaedica Scandinavica* (February 1978, 49(1):49-53) sounds almost identical to the Micheli case, except that Lourdes did not enter into it:

> Spontaneous regression of a malignant primary bone tumour: A histologically confirmed malignant, primary bone tumour in the [left] pelvis, presumably an osteosarcoma, underwent spontaneous regression. The large tumour was inoperable and gave rise to severe pain as well as

difficulty in walking. After 2 years of progression, with increasing destruction of the pelvic bones, the clinical and radiological condition improved spontaneously, and at present the patient is alive, almost symptom-free, after 6 years follow-up.

In this case, the patient had almost precisely the same condition as Micheli, so much so that I had to refer to the original report to determine that it was not his case being described. In this case, too, no medical treatment was reported. Both recoveries took place in the same way, with the same end results.

But let's get back to the religious magazine that ran the story of the Micheli case. The caption on the first X-ray reads:

X-ray taken in 1963 when Vittorio Micheli . . . went to Lourdes, shows complete destruction of the left pelvis hip socket and left thigh bone.

The date marked on that X-ray, used as evidence by the Lourdes team to establish their miracle, is "23.VIII.63." The X-ray was made *three months after Micheli was "cured."* Yet in June 1963, *two months before* this "complete destruction," the medical record says that "he could walk . . . without crutches, without pain." Are we asked to believe that he walked *without a left hip*?

We must consider as well that in the early days of the medical bureau at Lourdes, almost 80 cures a year were officially accepted as "inexplicable." Since 1947, with improved diagnostic tools and a better understanding of medicine, less than one cure a year has been accepted in that category. We now know much more about the remarkable defenses and repair facilities of living organisms. We know, for example, that our bodies are invaded all the time by various malignancies that are never manifested because they are fought off and killed by the body's natural defense mechanisms. As Ellen Bernstein, editor of the *Medical and Health Annual* of the *Encyclopaedia Britannica*, points out:

Miracles . . . are conditional; they depend on time, place, what is known, and what is not known. As medical sophistication increases, miracles necessarily decrease, which may mean that the days of "miraculous cures" at Lourdes are numbered.

The Latest Official "Miracle"

In 1970, miracle sixty-four was officially recorded at Lourdes. Serge Perrin, 41 years old, claimed that he had recovered from "recurring organic hemiplegia" (paralysis of one side of the body) and recurring blindness in one eye. The Lourdes medical team declared the case "miraculous." But an American team examined the data and discovered that the necessary tests—a spinal tap and a brain scan—had not been done to properly establish the *cause* of the condition. In fact, the American doctors said, Perrin's symptoms are classic signs of hysteria; in the absence of appropriate medical tests, that was a much more probable diagnosis. Furthermore, hysteria is known to respond favorably to highly emotional circumstances like those encountered at religious ceremonies.

Bernstein found that Lourdes officials were not helpful in supplying evidence, being more concerned with her intent and attitude. She commented on their qualifications:

> If Serge Perrin's case is representative, there are good reasons to be distrustful of officially declared miraculous cures at Lourdes. There are also reasons to question the allegedly rigorous system for recognizing them. . . . The expertise and skills of the doctors are at best a matter of chance since being present at the shrine and being a certified physician are the only requirements for joining the medical bureau.

Summing up on the status of Lourdes itself, Bernstein wrote:

> Lourdes has never swindled the sick with false promises. Nonetheless, a better effort could be made to convey to the world what the shrine really has to offer: Lourdes is *not* a miracle mill; it is *not* a spa; and the water does *not* have healing powers. Lourdes *is* a unique international meeting place and there is every reason to believe that the sick, the frail, and other sufferers derive innumerable psychological and spiritual benefits from their visits. Wonders *do* occur when pilgrims discover their own strengths and learn the art of living with their maladies.

2
Faith-Healing in Modern Times

The present-day Christian claim that certain people can heal the afflicted by the "laying on of hands" originated with nineteenth-century American and European evangelists. The Reverend William Branham, a former game warden from Jeffersonville, Indiana, is often credited with bringing the modern evangelical/fundamentalist healing movement into existence in the 1940s. Pastor Branham was a fire-and-brimstone Bible thumper who offered his audiences spectacular performances and grand promises. He also was quick to blame his victims for their failures. In June 1947, in the town of Vandalia, Illinois, he apparently had cured Walker Beck, a deaf-mute. When he heard the next day that Beck's condition was as bad as ever, Branham replied:

> I hear that Walker has smoked a cigarette after
> I told him that he would have to give them up.
> Because of this he will not be able to hear or
> talk and in all probability he will be afflicted
> with some greater trouble—perhaps cancer.

Tobacco seemed an unlikely cause for Beck's deaf-mute condition, since he had been *born* in that state.

Branham was so convincing a preacher that, when he died in a 1965 automobile accident, he wasn't buried for four months because his flock expected him to rise from the dead at Easter. He didn't.

The Pattern Is Established

Following Branham's successful format, dozens of imitators appeared. They showed up in every local vacant field in much the same way that traveling carnivals did, playing the towns regularly during the "season." They toured the countryside, erecting their tents, cleaning up and cleaning out each hamlet, then moving on with echoes of "Hallelujah" still ringing faintly from the hills.

The advantages of radio, seized upon early by such entrepreneurs as Rex Humbard and Oral Roberts, enlarged their potential audience enormously. It is still used by many evangelists, and can be said to have brought the profession into full bloom. Protected by the First Amendment, anyone capable of speaking in public became eligible to dispense interpretations of holy writ and to claim healing powers. An occasional individual took his or her inspiration from vaudeville, applying psychological techniques and razzmatazz to build an act that the IRS would never trouble, Congress would never question, and the law would find insulated by the Constitution against charges of fraud and deception.

A Similarity to Witchcraft

Faith-healing, especially today, is difficult to differentiate from witchcraft, which in its healing aspects is involved with expelling evil spirits from the body. The modern witch doctor in Africa still applies primitive show biz when he "pulls the thorn" by applying his mouth to a wound or the ailing portion of the body, producing by sleight of hand a thorn, stone, or sliver that is said to be either the actual cause of pain or a material representation of a demon or devil. Anthropologists have spent much time examining these methods, and as we shall see, one of them has compared these primitive methods to those used by today's more civilized practitioners. There may be a lot of information in these practices that can benefit medical science; much of today's medical knowledge came from similar sources.

In spite of this close resemblance of faith-healing to witchcraft, thousands of doctors and nurses in the United States have revitalized the International Order of St. Luke the Physician, an Episcopal group stressing a spiritual approach to the practice of medicine, thus identifying with if not actually joining the witches. This order experienced dramatic new life as a result of evangelist Oral Roberts's success in the 1950s. At that time, a Presbyterian minister, John Pitts, commented:

Today, interest in extramedical methods of healing men's minds and bodies is widespread and deep-seated, and the phenomena of Faith-healing can no longer be dismissed with a shrug of the shoulders, a snap judgment, and a clever

Witches involved in making folk medicine, an early attempt at pharmaceutical chemistry.

phrase, either by the church or by the medical
profession. . . . There seems to be more than
enough evidence to affirm that spiritual healing
is a fact.

Lacking any firm evidence of faith-healing, responsible skeptics *do not* resort to a "snap judgment" or a "clever phrase."
They simply do not accept wishful thinking as enough evidence to
prove a highly unlikely claim. It is the believers who get most of
their exercise jumping to conclusions.

An Orthodox Service

At St. Stephen's Episcopal Church in Philadelphia, headquarters of
the International Order of St. Luke the Physician, Father Roy
Hendricks conducts two healing services for the order every
Thursday. These services are so low-key and so close to orthodox
in nature, in contrast to those held by TV preachers, that the
New York Times told readers that the procedure at St. Stephen's
"exudes a well-bred approach that would shock Oral Roberts out
of his snap-on microphone."
    Though St. Stephen's has been offering this ministry since
1942, the Order of St. Luke the Physician was founded in 1947
and is now represented in 87 countries. At St. Stephen's, they
claim cures for afflictions from clubfoot to glaucoma. Unlike many
other claimants, they say that some of their cures are instantaneous and that others take many months, unlike those related in
the Bible. In December 1986, I wrote St. Stephen's requesting an
account of these cures, particularly of the clubfoot case. I have
received no response. If that cure did take place, this would be
the first such recorded example in history. I find it strange that
the order does not wish to share this miracle with my readers.
    Today's practitioners of faith-healing, graduated from the
small churches and the tent shows, have taken to television and
high tech to reach and influence much wider audiences than ever
before were possible. Television, much more than radio, has provided them with a means of almost equaling the impact of in-
person contact with victims of this particular flummery. Evangelist
Rex Humbard, a close friend of Oral Roberts who began television
broadcasting early in 1952 in Akron, Ohio, is largely responsible
for the television format now employed by faith-healers. Roberts,
inspired by Humbard's success, followed him onto the television
screen in 1955 after an earlier, abortive attempt at the medium.

Today, it is estimated that televangelists are seen by tens of millions of Americans weekly.

It's Magic

Reduced to its basics, faith-healing today—as it always has been—is simply "magic." Though the preachers vehemently deny any connection with the practice, their activities meet all the requirements for the definition. All of the elements are present, and the intent is identical. *Webster's Third New International Dictionary* defines "magic" as

> the use of means (such as ceremonies, charms, spells) that are believed to have supernatural powers to cause a supernatural being to produce or prevent a particular result (as rain, death, healing) considered not obtainable by natural means . . .

And the second edition of that dictionary comments:

> Magic is not clearly differentiated from science by primitive peoples. It is a part of most primitive religions.

David Alexander, a prominent investigator of paranormal claims and a valued colleague of mine, has observed:

> Take these evangelists away from their silk suits, well-coiffed hair and fancy limousines and put them in animal skins with a few rattles and beads. You've got a Cro-Magnon shaman, complete and ready to go to work.

Professor Morton Smith of Columbia University, long concerned with the role of magic in history, has pointed out that early Christians were actually violating the law of their time:

> If the Christians were an innocent sect practicing pure benevolence, why did the Romans make such strenuous efforts to stamp them out? It was because the Christians engaged in magical practices, and magic was a criminal act.

Sacred Babble

Healers W. V. Grant, Pat Robertson, Oral Roberts, and other TV
evangelists encourage their audiences to engage in "speaking in
tongues." This is an exact use of magical spells and incantations,
an intrinsic part of magical methodology, and is indistinguishable
from it, though it is called "religion" by the modern-day priests.
While "speaking in tongues," performers (both preachers and
worshipers) mumble gibberish which is believed by the faithful to
be a secret prayer language understood only by God—and his
Anointed Ministers, of course. (Some of W. V. Grant's magic words
transcribe as "Quah talah mokos! Stee keekeenee bahkus! Dee!")
The fact that each person mumbles differently matters not a whit.
God, angels, and Anointed Ministers, we are told, are able to
understand.

Technically, this psychological phenomenon is known as glossolalia. Early Methodists, Quakers, Shakers, and Mormons adopted
it, then de-emphasized it. Until recently, there was not much
emphasis on it in Christianity, and it fell into disuse until about
1830, when it reappeared in England, among "females of excitable
temperament," and now the Pentecostal sects have revived it.
Scripturally, glossolalia is traced back to Acts 2:4, and a meeting
of the Apostles, wherein

> they were all filled with the Holy Spirit, and
> began to talk in other tongues, as the Spirit
> gave them power of utterance.

Non-Christian glossolalia is difficult for Christians to explain.
It predates them considerably, being described in very ancient
religions and known in primitive societies untouched by Christianity. It was known to Plato, who described it in use in his day:
Greek and Roman oracles spoke in tongues. Virgil wrote about a
Roman Sibyl who babbled that way, in the *Aenead, Book Six.*
Moslems embraced the idea, too. Non-Pentecostal fundamentalists
believe that their Pentecostal brothers might be inspired to glossolalia by Satan. Who knows?

There is a biblical explanation of the fact that no one is able
to understand this chatter. We are told (I Corinthians 14:2) that

> when a man is using the language of ecstasy he
> is talking with God, not with men, for no man
> understands him . . .

A Minor Test

However, some preachers ignore that declaration and offer their audiences immediate interpretations of these rantings. The interpretations are almost always snatches of scripture, truisms, and generally flowery phrases that most people believe could be sacred utterances. Many years ago, I tested a preacher in Toronto, Canada, for his ability to interpret these sacred declarations. I played for him a tape of a long discourse in a "secret tongue" which I'd recorded in a church service, delivered by one of the congregation. The eager preacher gladly provided a running translation for me, only to find—to his dismay—that I'd made that recording two weeks previously in his own church—and his translation at *that* time had been very, very different indeed. He blamed the whole thing on "Satanic influence," and retired hurriedly to pray over the matter.

The Most Important Ingredient

There are other aspects of faith-healing that are congruent with the magical process. Belief is considered necessary for a healing to take place. More than that, the healers impress upon their subjects that initial belief must be expanded into an absolute, unquestioning faith before any result will be forthcoming, and that faith must be maintained from that moment onward or the charm will be broken. This gives rise to a perfect explanation for the subsequent failure of the process: The recipient of the healing ceremony was unable to "keep the faith."

That is the most disturbing aspect of all. Today's faith-healers impose a heavy potential burden of guilt on their victims. People are told that any failure of the healing magic is due to lack of *their* faith. They, not Jesus or the healer, must take the blame. David Paul, one of the more energetic of the modern evangelist/healers, launches into a wild tirade before those in his congregation, calling them "miserable, wretched creatures" who cannot make decisions, cannot prosper and cannot survive—he says—without "Jeeezuz" on their side. And that, he says, calls for total, unquestioning surrender, which preachers such as Paul can supervise because of their great wisdom.

There are a few important bits of specialized behavior that are expected of both preacher and congregation in modern charismatic religious rites. One recognized antic requires that the preacher strike on the forehead persons singled out for healing. Sud-

den shouts of "Be *healed!*" or "*Praise* Jesus!" usually go along
with this. In response, those so struck are expected to fall back
into the arms of waiting "catchers" skilled at intercepting them.
Anything from a short exclamation of ecstasy to a full-throated
roar of spiritual exultation—from the falling devotee—is also expected to accompany this "slaying in the spirit." Of course, the
occasional celebrant, finding the sudden attention too attractive to
resist, will cartwheel out of control, flailing about and screeching.
Short of hosing him down with cold water, there is little that can
be done for the afflicted until the ecstasies subside.

A Trick with Biblical Roots

The most impressive of all the show-biz stunts used by the evan-
gelist/healers is the trick of "calling out" members of the audience. It consists of wandering about the audience, picking out an
individual apparently at random, and calling him or her by name.
A street address may also be given. A doctor's name is usually
announced, and an account of the person's affliction goes along
with it. Other details, from a pet's name to the fact that a relative is in prison, can be thrown in. Most evangelists will go to
great lengths to assure viewers repeatedly that they have never
spoken to or questioned those whom they address with this information. Needless to say, the audience members are greatly influ-
enced by this seeming miracle. To them the only explanation of
this phenomenon is that the performer has learned his information
from God, as he claims.

Evangelists, particularly Pentecostals and charismatics, often
quote from I Corinthians 12, wherein the "Nine Gifts of the
Spirit" granted by God to special adepts are described. Two of
these are the Gift of Knowledge (the ability to "call out" folks
for healing) and the Gift of Healing itself. To today's faithful, it
appears that such people as Pat Robertson and the others possess
these gifts, because they apparently can and do demonstrate them,
both in person and via television. It must be added that fundamentalists, by and large, do not embrace the use of the Gifts by
preachers.

We are faced with two basic questions. First, are the televangelists offering proof of the Gift of Knowledge when they
"call out" individuals in the audience? No. But different preachers
use different methods to provide this illusion. I will describe here
the method used by W. V. Grant, a prominent healer/evangelist
who will be discussed later in detail in a chapter devoted to his

ministry. Other methods used by other preachers will also be discussed in chapters devoted to them as individuals. Second, are they producing actual healings—by whatever means, and by whatever attribution—that can be verified? This question will be addressed in detail in Chapter 16.

The "Gift of Knowledge"

Let us consider the process of "calling out." Here's how it works.

I visited several evangelists who perform this stunt as part of their acts. My team and I sat through endless mind-numbing hours of repetitious, trite sermonizing to determine all the details of the process. Most of that sermonizing was designed to apply "operant conditioning" to the audience. The audience participants were actually being given a crash course in how to react to the various bits of emotional stimuli that were being presented to them and that would be reintroduced again later. The preacher would ask inane questions like, "Anyone here understands that?" and "Anybody here can say, 'Praise the Lord'?" By eliciting constant, easy, affirmative responses, the pattern was laid for continued positive responses. Later, when important questions like "Anyone here going to give the largest bill they have to Jesus?" were asked, the answer was likely to follow the pattern.

I discovered that obtaining the information about the victims for the "calling out" process is the easiest part of it all, and is accomplished simply by *asking* them! Because people are admitted to the auditorium many hours before the performances, I had my team of observers with me at the moment the doors first opened at every one of the episodes we investigated. We spread out in groups of two or three and waited patiently until we were approached by someone from the evangelist's camp.

We saw those workers striking up casual conversations with early arrivals, determining the needed information, noting the seating location and a brief description of the person involved, and then hurrying backstage to record that data. Most of these preachers send their wives to wander around and gather information, and all of them send their "front men" for that same purpose.

A Smooth Act

W. V. Grant's act is dependent upon this gimmick, so I will describe in detail how he works the stunt. At Grant's meetings, his wife, Shirley, and other acolytes were seen wandering around in the audience before every performance hustling up information for the boss to use, and even Grant himself was out there gathering information in person. Recorded at one Brooklyn revival meeting, his questioning went like this:

> Hello! I'm Reverend Grant. Good to see you here today! Is Jesus going to heal you today, brother? Good! What—what's—your—(long pause) problem? I see. Well, Jesus will heal you. I'm going to call you today. Uh—what's—uh—what's your doctor's name? Uh-huh. I see. Well, God bless you, brother. God bless you.

And that's it. Short, simple, and bold. He has the required data, and he'll use it.

In addition to this method, "healing cards" are often used. These cards are handed to all who enter, and recipients are told that specific information concerning "prayer needs" of the individual is to be written down, plus names and addresses. The cards are gathered up early and taken backstage, bearing the same sort of data that can be obtained by the straight questioning gimmick.

The Family Bible Tells All

Much to my surprise, my team noted two other previously unsuspected methods that W. V. Grant used. In one, a Grant associate was seen standing at the back of the auditorium supplying hand signals. He was pointing to parts of his own body to indicate where the subject Grant was handling was afflicted! He had his own crib sheets, and was perhaps only there to remind Reverend Grant if the mnemonics began to fade. (The term "mnemonics" refers to a memory system which I will explain up ahead.)

The other gimmick was spotted when Grant took a massive Bible from one of our workers. He admired it and casually opened it at the inside front cover, glanced there for a moment, and then returned the book to its owner. He was apparently aware that many families record births, marriages, and deaths inside their Bibles. Later, during the "calling out" procedure, information Grant had learned from that brief perusal was fed back by him to our colleague. Unknown to Grant, the information written there was false, and Grant had been allowed to see it in hopes that he would use it.

A Disclaimer

Grant specifically states that there is no trickery used in his "calling out" stunt. In his broadcast of March 23, 1986, from Mobile, Alabama, he said, in typical evangelist style—the very longest way possible:

> What you see at these services is not ESP. What you see at these services is not mind power. What you see at these services is not fortunetelling. What you see at these services is not magic tricks. What you see at these services is "HSP": Holy Spirit Power! Paul called it the Gifts of the Spirit.

He then asked someone in the audience, "If I told you God told me something about you, would you believe it?" And he proceeded to do his vaudeville act, telling the victim details already known to the preacher by any of several means, none of them connected with heavenly voices or powers.

There is no question whatsoever that Reverend W. V. Grant gives the impression to his audiences, live and via TV, that his "calling out" is a divine event, and not a trick. To quote from an excellent and devastating *Cincinnati Enquirer* investigation of Grant by Camilla Warrick, which appeared in June of 1983:

> It was at the Texas Bible school, Grant says, that "God began to use me" and he started to call out the names of strangers during services.
>
> "It doesn't take any faith for God to show you somebody's name or somebody's doctor's name," he explained. "It takes faith for you to go ahead and say it after God shows it to you, because just as sure as you say someone's name . . . the old devil says, 'What are you going to do if it isn't?' "
>
> Grant's ability to call out names is a reflection, he says, of just one of nine gifts of the spirit that he possesses. But it doesn't manifest itself in all occasions for all people. "I can't see into anyone's life," he said, "unless the anointing is upon me."

Grant has committed himself many times during his services to declaring that his "calling out" process is divine. In Oakland, California (see Chapter 9), at a crusade in which he "healed" a confederate of ours, he several times reinforced the notion that he had no way except divine inspiration to know anything about those he would "call out." Excerpts from his statements at that meeting:

> . . . Don't be talking to me or asking me to pray for you or I can't call you out after a while, and ask you if I've ever talked to you before. How many understands that?
>
> So don't tell me anything. I may wanna ask you if I've talked to you and then if I ask you that, well, ahhh, you're gonna have to be honest. How many knows that?
>
> How many knows God knows all about you? Don't tell me a thing. That way, if I call you out later, you can say you hadn't talked to me.
>
> How many will lift your hand and say, "Brother Grant, I know because of what I'm seeing here tonight that Jesus is real. I know he knows my name and my doctor's name and my affliction. Lift your hand and say, "I know it's not you. It has to be God."

In his own publication, *Dawn of a New Day*, in the issue of Fall 1983, it says clearly that at a Tulsa meeting

> Brother Grant, ministering under a very unusual heavy anointing, called out and ministered to thousands. Through the Gifts of the Holy Spirit, he would reveal not only their condition and affliction—but also their names and doctors' names many times.

An Old Act

If you think the description of this "calling out" act sounds like that offered by mentalist Kreskin, take ten points for perception.

Kreskin, however—like his model, Joseph Dunninger, the greatest mentalist who ever lived—offers his act as entertainment, not religion. The methods are somewhat different, but the effect is the same. W. V. Grant, actually denying from time to time that what he is doing is a "magic act," not only gains the full attention of his audience with these tricks, but also convinces them of his closeness to God.

Of course, each of these information-gathering systems—personal questioning and written information—has its advantages and drawbacks. For example, the vast majority of the audience, not arriving until just before the scheduled performance, cannot know about the much earlier personal questioning. Using the "healing card" method, the preacher cannot easily know the location of those who made out the cards. He has to ask them to identify themselves, or be guided to them by another means. But how does Grant recall all this complicated data while he runs up and down the aisles? He carries no note pad, yet he appears to be aware of each set of data as he needs it. He uses a mnemonic system, a method of memory by association, to store his information. Memory expert Harry Lorayne perfected the mnemonic system and wrote definitively on it many years ago, and he has verified that it could easily be used for this purpose. Grant associates the face with the name with the doctor with the disease by means of certain simple procedures. He can easily store away some 30 sets of data, enough for any revival performance. Other data go on "crib sheets" carried in his pockets.

The Art of Mnemonics

There is a simply fascinating technique used by many actors, public relations people, politicians, and others who need to exhibit proficiency in recalling names, faces, and figures. The word "mnemonics" comes from the Greek word for "memory." It is a simple but powerful association system which allows the user to recall details that regular long-term memory might find difficult to supply.

Lorayne, the leading authority on mnemonics, has written a number of instruction books on the subject. It works thus: Suppose that you must remember the names of several persons to whom you are being introduced. Applying Lorayne's system, you would pick out some prominent feature of each person's appearance (facial details, dress ornaments, marks, etc.) and then associate that detail with either the sound or some other characteristic of the name. For example, you are at a party one evening and you have met a man with a Band-Aid on his cheek, and you are told that his name is Carter. You might choose to picture the Band-Aid as having a tiny cartoon of Jimmy Carter—with lots of teeth, of course—drawn on it. The connection has been made—and the sillier or the more bizarre the connection, the better. When you later see that man wearing his Band-Aid, you will have no difficulty making the connection, and you will recall his name.

A woman might be wearing outlandish rhinestone glasses and be named Alexander. In this case, you might choose to imagine the name Alexander written out on her forehead in rhinestones, and the tune *Alexander's Ragtime Band* being played. Next, you are introduced to a man wearing a loud checkered vest and you learn that his name is Hershey. Think of that vest with Hershey's chocolate syrup poured over the front of it, and that man will not be difficult to identify later on. This is the kind of outlandish imagery that will make mnemonics work for you.

Such systems are not at all hard to master, and I learned that "healer" Peter Popoff, after I had blown away his alternative system of identifying people in the audience (see Chapter 9), was seen reading a Lorayne book aboard an aircraft taking him to one of his crusades.

Pause. Without looking back to the pertinent paragraph, let's test the efficacy of the mnemonic system that has just been described. (I suggest that you cover the upper half of this page with your hand.) Imagine that it is later in the evening, and you have run into those same three people, in a different order from when you first met them. You wonder if you can recall their names, which you have committed to memory by means of the system. Now answer these three questions:

> (1) How do you address the lady with the rhinestone glasses?
> (2) You see a chap wearing a Band-Aid. What is his name?
> (3) Who is the guy with the checkered vest?

I think, from this example, that you will see now how easy it can be, even for one who is only slightly acquainted with mnemonics, to use this art. With some experience and practice, mnemonics can be a very handy and very powerful tool. It has made fortunes for W. V. Grant, among others.

All Sorts of Trickery

In investigating modern faith-healing, I came upon every common method of technical, psychological, semantic, and physical chicanery that one can imagine being used to deceive the public—and some new ones, as well. I was aided in my investigations by some of the finest minds in the conjuring business, and the names of those persons will come up in the discussions that follow. My own expertise is very much centered in the "mentalism" aspects of conjuring. In the early days of my career as a conjuror, I specialized in that field. Because of that specialization, I am able to spot signs of trickery that many "magicians" might miss. Indeed, I ran into several fellow conjurors who told me that they believed at least some of the faith-healers had genuine powers. A few of the former colleagues of the faith-healers themselves, even though they had been exposed to the actual methods used, had been fooled by some other aspects of the act and thus had retained some belief in the powers claimed.

We will turn next to the attitude of the "orthodox" churches concerning faith-healing. I will not attempt to define the term "orthodox," because each reader will have his or her own opinion about that matter.

3
The Church View

Is one of you ill? He should send for the elders
of the congregation to pray over him and
anoint him with oil in the name of the Lord.
The prayer offered in faith will save the sick
man, the Lord will raise him from his bed. . . .
(James 5:14)

Every denomination, sect, and cult of the Christian religion has
attempted to explain, condone, deny, embrace, or denounce faith-
healing. One evangelist, Glen Cole of Sacramento, California,
claimed in his television broadcast of May 24, 1987, that all
manner of instantaneous cures occur at his fingertips. He poured
forth a quite astonishing view of faith-healing. Briefly, here is a
summary of what he used ten times the necessary number of
words to say: Sickness started at the moment that Eve tasted the
fruit of the tree of knowledge. Because of her disobedience, our
species was doomed to die instead of living forever. (I am tempted
to invoke a picture of this planet with human beings piled a mile
deep over every square inch of surface, and continuing to reproduce in accordance with the scriptural admonition to do so, but I
am determined to resist that inclination.)

Pastor Cole pointedly ridiculed those who were so silly as to
go to their medicine cabinet seeking a cure for illness, instead of
running to a preacher. Sickness and dying, he said, can be stopped
by anointing, laying on of hands, and faith. Why do some people,

following the rules given, still get sick and die? Not to worry, he
tells us. It is an exchange of this mundane life for heaven. It is
"*the ultimate healing, death.*"

Let Pastor Cole's colleagues squirm their various ways out of
that mess. Perhaps, to them, it makes some sort of sense; to me,
it is dangerous and juvenile thinking.

More Orthodox Views

The United Church of Canada, in common with many other major
religious groups, looked into the claims of the faith-healers and
issued an official report in 1961 that said:

> Faith-healing is not a legitimate ministry of the
> Church and should be actively discouraged and
> resisted wherever it is practiced.

By 1967, that opinion had changed. For whatever reasons,
church authorities had now decided that there existed both authentic faith-healing and spurious faith-healing, and "discrimination
between [them] is not easy but important." The spurious variety
was attributed to people such as Oral Roberts. The United Church
of Canada's major criticisms of Roberts's variety of evangelism
were:

> (1) It is based upon an inadequate theology
> which often assumes sickness to be a divine
> judgment.
> (2) It has a naive view of the distinction
> between "natural" and "supernatural" healing.
> (3) It works—when it does—usually by suggestion
> and hysteria, and the patient may suffer a
> relapse that leaves him worse off than he was
> before.
> (4) People who are not healed may feel that
> God has rejected them and suffer morbid guilt
> feelings and spiritual shipwreck.

I note that the United Church of Canada report did not cite one
genuine, proven case of healing, and I may surmise that the
church changed its mind because the existence of scriptural references to such wonders was pointed out to it.

The Reverend Carroll R. Stegall, Jr., writing in *Presbyterian Outlook* early in Oral Roberts's career, reported his conclusions on this subject:

> So far from glorifying God with this, [the faith-healers] cause His name to be blasphemed by the world by their excesses. So far from curing, they often kill. Far from blessing, their arrival in a city is rather a curse, a misery, a racket, a destruction of faith in simple people.

The *Christian Century*, an Episcopalian journal, warned the faithful that it is "a profound heresy [to believe that God] is susceptible to such pushing around by man."

How Do Their Associates Feel About the Faith-Healers?

It has to be wondered just what the colleagues of the faith-healers think about their operations. They surely must suspect that tricks are being used. In some cases, they are absolutely sure of that fact. The first director of the Peter Popoff TV show was Paul Crouch, Jr. His father is the head of the Trinity Broadcasting Network (TBN), which in some areas of the United States provides 24 hours of Christian-style TV, seven days a week, to the faithful. We discovered that Crouch Jr. had dropped out of the Popoff gang for ethical reasons when he discovered the nature of the operation, but when my colleague David Alexander, an investigator for CSER, suggested to Crouch Sr. that he should have told his TV audience of Popoff's methods, Crouch showed no interest at all. Crouch might have felt ethically bound to warn his viewers but decided to commit what we might call the sin of silence. TBN chose not to protect Christians from being exploited, and Popoff was allowed to work his TV game for many years. That's no surprise to a veteran of the business, musician Bill Williamson. Says he: "You don't say anything when you find out something bad. You hurt one, you hurt them all." That was well before PTL blew up in a series of scandals and Oral Roberts became the clown prince of TV evangelism by threatening to die unless the faithful sent him more money. Now, all the evangelists are at one another's throats and accusations are as plentiful as "miracles."

The American way allows us to take advantage of the free capitalist system. There is nothing wrong with making money at a chosen profession. Most of us are required to account for our

income and pay taxes for our share of the financial burden of
government. But not all of us. Religious organizations are not
required to. Though the U.S. Constitution does not say specifically
that churches should be exempt from taxation, the statement
"Congress shall make no law respecting an establishment of religion" has been interpreted to mean just that.

Many churches and religious organizations choose to register
with the Internal Revenue Service as nonprofit organizations,
though they are not required to do so. Many evangelists, such as
Billy Graham and the Wycliffe Bible Translators, have joined the
Evangelical Council for Financial Accountability, a 350-member
Protestant group founded in 1979 by those who chose to publish
their financial statements for public scrutiny. One of the founders
was Jerry Falwell, who dropped out shortly afterward. W. V. Grant
and Peter Popoff, among other faith-healers, are not members. If
they were, we would have some way of knowing how much money
goes into the plastic trash bags that line the wastebaskets carried
about by their ushers at revival meetings, and how much is de-
posited by the mailman daily at all of the post office boxes and
street addresses where they do their mail-order business.

Caution: Demons at Work

The churches have had to deal with the problem of accommodating
medieval thinking and modern science, and living with both. The
two entities are quite incompatible, but both must be accepted if
the religious philosophy is to survive. Anthropologist author Kaja
Finkler looked into this strange marriage of opposites. Writing on
the subject of faith-healing in Mexico, she said that, in her
opinion,

> science and technology are destroying the fabric
> of society. With this have come various move-
> ments, preaching an antagonism between Reason
> and Feeling, exalting the latter at the expense
> of the former.

Finkler also recognizes that biomedicine cannot provide a patient
with a satisfactory relationship between pain and some "symbol"
—while faith-healing can and does. The most common symbol of
pain and disease provided by the faith-healers is the demon, which
can be exorcised by magic, that is to say, by proper incantations,
gestures, and—most important—offerings.

That last requirement was emphasized by Reverend Don Stewart, the preacher who eventually took over the A. A. Allen empire in Miracle Valley, Arizona, after the scandalous demise of the founder. Stewart said, exhorting the crowd waiting for A. A. Allen to appear:

> You got to promise God, and you got to keep
> the promise. If you want him to lift your pain,
> to make you whole, to bring you joy, you got
> to have faith. And faith is to vow and pay.

This simple faith-plus-payment formula is very appealing to many who misunderstand the profession of medicine and the nature of the organic healing process, and who are prepared by their religious training to accept the demon symbol without question.

These observations are echoed by Dr. Allan Bloom of the University of Chicago in one of the most talked-about books of 1987, *The Closing of the American Mind*. Professor Bloom says:

> The ideology of passion has come to dominate
> America's young. They generally believe that
> feelings are deeper than reason and that the
> two are in opposition—not that they develop one
> another, which was the old idea. They think
> that reason can't help you decide whether to
> believe in God or not, whether to like democ-
> racy or monarchy.
>   Even in the rhetoric of conservatism there
> is the notion that reason can't provide values.
> So there is a turn to religion. I'm not sugges-
> ting religion is unnecessary, but there is a
> widespread belief that religion can decide values
> and reason can't. On the left, many young
> people turn to rock music. They say it's deeper
> than words—that they don't have to explain
> what role it plays in their lives. They just say:
> "That's my taste. That's the way I feel about
> it."

I would add to that my opinion that not only is there "the notion that reason can't provide values," but there is a feeling that religion provides firm, inarguable values that are predigested, infallible, eminently acceptable (within the believer's immediate social milieu), and satisfying. In addition, no intellectual effort is required to adopt them, and the pressure for adopting them is very strong. The pressure may be the strongest influence in the lives of some people. Dr. Bloom goes on to comment:

> There used to be an intellectual class in America. . . . These people kept the world of ideas alive. But today the distinction between intellectuals and nonintellectuals doesn't make any difference; celebrity is the only standard. . . . Everybody has become a talker of cheap philosophy that anybody can pick up.

The celebrity status that the TV evangelists have attained merely by purchasing air time and putting on a good show gives them the charisma that attracts the faithful moths to their deadly flames.

Send in the Demons

Only one who has not looked into the state of modern religion can possibly fail to know that the Dark Ages, in many respects, are still with us. To millions upon millions of otherwise sensible people, demons, devils, imps, and various other supernatural critters are quite literally real. Evangelists such as Roberts, Robertson, Grant, Popoff, Shambaugh, Humbard, Swaggart, and dozens more regularly perpetuate this superstition. Oral Roberts has even provided us with a detailed explanation of how he recognizes and casts out demons. He says that he sees demons in the eyes of the possessed. After all, he says,

> the eyes, as you know, are the windows of the soul. And personally, when I'm in the presence of a person with demons, I can see the leering and gleaming in the eye of the individual.

He also smells out demons "by the breath or odor of the body." If that fails, he picks up his clue by "vibration" when he touches the afflicted.

The Roman Catholic Bestiary

It is not only the fundamentalists who wish to stop the acquisition of knowledge at the point it reached in early medieval times. Such

St. Mathurin, circa 1489, exorcising a demon.

supposedly advanced people as educated Roman Catholics also fear
these beasties. In 1928, the Reverend Montague Summers translated
into English the infamous *Malleus Maleficarum*, a 1487 book that
outlined the official Catholic view of witches, demons, and heresy
and was written by two inquisitors. Basing his statements upon
this 450-year-old document, and determined to remain in the Dark
Ages intellectually, Summers chastised those who adopted an
attitude about demons and devils that was more in line with
modern thinking:

> . . . Those err who say that there is no such
> thing as witchcraft, but that it is purely imag-
> inary, even although they do not believe that
> devils exist except in the imagination of the
> ignorant and vulgar, and the natural accidents
> which happen to a man he wrongly attributes to
> some supposed devil. For the imagination of
> some men is so vivid that they think they see
> actual figures and appearances which are but
> the reflection of their thoughts, and then these
> are believed to be the apparitions of evil spirits
> or even the spectres of witches. But this is
> contrary to true faith, which teaches us that
> certain angels fell from heaven and are now

devils, and we are bound to acknowledge that
by their very nature they can do many wonderful things which we cannot do. . . . Because
infidelity in a person who has been baptized is
technically called heresy, therefore such persons
are plainly heretics.

Speaking as recently as 1972, Pope Paul VI affirmed this statement:

Sin, on its part, affords a dark, aggressive
evildoer, the Devil, an opportunity to act in us
and in our world . . . Anyone who disputes the
existence of this reality places himself outside
biblical and Church teachings.

Perhaps inspired by this declaration, in 1976 West Germany's
Bishop Stangl instructed two priests to perform the rite of exor-
cism upon a 23-year-old epileptic Bavarian girl, Anneliese Michel.
The local newspapers reported that the church had decided her
body was being inhabited by various demons, including Lucifer,
Adolf Hitler, Judas Iscariot, and Emperor Nero. Anneliese, an
epileptic, died in the process of being exorcised, and the autopsy
showed she suffered beating and starvation. Her parents and the
two priests were convicted of negligent homicide and given suspended sentences.

Significantly, when Bishop Stangl died during the trial, his
death was attributed to a stroke, not to demonic possession.

Christianity and Voodoo: Are They That Different?

Recently, a U.S. television news series told of a serious problem
that has arisen with the Haitian-born residents of southern Florida. An astonished news commentator told his audience that the
Haitians remained faithful to their voodoo heritage, believing that
disease, bad luck, and poor finances were brought about by various
demons which can be propitiated by appropriate ceremonies and
sacrifices. The newsman then described how the disease AIDS was
subject to periodic, temporary remissions, and said that Haitian
victims of the disease frequently experienced such remissions
following voodoo rites, though no cause-and-effect relationship
was implied. Having assumed that the voodoo had been effective,
most Haitians were then resuming their sexual lives and thus

bringing a serious threat of infection to their partners. What surprised the newsman was that these folks actually believed in the existence and effects of demonic possession.

He need not have been surprised. It is not only voodoo worshipers who believe such medieval nonsense; *all* Christians who believe in the Holy Bible must also believe in demons, devils, and other such creatures, and they must believe that those entities cause disease and that they can be "cast out" by proper ceremonies, simply because it's in the Book. If they deny the reality of those creatures, they deny the Bible, and thus their faith. It is not a matter of choice, but dogma.

An Early Skeptic

Johannes Weyer, a sixteenth-century physician also known as Piscinarius, was an early skeptic of the belief that ailments were supernatural in nature. He observed:

> The uninformed and the unskilled physicians relegate all the incurable diseases, or all the diseases the remedy for which they overlook, to witchcraft. When they do this, they are talking about disease like a blind man does about color. Like many surgeons with their quackery, they cover their ignorance of our Sacred Art with the playthings of magic malefactors and they themselves are the real malefactors.

Weyer was, for his day, an unusually enlightened man who vigorously pursued various claims of magic and witchcraft, showing that they had no basis in fact. He met the claimants on their own terms and defeated them. He investigated one of the most famous of all "possession" cases, that of the Nuns of Cologne in 1564. Weyer solved that matter by determining that certain rather robust convulsions entered into by these virtuous ladies had been brought about, not by religious visions, but by visitations of neighborhood dandies who had favored them with their attentions and subsequently induced various raptures in the ladies by their very efforts at negotiating the walls of the convent. The ladies had turned heavy romance into religious exultation.

For his labors, Weyer was castigated by the church and his own profession. Complained one well-known physician of the time:

Oh, if only such a man had never been born, or
at least had not written anything! Instead of
which, he gives many people through his books
the opportunity to sin and to enhance the
Kingdom of Satan.

Johannes Weyer.

Fear of the truth has often led such people to pronounce
dreadful death sentences upon those who dared to deny supernatural claims. It happened often enough during the Inquisition.
Weyer, however, managed to survive to the then-surprising age of
73, and was accorded a proper Christian church burial. To many
modern historians of medicine, he is looked upon as one of the

founders of modern psychiatry; he is certainly one of the first philosophers to record a rational view of various human mental aberrations, many of which are believed even today, by the uneducated, to be caused by demons, witches, and other fanciful inventions. Weyer knew better and had the good common sense, intelligence, and fortitude to say so.

Anointing by the Anointed

One of the minor results of the Vatican II conference was that a Roman Catholic ceremony formerly known as Extreme Unction became officially known as the Special Sacrament of the Anointing. Its name was changed, but not its purpose. Usually associated with the deathbed, this ceremony is an insurance that the guardians of the Pearly Gates will recognize the applicant's commitment to the faith—a last-minute rededication. In a Catholic publication titled *Anointing of the Sick and Elderly,* author Sister Marie Roccapriore outlines the official aim of the rite, and gives the official point of view concerning suffering:

> Two particular states of life which are difficult to face are sickness and old age. Especially in our nuclear society, the sick and the aged seem to disrupt the normal pattern of everyday living. Too often the burdensome responsibilities of those who must care for them are accentuated by an almost callous disregard for their suffering. A lack of sensitivity to the basic needs of the sick and the elderly who yearn for companionship and loving attention, frequently leads to setting them apart from the normal gatherings of family, local functions of community or other forms of involvement in society.

In this statement—to this point at least—I can agree with Sister Marie. Then she continues:

> But faith-filled people are able to sustain themselves in the face of such painful experiences. Moreover, by fighting the physical evil which threatens to overwhelm them, by accepting their sufferings with resignation, and by becoming an inspiration for others in their

patient surrender to God's will, they participate
actively in the Church's mission in the world.

Here, I strongly disagree with all but the part about "fighting the
physical evil." It is interesting to see that the magazine *U.S.
Catholic* tells its readers: "[The Special Sacrament of the Anoint-
ing] is crucial for allaying fears and putting to rest skepticism."
How it can possibly accomplish that, I cannot tell. But note that
"skepticism" is designated as a fearsome attitude—perhaps because
it leads to realization of a real world. Healthy, rational, and
informed skepticism is not an enemy.

The Catholic church has leapt aboard the fast-moving—though
rickety—faith-healing bandwagon by officially endorsing certain
priests as healers. I will discuss this in detail in Chapter 13.

Faith-healer/evangelist W. V. Grant disagrees with the official
Roman Catholic view of fate and duty. He denies that the faithful
are expected to suffer endlessly in submission to divine will. He
preaches that suffering is *not* prescribed by the Bible, and that
God *must* fulfill His scriptural promise to grant any asked-for
favor, including the right to receive divine healing, and Grant can
quote scripture by the hour to prove it. He points out what a
great friend he is to have brought this contractual obligation of
the deity to the attention of the ailing who seek him out. And
payment for all of this requires only endless paeans of unceasing
praise—and financial support of God's ministers. W. V. Grant
constantly reminds his TV flock that he is one of God's ministers.

Grant is fond of the idea of anointing and has turned it into
a commercial gimmick. On his television programs he offers tiny
vials of "holy olive oil" from "Iza-rull" to his followers in return
for a certain minimum donation by mail. We learned, through
former employees of the Grant organization, that at least the oil
that he sends out is real olive oil, though it is from Italy, not
Israel. Peter Popoff, being more imaginative, was sending to his
correspondents common olive oil scented with Old Spice Shaving
Lotion. I have several vials of pink-tinted oil that managed to find
their way out of the Popoff stronghold in Upland, California.

A Lutheran Point of View

In 1962, the U.S. United Lutheran Church Committee, consisting of
physicians, ministers, and theologians, looked at what they called
the "religious quackery" of some faith-healers. They summarized
their findings:

(1) [The faith-healers] blame any failure of the healing ceremony on the subject's lack of faith.
(2) They ignore any attempt at the use of scientific methodology in their work.
(3) The motive is simply a desire for money and the personal power to exploit.

I believe this is an excellent brief summary of my own findings.

4
The Financial Aspects

> Provide no gold, silver, or copper to fill your
> purse. (Matthew 10:9)

The faith-healers are very much concerned with money. It is as large a concern to them as the healing process they are involved in. In fact, healer/evangelist A. A. Allen used to tell his audiences that, in many cases, poverty itself was a disease caused by specific demons. Needless to say, the preacher had discovered a solution to this demon infestation. It consisted of giving money to Allen, in large quantities and by whatever means could be managed. This also cured any vestigial poverty that Allen himself might have been suffering from, though that was not an obvious ailment with him, even to very astute observers.

The amounts of money asked for and received by religious figures are enormous. Moreover, it is banked tax-free. The IRS has declared that all such money—except for the preacher's declared personal income—is exempt from taxes. June Smallwood, an IRS exemptions officer, revealed that by IRS rules, churches do not even have to *apply* for recognition of their exemption. A church need not even file an annual information return, though some churches do so on a voluntary basis. The only requirement of the IRS is that the "main activity" of the exempted organization must be "running a church." And—more interesting by far—when asked how the IRS would know if an organization's major activity would meet that requirement, Smallwood replied:

> We wouldn't actually know unless the church
> applied for exemption.

And, she added, there is no surveillance of organizations that claim religious tax exemption

> where the organization does not come in for
> formal recognition. . . . It all boils down to a
> constitutional question.

The eminently sensible thing for churches to do, it seems, is to simply say nothing, do not pay taxes, and relax.

God as Terrorist

The accumulation of wealth by the faith-healers—and evangelists in general—would appear to be in direct opposition to the biblical admonition that specifically directs priests to eschew such mundane pleasures. But, as with any such inconvenient scriptural directive, the inventive preachers have found ways to circumvent criticism on this point.

None has been so much in need of this rationalization as evangelist Oral Roberts, who recently made yet another dramatic appeal for funds that managed to get him rather wide attention. Roberts is very preoccupied with his own demise. (This strange condition is known as "thanatomania.") He frequently announces to the faithful that God has spoken to him about his death, and he says that on more than one occasion

> I've asked [God] to take my life, and He won't
> do that. And I apologize for that. I shouldn't
> ask the Lord to take my life.

It appears that the idea of "seed-faith" giving was originated by the Reverend Gene Ewing, a man who has designed many such ideas for himself and other preachers. The system was first used seriously by Roberts, who suggests that by "planting" a financial "seed" offering, his followers will see their money multiplied—not by Oral, but by God—but only if the giver generates sufficient faith. A nonfalsifiable situation is thus generated, with some few donors getting lucky and attributing it to God. Others get unlucky and, accepting that God's mind is unfathomable, attribute *that* to Him, too.

The seed-faith system is currently popular among the TV gurus for extracting funds from the faithful. (See Appendix IV for a sample from Oral Roberts.) Even the language used by Brother Roberts to describe the process is invented to order. Contributors are told:

> God didn't tell us to come to Him and he would put us in poverty. He said, "I'll prosper you." We're not out to get your money, but we're sure out to get your money increased. We're sure out to get you prospered.

In earlier days, Roberts (or God, because Oral speaks for God) could afford to make colossal financial blunders while running his $500 million empire, and he (or He) did. Still, the operation flourished and grew fat. Inevitably, such success was noticed by less fortunate evangelists, and as a result Roberts inadvertently created his own competition. He showed other tent-show evangelists how the media and a cleverly constructed, carefully used mailing list could be put to work to attract money; and when those observers left their tents and put their own machines into operation, Roberts's share of the charismatic pie suddenly shrank.

Eyes brimming with tears, Reverend Roberts announced on January 4, 1987, to his vast TV audience that if he were unable to raise the remainder of what he said was a much-needed $8 million by the end of that March, God would call him to heaven before his time. Why he would need such a relatively small sum, in view of the immense wealth of his organization, we will never know. He easily could have raised most of that sum just by selling any of his homes in Beverly Hills, Tulsa, or Palm Springs, or by putting his Angus cattle up for auction. His son Robert might have held back on his purchase of the 7,100-square-foot mansion he was just then moving into. The two $600,000 winter homes Oral has in California might have been sold. There were so many ways.

Immediate objections to this maneuver were heard from almost everyone in the business and from the media, who were finally becoming aware of what is known as "the Gimme Business." Florida newspaper columnist Gary Stein, commenting on the brouhaha, suggested that if Roberts were not dead by March 31, the evangelist would meet the press the following day to tell them "April Fool!" The *Tulsa Tribune*, always a gadfly to Roberts, ran a headline that demanded, "Come off it, Oral!" then snorted, "The time has come to laugh," and called his threat "emotional blackmail." A number of TV stations announced that they were dropping the Roberts program. Others rebroadcast old Roberts videotapes rather than airing the outrageous appeal, and many warned him to cease his continual high-powered begging via their facilities. One brother evangelist, Pat Robertson, opined that God was not the sort to hold a person hostage against donations. Another called Roberts "a religious extortionist." These comments may have been suggested by the then-current success of the Arab religious fanatics who had discovered the profitable business of snatching hostages for ransom. The parallel was not lost on the public, and might even have inspired Roberts—subconsciously—in the first place.

This was hardly the first time Roberts had used this extortion ploy, though the media seemed to think it was. Eighteen months previously, he had sent out a mailing that told the faithful:

> For many days, God has been speaking to me.
> *This time it means life or death for me.* (Italics
> in original.)

He went on to say that if he didn't have $8 million by July 1985,

> I won't be on this earth much longer. . . . My
> life depends on what you do. . . . God has said
> to me that we must fulfill this vision or my life
> will be over.

Either God forgot about His threat, or He gave Oral an additional eight months to get up the cash before He would vaporize him with His celestial wrath. It reached a point where bookmakers in Las Vegas actually had "Oral's Countdown to Death" listed on their betting rundown. Bets were placed on whether he would live to see April 1. Odds were highly in favor of his survival.

But the Reverend Roberts had yet another dramatic episode with which to regale the media, hard on the heels of this latest death wish. He told his TV audience breathlessly (pun intended) how he had been awakened one night by Satan (not just *any* demon, but the top demon himself) sitting on his chest strangling him with both clawed hands. Said Oral:

> One night, the Devil came in my room—just a
> few nights ago—and I felt those hands on my
> throat, choking—trying to choke my life out of

> me. And I yelled for my wife, Evelyn, "Honey,
> come!" And Evelyn laid her hands upon me and
> rebuked the Devil and commanded him to get
> out of mah room. And I began to breathe, I
> came out of that bed and—strong in the Lord.
> Let me tell yuh, there's *nothing* that can take
> yuh down when you have the power of God in
> yer life!

What had actually happened to Oral Roberts to produce this
unlikely tale? Indigestion? Maybe his fears of impending death
brought on a nightmare. Or perhaps the reverend gentleman was
just testing—again—to see how big a whopper his audience would
swallow. But has it occurred to him that he doesn't have many
friends in high—or low—places? When both God *and* Satan are
trying to do you in, there's a message in it somewhere. Besides,
Oral had declared back in 1963 that he is thoroughly protected by
God, at least in respect to infections:

> . . . In sixteen and one-half years of laying my
> hands upon hundreds of thousands of the most
> miserably ill people on earth, God has let none
> of their diseases come upon me, and that is a
> testimony of His being with us.

To those who have followed the strange meanderings of Roberts's mind over the years, his tall tales are not surprising. The
faithful are prepared, by the literature issued from the ministry,
to accept these Munchhausenian yarns. In *The Miracles of Christ,*
a book that serves as a primer on accepting the incredible, Roberts demotes reason and makes blind faith a Godly virtue:

> It requires faith to believe God can [perform a
> miracle] . . . It takes faith because it goes
> against all human reasoning. It goes against
> everything our mind has been taught by Man's
> reason.

Saved from the Unthinkable

Springing to his father's aid, Richard Roberts pleaded to viewers
of his own TV program: "Please don't let this birthday be my
father's last." At the rate of $160,000 a day, currency once again

began filling the mail room and a few days before divine thunder-bolts were scheduled to crease his brow, Oral announced that Jerry Collins, the owner of a dog racing track in Florida, had anted up $1.3 million to save him. At least for the time being, the world could relax, no longer faced with the dreadful possibility of having to do without Oral Roberts.

But Oral wasn't finished. Recognizing a winning hand, he next announced that God was now demanding a similar $8 million a year *in addition to the regular tithes from Roberts's flock*, to be collected "every year until Jesus comes"! Furthermore, in spite of all he had actually said and written in reference to the March 31 death threat, the reverend gentleman declared that he had never said he'd die, and that any such notion was merely the invention of a hostile press. The mind boggles at Roberts's ability to deny his own words.

(This whole event was all the more newsworthy because it immediately preceded the tremendous upheaval in the evangelism business that resulted when Jim Bakker and his wife, Tammy Faye, revealed that a mixture of blackmail, sexual shenanigans, and drug addiction was forcing them to hand over their $130-million-a-year PTL operation to Jerry Falwell, admittedly to keep it out of the hands of Jimmy Swaggart, a high school dropout dubbed the "Weeping Pastor" of television.)

What happens to those millions that are poured into the Oral Roberts ministry is still a mystery.

Gold Bars and Cut Diamonds

Concerning the fortunes brought in by the Peter Popoff ministry of Upland, California, no such mystery need trouble us. Popoff was never shy about such matters with his close friends, delighting in showing off his wealth at every opportunity. His home in Upland (assessed at just under $800,000), which he put up for sale after I exposed his tricks on the Johnny Carson show in February of 1986, boasted both a walk-in vault and a jewelry display room measuring six by eight feet, with illuminated display shelves. Said former Popoff controller Ira McCorriston:

> [It] looks like a jeweler's store when you walk
> in it, all the lights and the glass cabinets and
> all the gold bars, the silver and the diamond
> collections and all that, laid out like you walk
> into on Fifth Avenue . . . That's one part . . .

then the other part is this door. It's like a
bank.

Ira says that he never got into that part of the "bank," the
section protected with steel armor-plate and a combination lock,
but reports from inside were that Popoff had $2 million in cash
stashed away in there against bad times, and had boasted about it.

There were three main sources for the Popoff income. As with
all these operations, the mail contributions were by far the major
source. This money came in from appeals made via the 55 TV
stations and 130 radio stations on which Popoff appeared weekly.
Then there was the Inner Circle Club money, a method of continuing to extract money from selected individuals who had already
sent him large cash gifts, though that system was only put into
operation shortly before my TV exposure of Popoff began to take
effect. The in-person crusade money was substantial, too, and was
far more maneuverable because much of it was in cash.

Cameraman Gary Clarke worked on the videotaping of some of
the early Popoff crusades by All-American Video, W. V. Grant's
production company. (It was later renamed QC Video when Grant
moved to Cincinnati.) Clarke witnessed an event in Atlanta, Georgia, on Christmas Eve that showed him just how enormous the
profit was from these shows. It is something that he cannot
forget. One of Popoff's "money men" was backstage heading for
the truck to join the others for a count of the take for that
meeting, and Clarke watched as the man struggled to get an
enormous wad of cash out of one of his pockets. Another employee had to help him. Cash was strewn about the floor, and they
were picking it up like so much litter.

A Very Private Matter

Controller McCorriston averred that he never saw or counted any
of the Popoff crusade proceeds. He was only concerned with the
mailed-in money, along with the donations ($100 each) that especi-
ally generous people sent in to become members of the Popoff
Inner Circle Club. "[Popoff] doesn't bring any of the field [cru-
sade] money back [to the office]," he said. The plastic trash bags
of cash and checks went backstage to Popoff's wife, Elizabeth,
where the loot vanished. At the end of the service, Liz would
emerge with a large locked suitcase which went directly to the
limousine and thence home with the Popoffs. Popoff's former
assistant, Mike Delaney, says that at those crusades:

> [Rod Sherrill] collected [the money], took it in
> the room, and counted it up . . . Peter would
> take the money home. I'd see him the following
> Monday. He'd come back and bring the suitcase
> [containing] the [checks], the donations.

The Mail Operation

According to McCorriston, the average mail income *alone* was about $1.25 million a month. But after the fateful Carson show, the two full bags of mail they received daily dropped to a quarter of a bag. Within a few months, the monthly mail income had dropped to less than $300,000, and by the time McCorriston left in the last week of October 1986, it was down to a mere $200,000.

Expenses at the Popoff organization were rather substantial. There were 50 to 60 employees, varying according to how much mail had to be opened. Payroll alone was about $80,000 a month. Then there were office expenses of some $9,000 a month. A special "house allowance" for the Popoffs to pay for maids, mortgage, and utilities amounted to $11,000 a month. A check for $16,000 was sent each month to Upland Management as rental for the 19,000 square feet of office space occupied by the Popoff mail operation. (Interestingly enough, Peter Popoff also *owned* Upland Management.) Elizabeth Popoff received a salary check separate from Peter's. According to former director Rod Sherrill, the monthly budget for TV production was $40,000, but McCorriston says that TV plus radio production and distribution ate up $200,000 to $300,000 monthly, the difference perhaps being due to travel and advertising costs. Postage alone amounted to $100,000 a month, and the special four-letter mail campaigns to bring the faithful out to the crusades in any area cost another $100,000 a month.

Peter Popoff's personal expenses included a monthly payment of $5,000 to one of L.A.'s most expensive interior decorators, to apply to his $300,000 bill for redesigning the Popoff residence. But that amount didn't come out of the Popoff pocket; the Peter Popoff Evangelical Association paid the bill every month, McCorriston says. But that's not too difficult to understand when you know who constitute the entire board of directors of the association. Let's see, we have Peter Popoff, his father, Peter George Popoff, his wife, Elizabeth Ann Popoff . . .

A neighbor of the Popoffs told me:

When they moved into the $400,000 house down
the hill we all thought he was a Cadillac dealer.
There were always three or four custom Caddies
parked outside. Then he moved up the hill to
the $800,000 home, and started building the
extension on the house and bought some more
property out the back. Then we found out who
he really was.

The Reverend and Mrs. Popoff were accustomed to living well.
They shopped on exclusive Rodeo Drive in Beverly Hills, and every
now and then they traveled by rented limousine into Los Angeles
at $145 a trip (including on-board champagne, which is what he
drinks exclusively) to enjoy a $200 dinner. Invited occasionally to
share that dinner with the Popoffs, McCorriston told me he would
sadly reflect that it was being purchased with a number of $5 and
$10 checks from older folks surviving on Social Security payments.
But the champagne *was*, after all, the very *best* that their money
could buy.

Living High on the Hog

The Popoffs were great party folks. Valet parking was supplied for
guests at the Popoff mansion. These were neighbors and other
"nonreligious" persons who lounged around the Popoffs' 12-foot-
long bar sipping $100-a-bottle champagne, according to McCor-
riston. Rod Sherrill and Volmer Thrane, two easygoing buddies of
the Popoffs, were there frequently. As controller of the Peter
Popoff Evangelical Association, McCorriston was shocked at the
way money was wasted on these affairs. "It was terrible the way
[Popoff] threw it around," he lamented.

Popoff established this lavish style early in his career. Only
six months after he started the TV operation, at Christmastime in
Atlanta, he suddenly announced one night that he was taking
everyone in sight to dinner at the Hilton. Rod Sherrill, who was
then in charge of trying to curb Popoff's spending, could only
groan at this generosity, which had been sparked by an exception-
ally dramatic sum donated at that evening's performance.

In spite of the enormous amounts of money passing through
their hands and into various accounts, most of the faith-healers
get severely into debt simply because they don't pay their bills.
Popoff was thrown out of Channel 46 in southern California,
where he did his TV editing, because he refused to pay his debts;

by the time McCorriston left the organization, Popoff owed Channel 46 more than $40,000. He also owed IBM Corporation $150,000 for the rental of $1.5 million worth of computer equipment that was used to generate his high-powered mail solicitations. His total indebtedness came to about $2 million as his empire was collapsing in October of 1986. The Popoffs have abandoned their Uplands home and are now renting in Anaheim.

Religion, Texas-style

W. V. Grant is not far behind Popoff in financial excess. In 1979 he purchased a mansion next to that of his sidekick, the Reverend Glen Cole, at 1944 Mount Vernon Drive in Fort Wright, Kentucky, right across the river from Cincinnati, Ohio. The price was $153,000. That would make it worth roughly $250,000 at today's real estate prices. The property was actually purchased by "Health and Healing, Inc.," one of Grant's many corporate names. That corporation is not registered in Kentucky. Nor are any of Grant's Cadillacs, his Mercedes-Benz, or his wife's Porsche registered in Kentucky, at least not under their names.

The Grants had their own front-row reserved seats at the exclusive Columbia Auction Gallery in Cincinnati. In 1983 Peggy Palmer, a local woman who frequented the better auctions, watched the couple spend $20,000 in one day on oriental rugs, art objects, and furniture. They outbid everyone, Palmer says. Later that same month, Peggy came upon the Grants at the Cincinnati Convention Center, where they were buying gold jewelry in large quantities. In fact, said Peggy, the Grants were conspicuous wherever they went for the amount of gold they wore. "Not your ordinary $100 gold chains," she says, "but really heavy stuff." She was "really angry" to know that poor people with $20 they could not afford to give were nonetheless dropping that money into the collection baskets at the Cathedral of Compassion and the Grants were buying luxuries with it. She notes that other bidders at the auction were whispering, "Where are these people going to put all this stuff?" The furniture alone would have filled several houses.

Revelations of a Decorator

Raul Mitchky, an interior decorator, told Camilla Warrick, the *Cincinnati Enquirer* reporter, that he had moved a bookcase in the study at the Grants' Fort Wright mansion while he was working there, and a bundle of $20,000 in $100 bills fell at his feet. At that point, he'd been working in the house for only four days and didn't know that "Dr. Grant" was the evangelist W. V. Grant. He wrote across the wrapper: "Thank God for honest paper-hangers!" and replaced the money. He described to me his impressions of the Grant house:

> There was a lot of old furniture in the house, a very lavish home with lots of antiques. . . . One time, [Shirley Grant] came in and she'd just bought a $25,000 painting, and they had antiques like you wouldn't believe and the whole house was—their *cars* were worth three times [the $24,000 a year Grant claimed was his income]. . . . I had to move 60 pairs of shoes out of *his* closet. . . . And jewelry! I've never *seen* so much jewelry. Gold! There was more on their dresser top than in a jewelry store! [About Shirley Grant]: She had more gold on her than I've ever seen on anybody in my life. And she had three closets of clothes for her fat, intermediate and skinny stages.

More Real Estate

In addition to the Fort Wright mansion, Grant maintained a penthouse apartment at 1 Lytle Place in Cincinnati, renting for $30,000 a year. Russ Grant (no relation) installed a burglar alarm system there, and estimated that they had $200,000 worth of antique furniture. Those prices are circa 1979. Mitchky was called in to do the interior work on this new residence. He told me:

> [Grant] was taking this place just to have a place to spend the weekends. There was going to be an installation of about 60 rolls of [wall]paper. They chose *really* expensive wall coverings for their homes. It could have been anywhere from eight to nine thousand dollars just for the cost of the paper. That's not including the labor. They bought all new bedroom and dining room furniture, and lots of other stuff.

High Living in Texas, Too

Recently, Grant moved the whole operation to Texas. His scale of living did not suffer from the move. The new Grant mansion outside Dallas cost $800,000, plus another $200,000 for the play area, outdoor night lighting, swimming pool, patio, and assorted electronic pinball machines, which Grant adores. One night shortly after Grant moved into the estate, during a discussion of the new stereo equipment he had just had installed, he noticed that it did not include a cassette player. He called to "Reverend" Larry King, his truck driver, and handed him a fistful of cash with instructions to go out and buy him a player, "something you think I'd like." He could easily afford it. At that point in his career, W. V. was taking in some $25,000 a crusade.

The Reverend Grant pleads for donations to keep his show, "Dawn of a New Day," on television, basing his begging on his claimed $8-million-a-year cost for air time. Between October 1985 and October 1986, he was spending $375,700 ($7,225 each week!) on one TV station alone, KHJ-TV in Los Angeles. But that was his single biggest market. It was also his most expensive by far; some small UHF stations can sell that same half-hour for as little as $500. The Los Angeles bill represented about 10 percent of his annual air time budget. Actually, the total cost was just half what he claimed, or $4 million. The week after I exposed his operation on television, RKO affiliate KHJ-TV dropped his show.

Grant does not even show up in the top ten of the 87 syndicated U.S. religious television programs listed by Arbitron, the media research group that monitors such matters. Evangelist Rex Humbard, who never had a day's schooling in theology and was simply appointed as a "reverend" by his father, was performing as a TV minister before some present incumbents were out of puberty. He claims there are some 1,100 television preachers operating today, though this estimate may be inflated and surely covers every 10-watt local station. Robert Schuller's "Hour of Power," conducted from the $15 million space-age Crystal Cathedral, commands the number-one position in that competition, spending $30 million a year on TV production costs alone and reaching 1,123,200 households.

Jim and Tammy Faye Bakker, formerly of television's "PTL Club," established in the mind of the public that money-hungry evangelists can flout every standard of moderation that has been established in civilization. The pharaohs of ancient Egypt would have envied some of their excesses. An air-conditioned doghouse, a

50-foot-long clothes closet with three cut-glass chandeliers hanging in it, and a breathtaking selection of mansions supplied by their ministry all came to light when the media finally decided that religious figures were, after all, fair game for investigation. Bakker even built himself a new studio dressing room enhanced by a sauna and an array of gold-plated fixtures. The gold plating alone cost his contributors $27,000.

A Bold Admission

Ex-convict and faith-healer Leroy Jenkins, in full makeup, stuffed into a flashy powder-blue suit and crowned with a rather bad hairpiece, was asked in June 1987 on a CNN-TV interview about the Bakkers' reported extravagance and misuse of the ministry's money. He defended them vigorously by explaining how he handles his funds:

> The contributors didn't ask where [the money] was goin'. They don't ask *me* what I'm gonna do with the money, and if they did I'd tell them, "None of your business!" I'd say, "You gave it, and that's as far as we go. God blessed you for givin' and He didn't bless you for tellin' *me* what to do with it.

At least Leroy tells it like it is: The evangelists take the money and spend it. There's lots of it, and a lot more where it came from. It's as simple as that.

It appears that the easy, foolproof way to get rich in America is to learn about twenty quotations from the Bible, dress in an expensive suit with lots of gaudy jewelry, and rent an auditorium. Tell all the lies you want. Exaggerate your history or invent it entirely. Label all your opponents as "tools of Satan." Answer any and all arguments and objections by quoting scripture. Beg for money, incessantly. Oh. I almost forgot. Ordain yourself as an Anointed Minister of God. Then watch the money roll in.

It's tax-free, and you can use it any way you want.

5

The Mail Operations of Faith-Healers

I Have a Little List

It would be well to understand something about the mailing list business. The selling of names and addresses is a well-established and legitimate pursuit. Those in the mail order, service, and specialty businesses need selected lists for their mail campaigns. From various polls, surveys, and other sources, data are gathered on every imaginable aspect of individuals. This information is then sorted and coded into various categories. Religion, race, age group, gender, income, real estate holdings, hobbies, and dozens of other variables are recorded. Customers can purchase lists limited to, for example, males owning one or more automobiles—in order to sell them specific products or services. A swimming-pool maintenance firm can limit its list to those who own pools and have a certain minimum income, factors that would make them likely to purchase that service.

Similarly, evangelists can purchase lists for their purposes (selected for income, religious affiliation, and age, particularly) and will also create their own lists as new names come to their attention through their campaigns and "crusades." In the trade, there is a sub-list known as a "Code Seven" document. It is a carefully culled selection of names and addresses of those who have given substantial amounts to religious organizations and are likely to do so again. But while the swimming-pool businessman will pay only 6 to 10 cents for each name he obtains, the evangelists will give up to $4.00 each for the coveted Code Seven items. Those names can return small fortunes to the purchaser several times a year, year after year, for only the investment of a begging letter and perhaps a cheap wooden or plastic souvenir every few months.

A list is usually sold to a mailer along with the legal, limiting provision that it can be used only a specified number of times for the price paid. Lists are protected against further use by the insertion of "marker names" that are invented by the supplier. Should the list be used improperly, mail sent to those false addresses will come to the attention of the list vendor, and action can be taken. Substantial sums have been awarded in court for improper use of these lists.

Until automated, computer-personalized mailing systems came into use, the biggest mail operation in the evangelist business was run by A. A. Allen from his Miracle Valley, Arizona, headquarters. Allen employed 175 people there, sending out as many as 55 million pieces of literature annually. That was before 1970; but when modern technology brought swift, economical, highly efficient electronics to the business of mail solicitation, the Allen effort began to pale in comparison.

The Biggest Little Mail Room in California

Evangelist Peter Popoff had four high-speed printing presses, along with binding equipment and other machinery, at his extensive headquarters in Upland, California, with which he prepared the huge mailings (100,000 pieces at a time) that he sent out in response to the nine or ten full bags of "prayer requests" that came in to his ministry every week. Says Ira McCorriston, Popoff's former controller:

> Popoff works his mailing list very well. He hits them hard—two or three letters a month—and he'll send four pieces of literature out to advertise a meeting.

At least some of those letters would contain a "gimmick" of some kind. Prayer cloths, sacred gloves, shoe liners, or gold lamé ribbons would be included, along with some esoteric instructions on how to activate the magic charm for health and/or wealth.

One of the Popoff mailings in January 1986 contained a tiny packet of pink crystals and a nickel-sized round wafer sealed in plastic wrap. The letter that came with it (addressed to one of my pseudonyms) said:

> Let me say this first, generally, all through God's Word no one received a miracle from God unless they did something that seemed unreasonable to the carnal mind . . . So, God asks you to do that which is unreasonable, which doesn't correspond to your natural reasoning. That which you'd never think of doing. . . . As a BELIEVER take the wine and bread I was led to send you . . . then take the S-P-E-C-I-A-L PRAYER slip and write on it the urgent problems you face and the needs you have today. Next . . . put this wine and bread that I have prayed over in your Bible at Matthew 26: 26-29. Then put your prayer slip inside the enclosed envelope. And be sure to include your SEED-gift for God's Word. (The Lord spoke about $177.00. Pray about this.) . . . MAIL THE ENVELOPE TO ME. Don't let doubt enter your mind. Act today! James, after this prayer blessed wine and bread have been in your Bible three days take them out in faith. . . . Eat the bread, eat the health of the body of Jesus. . . . Then pour the wine into a small amount of water and drink it. (You will actually see the water become unfermented wine; the kind Jesus used.) . . . When you place your PRAYER SLIP in the envelope, try to include the amount the Lord put on your heart for His work. IT'S YOUR MEASURE OF FAITH FOR THIS IMPORTANT TIME! . . . YOU ALREADY KNOW WHAT TO DO.

Contrast this with a rather less ambitious mailing by Oral Roberts in 1983. He sent out a few wafers to his followers, saying:

> Now, Partner, I have enclosed this packet containing the bread, the symbolic element of the body, for our Holy Communion service on May 22 at 2 p.m. CDT.

If Roberts had had the imagination, he too would have included a few crystals of *artificially cherry-flavored Kool-Aid*. Yes, that's what the "unfermented wine" was that Popoff had enclosed in *his* mailing!

In addition, before every major public meeting, Popoff would have his office employees telephone selected individuals in the geographical area of each crusade, via the mailing list, and remind them to attend. Names of those people were obtained from a computer printout of all "Code Seven" people on his mailing list. Proceeds from such a meeting—much of it in cash—could run from $10,000 to $50,000, depending on the area and the season. And because only the Popoffs ever handled or counted this money, most of it in cash, according to McCorriston, "You never really knew what went on out there in the field."

The Eagle's Nest Mail Room

One of W. V. Grant's former employees gave an impressive description of his mail operation in Cincinnati:

> [Grant's] mailing room was incredible. It looked like a post office. It had these big tables with states labeled at the head of each one, where the mail was coming in from and going out to. Most of the workers were women. . . . I never knew how to act around those people. I thought you're supposed to be nice, wear a tie, talk pretty. But you'd go back there to QC Agency and you'd never have heard such foulmouthed language. Even the women in the mail room! The way *they'd* be talking! I'd think, *these* women are working for W. V. Grant?

The Tulsa Postman's Burden

Oral Roberts sends out more than 27 million letters and publications annually. The operation is so large that his mailing room has its very own zip code, 74171. This rather makes us doubt Roberts's assurance to the faithful that he personally reads each and every letter.

As an example of the high-powered rhetoric that Roberts sends out, consider the letter in Appendix IV. The signature is in blue ink, appearing to be handwritten. There are a number of subtleties here that I should point out. This letter was not just entered into a computer to keep in touch with the faithful. It was carefully designed by a master hand, and it was guaranteed to appeal to lonely, frightened people. The elderly have always been the major targets of the evangelists, and this letter is also worded to appeal to them. Note the inference that Roberts "sat down and wrote" to the recipient, the appeal to the "pen-pal" aspect, and the strong suggestion that Roberts has read the letter that was sent by the person receiving this one. The recipient is also invited to correspond with Roberts on a personal level. This could not happen, in view of the tens of thousands of responses Roberts could expect. The letters begging for money followed soon after this one was received.

Copying a Good Idea

Reader's Digest often sends out mailings that have the familiar alternate red-and-blue diagonal stripes along the envelope edges. This is usually used to designate an airmail letter, and at one time, before U.S. mail began delivering all first-class mail by air, envelopes so marked assumed greater importance than surface-delivered mail. To many, particularly to older folks, these envelopes still stand out, and this gimmick must be effective, because it is used by prominent mailing houses.

Evangelist Rex Humbard has carried this idea a bit further. In December of 1986, those on his mailing list received a letter in the red-and-blue design with a return address that read, "Hotel Inter-Continental, Jerusalem, P.O. Box 19585, Jerusalem." The apparent cancellation in the upper right-hand corner of the envelope read, "Seasons Greetings From Jerusalem." The impression given is that this letter arrived via airmail and that it was mailed from Jerusalem.

The smallest print on the envelope, in place of the stamp, read "U.S. Postage paid. Rex Humbard Foundation." In actuality, this was a bulk-mailed piece that was sent from Akron, Ohio, though there is no way the recipient could know this without having the means to refer to the postal permit number, since there is no real cancellation used on such bulk mailings. On the face of the envelope, apparently scrawled there in blue, it says:

> Please open immediately! In this letter is a
> beautiful gift for you ... from Jerusalem. The
> land of the Bible ...

ORAL ROBERTS

December 13, 1984

Mr. James Randi
51 Lennox Ave
Rumson, NJ 07760

Dear James,

I'm so glad that you sat down and wrote to me.

Through the years I've discovered there's something very special about two people writing to each other. I've seen so often that a closer relationship can be developed—in my situation, a deeper relationship in Christ. A letter, when it reflects true feelings and needs, helps me as a minister of the Gospel to serve you better.

I have long had a ministry of answering the letters people write to me. I always pray over what is shared with me, then I write back with something good from God's Holy Word. This continues to be a blessing to many people and I hope it is a blessing to you...especially to know that I have prayed that you will be totally healed of any problem with your blood pressure.

For the next 3 months, free of charge and with no obligation, I'm sending you our monthly publication, ABUNDANT LIFE, and one issue of our quarterly daily devotional guide, DAILY BLESSING. Should you be blessed by these magazines as our regular subscribers are, let me know that you want them continued.

I guess what I am trying to say is, I really want the Lord to make me a blessing to your life. Please feel free to write me any time and let me know what you are going through. I will keep it confidential. Then I will hold your name and needs in my hands and pray and write you back. This is a vow that God has helped me keep for these many years of this ministry.

I want to be your partner.

In Jesus' Name,

Oral Roberts

P.S. I'm enclosing my little pamphlet, "If You Need To Be Healed Do These Things." May God bless it to you.

A typical Oral Roberts computerized letter.

The "beautiful gift" was a simple, cheap paper bookmark printed by "Palphot," a West German printer. The gift was not *from* Jerusalem, and it was not *made* in Jerusalem. It was the usual junk come-on. The letter included with this stunning gift appeared to be on Hotel Inter-Continental stationery. It gave, scribbled across the top apparently by hand in the same blue pen, further assurance that:

> This beautiful Bible bookmark is a Gift from
> Maude Aimee and me ... We bought this in the
> holy city of Jerusalem ... Just for you!

The letter began:

> Dear Precious Partner,
>
> Just a few hours ago I completed my special
> time of prayer at the Seven Miracle Places in
> the Land of the Bible—the Holy Land.

And further on, it said:

> Maude Aimee and I purchased for you in Jerus-
> alem—the Land of the Bible—the enclosed book-
> mark.

The letter tells the recipient that an "urgent situation" has
suddenly developed back in Akron that requires "over $135,000"
immediately. Enclosed also is an envelope that seems to have been
hand addressed (again scrawled in blue pen) as an offering envelope. A further small note repeats the plea for money, and is
written (actually printed) on what appears to be a sheet torn from
a Hotel Inter-Continental scratch pad; the words "for the convenience of our guests" appear under the hotel's logo.

There is no question about it. This mailing is false, misleading, and mendacious. It is another cheap trick designed to part
the faithful from their money.

Faulty Computer Programming

Faith-healer W. V. Grant uses the system of dropped-in names and
personalized data in his computerized letter campaigns. Each
recipient believes his letter was specifically prepared for him. But
occasionally the programmer gets careless. One such example
occurred when Grant sent out a January 29, 1978, letter that read
in part:

> The Lord spoke to me last night at 4 a.m. I
> tossed and turned all night under the Spirit.
> and suddenly just before daybreak, the Lord
> revealed to me exactly why.

At this point, Grant appealed for $21,000 to pay for "church remodeling and air conditioning." He said receiving it would constitute "a miracle." The "miracle day," he wrote, would be February 23, 1978.

An astute victim of this appeal thought there was something familiar about that wording. Looking back almost three years to April 10, 1975, she found another Grant letter *with exactly the same wording, exactly the same appeal, and exactly the same amount of money asked for*! The only difference was that this "miracle day" was designated as April 21, 1975.

The U.S. mail is being used by faith-healers—and other evangelists—in a way that I believe is inconsistent with fair, proper, and legal procedure. I don't like it one bit, and I wish something would be done about it.

6
A. A. Allen and Miracle Valley

See! Hear! Actual miracles happening before
your eyes. Cancer, tumors, goiters disappear.
Crutches, braces, wheelchairs, stretchers discarded. Crossed eyes straightened. Caught by
the camera as they occurred in the healing line
before thousands of witnesses.

So said the television ads of 1957, all over the United States, as a
paunchy, hollering faith-healer dressed in iridescent lavender and
white patent leather boots, named Asa Alonso Allen, "God's Man
of Faith and Power," the best-known of his trade in the late
1960s, swept the country with his "Great International Miracle
Revival Training Camp and Solemn Assembly." When A. A. Allen's
traveling show was in session, balls of fire were said to hover
over the tent. Flames were reported dancing in the air over the
worshipers' heads, a cross of blood would be seen materializing on
Allen's forehead, and "miraculous mystery oil" dripped from his
fingers onto the faithful.

In 1958, he founded his own community on 1,280 acres donated
to him by rancher Urbane Lienen Decker. There was a single gas
station/store, a coin laundry, and a cabinet shop. But the big
business was religion. At the entrance to Miracle Valley was a
huge sign that made it plain just what was going on in that neck
of the desert. In red and gold, it proclaimed:

A. A. ALLEN REVIVALS, INC.,
MIRACLE VALLEY,
ARIZONA.

The Blind to See.
The Deaf to Hear.
The Lame to Walk.

SIGNS. GIFTS. WONDERS.

Miracle Valley, Arizona, is at the base of the Huachuca Mountains in the southeast corner of the state. There, Allen had his own airfield, a Cessna 150 aircraft, a record company (with 47 albums going), a 3,000-seat church, and a telephone prayer center. He appeared on 58 radio stations daily, and on 43 TV stations weekly. His radio program, "The Allen Revival Hour," was heard not only in the United States and Canada, but in several other countries, including the Philippines. A clandestine radio station beamed the show straight in to London, England, from an illegal offshore transmitter in the North Sea. Some 175 people were employed to handle the mail and publishing business, and real estate was sold to converts through the Miracle Valley Estates. The ministry had an annual gross of $3.8 million, but A. A. and the associate ministers took no chances. Their cuts came right off the top of that figure—before any bills were paid, and before expenses were covered.

A Disclaimer—Just in Case

Miracle Magazine, a monthly publication with a circulation of 350,000, was produced and printed at Miracle Valley. Allen was very careful to publish a disclaimer concerning the wild claims of healing that appeared in that periodical, sent in by enthusiastic "healees." Obviously advised by lawyers, and to cover the possibility that someone might look into one of those cases, the publisher of the magazine inserted this notice:

> Utmost care has been taken to assure the accuracy of all testimonies before publication and A. A. Allen Revivals, Inc. and "Miracle Magazine" assume no legal responsibility for the veracity of any such report, nor do they accept responsibility as to the degree or perm-

anence of reported healings, deliverances or
miracles since the Bible itself declares that for
those who do not continue to live for God,
even worse things may come (John 5:14).

(Evangelist/healer W. V. Grant, perhaps at the urging of his
lawyers, fumbled his own attempt to disavow responsibility for
such claims. He inserted a similar notice in his publication, *Dawn
of a New Day*, but it was a garbled sentence that really said
nothing. It read:

All healing reproduced herein is just exactly as
reported and no liability is assumed for their
veracity.

Because the reports are made by Grant himself, one wonders who,
if anyone, has been protected by this notice. It is printed in black
on a dark blue background, sideways, in the smallest type used in
the publication.)

A Colorful Start

A. A. Allen was born in Arkansas into the Methodist church,
switched to Pentecostalism and then began his career as a minister
of the Assemblies of God in his twenties. He worked at it successfully until 1955, when he jumped bail on a drunken driving
charge in Knoxville, Tennessee, and was defrocked by the Assemblies of God. In typical fashion, he immediately re-ordained himself and started up his big moneymaker, the Miracle Revival
Fellowship. He went "under canvas" and began touring with his
big tent show.

When Allen discovered radio and television, he abandoned his
tent and switched to the electronic media. By mail, he sold "prosperity cloths," pieces of his old tent, for $100 to $1,000 donations. The idea was that all those years of high-powered preaching
had impregnated the fabric and would bring a blessing to the
owner by radiation alone.

He specialized in visions, divine voices, and prophecies. At one
point, Allen advertised a plan to raise the dead, in accordance
with biblical instructions to the apostles to do the same. The
dreadful possibility that corpses would begin stacking up at his
Miracle Valley headquarters brought him to a quick stop on that
one.

A Tough Customer

Allen, who looked a little like James Cagney, was lampooned
mercilessly by the press for his bizarre behavior. He constantly
threatened retribution from heaven against those who offered him
resistance. When one newspaper ran a series of uncomplimentary
articles about him, he warned the reporters:

> I'd hate to be in their shoes. You just don't
> fool around with a man God has anointed. He
> will get them one of these days!

Allen tried to establish for his followers that this threatened
vengeance was actually being carried out by God. Robert W.
Schambach was Allen's right-hand man at that time. He was the
one who chuckled with success when the circulation chief of the
Fresno Bee died after a sister paper, the *Sacramento Bee*, published strong criticism of Allen. He also claimed that an earlier
earthquake in Eureka, California, and a flood were the results of
Allen's dissatisfaction with that town's reception of his preaching.
Schambach eventually went out on his own; he is still active in
this field and on TV, performing his Holy Ghost Miracle Revival
tent show to crowds of thousands in the Bronx.

Allen said to the *New York Times*, as late as 1970:

> There are no evangelists left that offer us any
> competition now. We've got the field. Back in
> the late '40s and '50s, Jack Coe, Oral Roberts,
> O. L. Jaggers and 200 others you know, there
> were 200 evangelists all praying for the sick,
> having healing revivals. Now they're nonexis-
> tent.

Well, he was dead wrong about Oral Roberts. That preacher is still
very much with us, demonstrating that he has the greatest endurance in the business.

The *New York Times* described the Allen performance as

> a combination of the traditional fire and brim-
> stone, organ-thumping, evangelical style, and a
> sophisticated awareness of the power of radio
> and television to carry the message from be-
> yond.

The Evidence for Healing

Though he was able to produce the usual mass of anecdotal material to try to prove his healing ministry, A. A. Allen proved only that he was operating on the same principles as all the rest. He crowed about 60-year-old Tom Jennings, a man in a wheelchair with a blanket over his legs, who Allen said had cancer that gave him "only six weeks to live." Allen said Jennings had the "cancer demon" and promptly cast it out, then told Jennings to wheel him (Allen) down the aisle. The crowd cheered Jesus for yet another miracle. But Jennings had never been told that he had only six weeks to live, wrote reporters from *Look* magazine in a 1969 article. And Allen himself had seated Jennings in that wheelchair and supplied the blanket. Jennings not only was able to walk, but had years ahead of him. As *Look* said, Allen's greatest miracle seemed to be separating bills from billfolds.

He was very good at that. In his heyday, he claimed he sent out 55 million copies of his publications from his mail room every year. He sold water from his Pool of Bethesda in Miracle Valley to customers all over the world. Said Allen of this commodity, "People are being healed instantly while they sip it as an act of faith."

Containers of plain old dirt from the valley were also sold, though no instructions went along with them.

The reverend displayed demons in glass mason jars, sealed up safely and looking very, very dead. Allen told the faithful that though those preserved specimens might look to some insensitive, unbelieving folks like ordinary toads, snakes, and spiders, they were actually disease demons. The faithful believed and marveled.

But not all were enchanted by Allen's Ozark baritone and pickled devils. A physician from the nearby town of Sierra Vista, Dr. Kenneth A. Dregseth, told an interviewer:

> I have seen no miracles. In fact, I've had to run diabetics to the hospital when they've stopped taking their insulin, believing they had been cured in Miracle Valley.

The Dream Ends

On June 14, 1970, listeners in the United States, the United Kingdom, and the Philippines were hearing a recorded message from A. A. Allen on his radio program saying:

> This is Brother Allen in person. Numbers of
> friends of mine have been inquiring about
> reports they have heard concerning me that are
> not true. People as well as some preachers from
> pulpits are announcing that I am dead. Do I
> sound like a dead man? My friends, I am not
> even sick! Only a moment ago I made reserva-
> tions to fly into our current campaign. I'll see
> you there and make the devil a liar.

At that moment, at the Jack Tar Hotel in San Francisco, police
were removing A. A. Allen's body from a room strewn with pills
and empty liquor bottles. The man who had once said that "the
beer bottle and gin bucket" should have been on his family coat
of arms was dead at 59 from what was said to be a heart attack
but was in reality liver failure brought on by acute alcoholism.

The King Is Dead

During the scramble to fill Allen's position, Miracle Valley went
through a series of owners, none of them having his organizational
genius. In 1975, more than 32,000 letters a month were still coming in when one of Allen's acolytes, Don Stewart, a former Bible
student from Clarkdale, Arizona, began running the operation.
Stewart eventually established his own following in Phoenix, and is
currently accused of arson and embezzlement by his church.

Things came to a close in Miracle Valley amid bankruptcy
proceedings in 1979, shortly after the all-black Christ Miracle
Healing Center & Church was founded there by the Reverend
Frances Thomas. The parishioners were blacks who went there—
mainly from Chicago and parts of Mississippi—"because God told
them to." There had been immediate conflict with white residents
and older residents of the area, who by now wanted to put such
phenomena as A. A. Allen behind them. Riots, bombings, and
murders followed the deaths of five church members. This was
characterized by Reverend Thomas as "God's will." Authorities
found it more difficult to believe that the agonizing death of 6-
year-old Therial Davis from a strangulated hernia was also "God's
will." Neighbors had heard the child's screams for three days
before the child finally succumbed, but they did nothing to inter-
fere with the parents' constitutional right to refuse medical assistance and wait for divine intervention. The spirit, if not the body,
of A. A. Allen was still alive in Miracle Valley.

7
Leroy Jenkins and the $100,000 Challenge

Leroy Jenkins is currently making a comeback in the evangelist business after undergoing rather serious reversals. As recently as June 1987, he was announcing plans to buy the $900,000 Coliseum in St. Petersburg, Florida. He had just held a huge crusade there. The *St. Petersburg Times* reported that he

> moved his audience to tears, to dancing, to shouting and to the front of the room. It was at the front of the Coliseum Ballroom where he accepted their money and laid his hands on each one.

But a security guard at the Coliseum was not deceived. Said he: "I think it's all bull. I think he's a con man."

Others who chose to believe in the colorful preacher were not at all fazed when the next day it was reported that he had been robbed of $900 in pocket cash and a $4,000 wristwatch. No one questioned why a preacher was walking about with that kind of valuable merchandise and "mad money."

A former antique salesman, Reverend Leroy Jenkins claims that he originally was converted to religion when he came to believe that he had been healed of a wound on his arm by none other than A. A. Allen. Thus discovering the faith-healing business, Leroy immediately lost all interest in the antique trade and took up the much more lucrative calling.

The Reverend Jenkins is not known to use any very fancy techniques to perform his act. As with the early tent-show performers, he appears to rely upon spotting symptoms in those he approaches, giving them general guesses, and putting words in their mouths. He is one of the old-timers in the healing business, and along with Ernest Angley has served two generations of cartoonists as a model for their southern Bible-thumper characters.

A Fortuitous Encounter

In 1960, Jenkins met a widow, Maudie Bartz, at one of his tent meetings in Dallas, Texas. The two "discovered" that Maudie was Leroy's long-lost mother, and she agreed to finance Leroy's ministry. Later, Maudie officially adopted Jenkins, his wife, and their four children. Leroy thus became her son, and stood to inherit her estate. The reverend's name was officially changed to Leroy Jenkins Bartz on March 14, 1961. Leroy used the new name for a while, but dropped the "Bartz" part when he and the family suddenly packed up and left Texas for California, without notifying Maudie Bartz. She philosophized to Anderson, S.C., *Independent* reporters:

> He just figured he'd milked this ol' cow dry
> and was goin' on.

Maudie Bartz was rich, widowed, and 99 years of age. She never saw Jenkins again.

Trouble in Paradise and a Touching Defense

Before long, Jenkins was screeching scripture at a huge audience from a Delaware, Ohio, church pulpit (he called it the Church of What's Happening Now) and via a radio and television ministry. In the 1960s, he attracted to his platform a number of celebrities, including Mae West.

In 1972, the *Columbus Dispatch* reported that Jenkins had been arrested on a drunk charge. Scores of vituperative letters followed that article, and the *Dispatch* published half a page of them. In order that we may more accurately assess the mentality of at least some of Jenkins's followers, here is an (almost) complete letter from Howard F. Davis of Newport, Kentucky. We are not privileged to know what words went into the blank spaces:

It's polite to start a letter, "Dear Editor." — —
— — to you, and or all of your writers, and the
whole paper.

This also goes for the dirty, rotten,
worthless police you back up in your dirty
town. It is a shame, a dirty shame, that all you
people that accuse brother Leroy Jenkins of
such a thing, are dirty — — — — . That's right
brother, dirty — — — — , to try to put a man of
God down. You will all join the devil in hell,
forever.

I'll tell you something, you and whoever
they are went just a little too far this time.
You can fight people, all you want to, you can
fight this and that, but brother you can't fight
God.

If any of you — — — — die tonight, you
will go straight to hell, (forever) and ever, and
ever, you know? That's a long time, because
you don't have a father in heaven so that
makes you — — — — .

Each and everyone of you will pay for
what you done to Leroy Jenkins.

It's too late to cover the damage done,
but it's not too late to save your sole [*sic*]. We
won't stop now, untill [*sic*] the lid is blown off
the dirty police dept., the mayor and whoever
is involved, because you have opened the hor-
net's nest, and all the hornets were in church
Sunday and got there [*sic*] stinger [*sic*] sharp-
ened and filled with toxin, with the exception
of five of your — — — — seated in church.

May God have mercy on your soles [*sic*].

The writer seems to have a fixation on the word "dirty," and
one can only hope that he does not represent the gentle, kind,
and forgiving Christian that we have been led to expect.

Suspicious Signs and Wonders

Jenkins's operation at Holy Hill Cathedral was hit on April 8,
1978, by a suspicious event—a dynamite blast—that did minor damage. Strangely enough, Jenkins had taken out a $1.2 million insur-

ance policy on the building one week before the explosion. In addition, only a few days before the blast, most of the contents of the cathedral had been removed. Tongues wagged.

Three weeks after the dynamite blast, a fire destroyed Jenkins's home. It was insured.

It was disclosed that just six days before the Reverend Jenkins went on television to appeal to his viewers for $300,000 to save his ministry, he had closed a deal on a new $230,000 home in an exclusive neighborhood in Greenwood, South Carolina. Tongues resumed wagging.

The ministry's official journal, *Revival in America*, claimed endorsements from all sorts of famous persons. Among those named were Liberace and President Jimmy Carter. Asked by reporters from the Anderson, S.C., *Independent* about the matter, both celebrities denied any connection with, or endorsement of, Jenkins. It seemed that Reverend Jenkins had been using his imagination liberally. More tongues went into motion.

A Man with a Lot of Enemies

The federal Bureau of Alcohol, Tobacco and Firearms began looking into these strange events. From what he believed was the inviolable safety of his pulpit, Leroy Jenkins attacked that agency, and threw in the FBI, local police, and the IRS as fellow villains:

> Most of them are as crooked as they can be.
> They're a bunch of liars and thieves. . . .
> There's not a law or a government or the FBI
> or anybody else that could take away from me
> what God gave me 21 years ago. When Jesus
> Christ hanged down from the cross at 33 years
> of age, people didn't lose their faith and res-
> pect for him. The government is what killed
> him, the same thing they're trying to do to me,
> the same thing they would try to do to you.
> You give them hillbillies a badge, honey, and a
> gun and it's dangerous; I'm scared to go out on
> the street. They don't have as much education
> as I do. Those little hillbillies will shoot you.
> . . . [The IRS] is very jealous of what I have.

Jenkins was fearless but unwise in his choice of targets when he attacked sin and the devil. As with all those who claim to speak with God's voice, he had no notion that he could be prosecuted or persecuted for his activities. As in the example given above, he managed to alienate every local and state official within reach, castigating them from his electronic pulpit for real and/or imaginary transgressions. It was a situation that could not long go unanswered by those he attacked.

It seems not unlikely that his claims of resulting harassment may have been quite true; his church was subjected to endless building inspections and repeated permit checking, and he suffered other aggravations. In 1977, probably to escape the immediate wrath of the authorities, he began moving the whole operation from Delaware, Ohio, to his childhood home of Greenwood, South Carolina, changing its name to the Spirit of Truth Church. The dynamite blast in the old church in Delaware occurred shortly after that.

At this point, the Jenkins ministry had become a multimillion-dollar operation, and it was growing daily. Jenkins was at the height of his power, and it seemed that nothing could stop him.

The Preacher in Prison

In April of 1979, Jenkins was arrested again. Though he had assured his congregation that he would not be convicted, he was, on two counts of conspiracy to commit arson, and one of assault, for attempting to have reporter Rick Ricks of the Anderson, S.C., *Independent* beaten up for certain comments he had made in that paper. It was revealed in court that Jenkins had hired two men to torch the home of a state trooper who had given Jenkins's daughter a traffic ticket. That home, and another in Anderson, were burned to the ground by two men Jenkins had hired.

Local rumor—and Jenkins endorsed the rumor—had it that the trooper also had taken advantage of Jenkins's daughter, but this was never brought out in the trial. If it did indeed occur—and Jenkins has been known to make statements and accusations that are not exactly true—Jenkins's offenses might be more easily understood. In his world, personal, direct vengeance is often preferred over legal procedure.

Jenkins began serving a 12-year prison term back in Delaware, Ohio. Behind bars, he managed to keep his evangelical operation alive, though only on a bare survival scale. But he continued to run afoul of regulations that lesser mortals may not ignore. In September of 1980, when two bottles of contraband Scotch whiskey were discovered in a room for which he carried the key,

Jenkins lost the valued "trusty" status he had until then enjoyed, and went into the regular lockup awaiting transfer to another, more secure institution.

Evidence of the vendetta against him by the authorities continued to surface. Though it would not have been unusual for the authorities to have granted him parole when he asked for it at several points early in his prison stay, it was repeatedly denied until June 1985.

However, Jenkins had already been freed on work release in December 1982. Though this was far short of a real parole, and he was severely limited in his travels and activities, it meant that he was able to get the ministry rolling again. One of his first actions was to sue television producer Jimmy Rea, Jr., proprietor of JR Productions. Rea had prepared Jenkins's broadcast films and tapes until the sudden demise of all the Jenkins shows in 1979 when the preacher went into prison. There was a feud over some $200,000 worth of electronic equipment used to produce the Jenkins show. Countersuits flew about wildly; theft and bad debts were claimed by both sides. But Jenkins's big problem wasn't the money involved in the lawsuits; he was more concerned with Rea's demand that he reveal in court how much money was being raised through solicitations by the Jenkins broadcast operation. To Jenkins's relief, that figure was never disclosed, and the case was settled out of court.

Enter a New Character, the Reverend Peter Popoff

Another comic episode in the Jenkins soap opera came to light in 1984, when he disclosed that some unnamed person had illegally sold his very valuable mailing list of potential donors to a rival, California-based evangelist Peter Popoff. Jenkins went to court over this matter too, and the National Graphics Corporation, which did Jenkins's mailings, was named as a co-defendant in the action. His Columbus attorney, Henry Eckhart, managed to have the court order Popoff to surrender the list and to immediately stop using it to solicit contributions. But, said Eckhart, the name of the mystery individual within the Jenkins organization who actually sold the list to Popoff would be disclosed only on order of the court.

Jenkins's reluctance to have that name known is quite understandable. While Daddy was in the slammer, his son, Danny, had been running his operation for him. And *he* was the one who had copied and sold the list to Peter Popoff through All-American Video television director Rod Sherrill. Danny and Rod were almost brothers. They had been raised together, Rod being an adopted son of Leroy. In fact, they had started up QC Video—W. V. Grant's operation—together. QC at one time was taping shows for as many as 20 different evangelists.

Popoff had paid Danny $25,000 for this list of 15,000 to 20,000 names, all of them "Code Seven" items. He told the court that he hadn't even recovered the cost of the list by using it. But his former controller, Ira McCorriston, described Popoff's income from use of the list as "unbelievable." It was $1.2 million to $1.4 million.

Caught in the Act

Of course the mailing list Popoff purchased from Danny Jenkins contained "marker names" (see Chapter 5) to ensure that only limited use was made of it. Soon after the Popoff court case, those marker names showed up, and Jenkins was alerted to the fact that his list was being used illegally by Popoff. Under the persistent delusion that he could not be touched by the law and was free to flout any court order, Popoff had continued to use the list despite the court injunction not to do so. Warned by his business manager, he said: "They'll never know, and besides, no one cares." However, in a feeble attempt to escape detection, he left out all the Ohio addresses when he used it, because Jenkins made his headquarters in that state.

Popoff's purchase of the list from Danny Jenkins was legal, but his continued use of it after the court injunction was illegal. In January 1987, after protracted legal procedures, the court finally ordered Popoff to pay $100,000 to the Jenkins ministry as a penalty.

Back in the Saddle Again

Meanwhile, Jenkins was still trying to rebuild his ministry after his prison stay. He taped shows before as few as 20 or 30 persons because he was unable to attract more. But his ingenuity came through for him. He instructed All-American Video director/editor Rod Sherrill, who had worked with him long before Leroy went to prison, to look back in their archives and come up with some old tapes showing large audiences. Sherrill then edited them into the new Jenkins shows to produce the illusion that he had appeared before packed houses. The result of this electronic manipulation was a series of heavily faked—but very effective—videotapes.

(Sherrill seems to have been very inventive on behalf of all his employers. The "enhanced audience" technique was only one example of his creative editing. On another occasion, for example, cameraman Gary Clarke, who first met Sherrill when they both worked for All-American Video, recalls an event at the studio in Columbus, Ohio, when Rod was editing a singularly dull section of videotape made during a W. V. Grant meeting. He came upon a shot of a woman expressing obvious disbelief in something Grant had just said or done. She was seen rolling her eyes upwards—as if to say, according to Clarke, "Come on, nobody would buy *that!*" Sherrill edited the shot into one in which Grant was tossing a broken cane up onto the stage, and it appeared that the woman's eyes were following the cane as it sailed through the air. "Rod was real proud of that one," Clarke reported, "and he showed it to everyone.")

Making good use of his jail experience, on one of the new (post-prison) batch of TV shows Jenkins told his audience that he had recently spent some time among "rapists, murderers, and kidnappers," according to Clarke. Jenkins didn't trouble the viewers with the information that he had been among those people as a convicted felon. He boasted that he had taught the miscreants how to make "real leather wallets," and that they had fashioned 5,000 of them "with scriptures engraved in gold." But unfortunately, he reported, these wallets had been lost somewhere, and it took a direct revelation from God to Jenkins to find them. Now that they were available again, Jenkins said, he wanted to send these wallets as gifts to the first 5,000 lucky applicants, and he would put a real $1 bill into each wallet "so that you'll never be without money again."

Forty-five minutes of videotape later, Clarke said, Jenkins threw in the harpoon. One of these lovely handmade wallets was to be "given" to each person who sent in a "love offering" of $100 so that the viewer could share the good fortune of "a woman in Atlanta" who, viewers were told, had gotten fabulously rich by accepting such a wallet from Jenkins. He sold them all.

As I did with all the healers I examine in this book, I challenged Leroy Jenkins to produce evidence of *one* healing he'd produced. On his TV show, and in newspaper advertisements, he had demanded that I attend his services and see his "calling out" performed without any tricks being used. On August 16, 1986, he published in the *Columbus Dispatch* a display ad featuring a vintage portrait of himself:

$100,000 CHALLENGE
I WELCOME THE "AMAZING RANDY" OR ANYONE ELSE
TO PROVE THAT I AM A PHONY
I BELIEVE THAT YOU OWE IT TO YOURSELF
TO COME AND SEE FOR YOURSELF!!
DON'T MISS THIS GREAT CRUSADE AT VET'S MEMORIAL
AUGUST 17, at 2:30 SUNDAY AFTERNOON
300 W. BROAD ST., COLUMBUS, OHIO
HUNDREDS WILL BE SAVED, HEALED, AND DELIVERED FROM DRUGS
THROUGH THE DIVINE POWER OF GOD!!
NEWSPAPERS CARRIED STORIES THAT
MY CHURCH WAS BOMBED AND BURNED TO THE GROUND
IF ANYONE CAN PROVE THAT THERE WAS EVER A FIRE
OF ANY KIND IN MY CHURCH
I WILL GIVE THEM $100,000
WATCH LEROY JENKINS CRUSADE
EACH SUNDAY AT 7 A.M. CH. 10

Well, as is usual with most of these challengers, Jenkins got it backwards. It's *my* challenge to *him* to prove that he is genuine. I'm not saying, nor have I ever said, that he is "a phony." I'm only saying that he has not proved that he's for real. I have nothing to prove. He has.

Several letters went out from my office offering to meet Jenkins to establish his validity. There was no reply until October 1986, when he wrote:

> I am not going to participate in any of your publicity stunts. You are obviously an atheist who is attempting to obtain publicity for your forthcoming book and I have no intention of helping you do so.

Was I surprised at this response? Not at all. One becomes accustomed to "Through the Looking Glass" kind of thinking while involved in these investigations. But when I read this reply to Dennis Jenkins, another of Leroy's sons, he assured me that his father would actually welcome being tested. I never heard from either of them again.

As I write this, Leroy Jenkins is busy defending the two top bananas of the Jim and Tammy Faye Bakker vaudeville show and simultaneously bad-mouthing Jerry Falwell, who took over the PTL ministry when the Bakkers' scandals hit the limelight. Jenkins likens the charges against the Bakkers to those against him. In a CNN-TV interview he said:

> [I was charged with] conspiracy to beat up a reporter, conspiracy to burn down a highway patrolman's house. And that's what the conspiracy was. Nothing to it whatsoever, and uh . . . it was a frame job, just like with the Bakkers. . . . The million, two hundred thousand people that I have on my mailing list that follow me believe also the same as I do.

My! How that little mailing list has grown!

A Simple Act to Follow

It seems that Jenkins is an excellent "cold reader." It also appears, from what little information I have been able to gather, that he uses no mnemonic system or other more technical means for his "calling out," though he undoubtedly makes use of any information that may come his way, whether by design or by chance. Many ailing people can be diagnosed even by an amateur, by watching their gait, their complexion, or their expressions. If Jenkins were obtaining names and addresses as well, without any data-gathering, I'd have to award him my prize. But I may never have that opportunity. As of this writing, he is still trying to collect from Peter Popoff the court settlement granted him, plus another $200,000 penalty. And, says Henry Eckhart, Jenkins's lawyer, Popoff still owes his Ohio lawyers their fees for defending him, and Danny Jenkins has left his father's ministry.

With all of his ingenuity, charisma, and showmanship, Leroy Jenkins is just another of the bombastic actors in the sad charade that passes before us. Lots of faith—from the victims—but no evidence whatsoever that he produces any healing.

8
W. V. Grant and the Eagle's Nest

Joseph Barnhart, professor of philosophy at North Texas State University, was one of those who gave me valuable assistance in my investigation of faith-healer W. V. Grant. As a result of his observations of this ministry and Grant's techniques, Barnhart suggested a scenario that I have come to accept—though with some difficulty—because it satisfies all the evidence and it has been confirmed by my subsequent investigations. He contends that the faith-healing service functions as a significant drama for those who attend. This explains their willingness to believe what others see as obvious delusions. He says that we cannot divide the participants into "audience" and "performers." The entire auditorium becomes a huge stage, with both the preachers and the believers taking part in the drama. A careful observer notices that almost everything in the drama leads up to the climax, the long-anticipated healing scene. It is a ritual of major magical importance to the participants.

Barnhart points out that the afflicted person *wants to get close to this magic*. By pretending—earnestly—and by refusing to entertain any doubt, on his or her part or on behalf of another, the subject maintains and reinforces the myth that *all of the actors* have agreed to believe in, for their own reasons. The faith-healing service is a sort of mutually accepted morality play that is participated in without doubt or hesitation, for fear of breaking the spell.

The Big Operator from Big D

Walter Vinson Grant is a tubby, 40-year-old faith-healer now based in Dallas, Texas, at a quite modest (500-seat) "cathedral" he calls the Eagle's Nest. He inherited his anointment from his father, a butcher turned tent-show preacher who was said to be very much against faith-healing. Grant Sr. wrote booklets full of trashy, juvenile, bigoted pseudo-religious pap that his son is still selling as if they were his own creations. The books rave about UFOs, demon possession, and psychic powers, predicting that men will never land on the moon because Lucifer and his devils live there. Winning titles among the 60 available (at 50 cents each) are *The Great Dictator—The Man Whose Number Is 666, I Was a Cannibal, Men in the Flying Saucers Identified, Faith for Finance,* and *Freedom from Evil Spirits.*

Grant dresses in expensive and well-tailored business suits set off by monogrammed shirts and elegant jewelry. As he performs on stage, equipped with a stammer that he seems unable to cure (though he claimed to have "healed" it 20 years ago), he looks like prosperity personified. He must have a highly elastic wardrobe, as his girth oscillates grandly between visits to a North Carolina fat farm and a spa near San Diego. It was at this spa that Grant says he was approached by—of all things—a young deer that uttered words of prophecy to him, sort of a Delphic Bambi. Grant wanted to announce this on his TV show, but director Rod Sherrill says he talked him out of it.

Grant runs his mail-order business from a post office box, selling a book titled *God's Answers for You* ("made to sell for $30" but available for $15, "gold gilted [sic] edges" and all), tape cassettes of sermons, Bibles ("half-price this month"), record albums, and eight-tracks. Also available is a Bible course ($64), which offers the subscriber a purple and gold diploma as a real "Reverend" with an "honorary Doctor's Degree" and a "license to preach" after certain "true-and-false [sic]" questions have been answered. Grant offers to take $2.00 off the price for anyone who gives him the "name of someone who wants this course."

Until recently, a popular item in his catalog was the "Jesus 8 Personalized Health Club Kit," said to be a mixture of herbs, vitamins, and "7 Magic Minerals of Youth." The accompanying literature promised to cure AIDS, among other problems.

Grant Jr.'s history is uncertain at best. Consider what Grant Sr. wrote about his son's early history and what the son recalls of his own youth. The father claimed that during one football game,

Grant "was knocked unconscious that night. He played for half the game while he was unconscious, scoring three touchdowns."

Well, I hardly think that myth needs to be debunked. We are accustomed to impossible claims from the Grants. Suffice it to say that the school young Grant attended was W. B. Adamson High School in Dallas, and those three touchdowns don't show up in the record books there. Grant Jr. tells reporters that he "led the state of Texas in scoring as a halfback . . . and I had 77 full NCAA football scholarship offers." He says that he scored an average of 22 points a game while at Adamson. These stories are firmly denied by the recollections of Adamson's former coach, James Batchelor, who now works with the Dallas Cowboys football team.

He recalls Grant well. "He was not the kind that would get 77 scholarships," Batchelor says. The fact is that W. V. Grant did not receive offers from even *one* school, let alone 77. And no football player in the history of that school has had the record Grant invented for himself. Batchelor says Grant's claims are "just not true," and he regrets having to blow the whistle on him.

Even Grant's college degree is phony. He claims that he obtained it from "Midstates Bible College" in Des Moines, Iowa, in 1972. He displays the diploma on his office wall. But Midstates wasn't then and isn't now registered with the Iowa Department of Public Instruction, as all parochial and public schools are required to be. It wasn't recorded with the secretary of state's office in Iowa as a corporation; nor was it listed in the county recorder's office. It didn't even show up in the telephone directory!

Diversity of Operations

Looking through the various publications put out by W. V. Grant and seeing the many mailing addresses he uses and lists in his television show credits, I noticed their variety and geographical separation. There is a mailing address at a post office box in Cincinnati. Then there are mailing addresses for W. V. Grant located in Dallas, Texas, both at a post office box and on Grant Street. His Bible course is attributed to five different sources: 21st Century Christ Ministry, Kingsway Bible College, International Deliverance Churches, TVD Bible College, and Faith Clinic Bible Correspondence Course. His television show is prepared and distributed by one or more of these entities: All-American Video, QC Advertising, QCM, QCI, QC Inc., and QC Video.

These are organizations listed for Grant:

> Eagle's Nest Cathedral
> Soul's Harbor Church
> World Headquarters
> Grant's Faith Clinic
> Faith Clinic School
> The Cathedral of Compassion (in Cincinnati)
> W. V. Grant, Jr., Evangelical Association
> Health & Healing, Inc.
> Voice of Healing
> Voice of Deliverance

Evidently deciding that consolidation of these enterprises would be a wise move, the reverend announced that as of January 1, 1986, all of them would be receiving mail (and offerings) at a single Dallas address, known officially as the Eagle's Nest Cathedral. One might wonder where Grant gets his imagery for this new name for his church, though the heights of Berchtesgaden spring to mind. At his services, he pushes the "eagle" theme strongly. In the process, he mangles zoology by preaching that "Eagles are part of the Dove family, while Ravens are of the Buzzard family." He further reinforces mythology for his flock by declaring that eagles are known to carry off sheep and goats weighing over 200 pounds at speeds of 200 miles per hour, and he encourages his followers to "be part of the Eagle family, not the Buzzards." As he frequently does, W. V. Grant tends to lose me somewhere about halfway into such a discourse.

The Elusive Truth

This Man of God, in common with his colleagues, tends to exaggerate somewhat, making statements that the most cursory examination will prove impossible, or at least very highly unlikely. For example, he claims that he flies 400,000 miles a year fulfilling his ministry, so a lot of his time must be spent close to heaven. A rough calculation, allowing for the fastest jet speeds, reveals that W. V. Grant claims he spends more than one month every year—24 hours each day of that month!—aloft in an airplane. Were he to fly a maximum of eight hours a day, he'd be flying a full three months a year! His claim of flying the equivalent of 160 coast-to-coast trips per year, while officiating every Sunday at the Eagle's Nest, should be hard for even the most devoted believer to accept.

The faithful who hear him deliver his message every Sunday apparently never trouble to even wonder about such fanciful figures.

It would be difficult to imagine how the Reverend Grant can explain the rather large discrepancies between his TV coverage claims and the facts as recorded by Arbitron, the New York-based company which since 1949 has been the nation's leading broadcast audience measurement organization. Its latest in-depth survey of the religious TV programs shows that in yet another respect Grant has not given us the right figures. He claimed in 1985 to appear on "more than 300" TV stations. Grant says he was seen at that time in more homes than Oral Roberts; the Arbitron report says that Grant covered 198,000 households, while Roberts appeared in 1,046,000, and Roberts was actually seen on 201 TV stations compared with Grant's 93.

Miracle Time

Grant holds what he describes as "two great miracle services" at the Eagle's Nest Cathedral every Sunday. He claims he has to spend more than $8 million annually for the TV time alone for his show "Dawn of a New Day." At his revival meetings, as he tours the United States from coast to coast, miracles seem to fall from his fingertips. He apparently fills dental cavities, straightens limbs, adds vertebrae to ailing backs, and cures tumors, deafness, blindness, digestive problems, "broken hearts," otherwise-damaged hearts, diabetes, paralysis, fractured bones, arthritis, gallbladder conditions, high blood pressure, colitis, obesity, bone spurs, kidney problems, and almost any other disease our species is heir to—all by mumbling some magical syllables ("speaking in tongues"), touching the sufferers, and grinding his teeth.

It seems he also reverses hysterectomies. Declared one woman:

> When they opened me up, they found all my ovaries and tubes were back and they just couldn't understand it!

In another case, an afflicted woman had her leg and foot problems remedied by the Reverend Grant. Her testimony revealed,

> I couldn't wear high-healed [sic] shoes for 13-15 years. I praise the Lord that I can now.

Is there no end to this man's good works as he solves such a heart-rending fashion problem?

At every revival meeting that Grant holds, people are commanded to get up out of their wheelchairs and run, not walk, up the aisle and back. Canes and walkers taken from cripples are dramatically broken and thrown up onto the stage while those who held them moments before trot about in ecstasy. It seems that the deaf hear, the blind see, tumors vanish, and bacteria are slain at a wave of his hand.

From the point of view of showmanship, Grant's act on stage is exceedingly dull and repetitious, so much so that he is known to play with his victims' hats and ties, according to his one-time director Rod Sherrill,. simply because he, too, is bored by it all. His performance is rather colorless when compared to that of another healer/evangelist, David Paul, who sweats, postures, bellows, and shrieks while performing some remarkable acrobatics. But at least Grant's method of "calling out" (see Chapter 2) requires a certain amount of skill.

How Blind Is "Blind"?

Faith-healers get great mileage out of appearing to heal the blind. But remember what "blind" really means. The dictionary says it means "unable to see," but the law has established a definition that enables a person who is able to see poorly to adopt the designation legally. Faith-healers are often deceptive—perhaps innocently—when using the term. The Center for the Partially Sighted, in Santa Monica, California, says that 94 percent of "visually impaired" persons and 75 percent of those termed "legally blind" have usable though limited vision. Certainly most of these can see the number of fingers held up before them, and many can see well enough to read, though with great difficulty. Thus, when a faith-healer holds up a number of fingers in front of a person "healed" of blindness, it is usually not difficult for the person to say how many fingers are being displayed. The audience is encouraged to believe that the "blind" individual was not previously able to perform this simple determination.

Grant is fond of that demonstration, and he has another trick he uses when confronted with a "blind" subject who can see well enough to find a seat in the auditorium. While walking about during his performance, he uses a cordless radio microphone. It broadcasts to the amplifying system. If he holds it to his own lips or to the lips of a subject, *only* his or that person's voice can be heard over the system and will be recorded on the videotape. But that person can hear Grant clearly if he speaks without the microphone. This gives rise to a trick he uses to be *sure* of the results. It consists of Grant asking the subject to tell him how many fingers he is holding up, then placing the microphone before the subject's mouth and *at the same time saying the required number out loud*, which the subject merely *repeats!*

Joseph Barnhart and I saw this trick used right beside us when we attended a Grant meeting in St. Louis, Missouri, on November 4, 1985. We were accompanied by members of the Rationalist Association, in St. Louis, who readily agreed to assist in the project by passing out 2,000 leaflets requesting people to contact us through the Rationalist Association *if they had actually been healed*. No reply—not one—was ever received.

A Careful Observer

In the "mentalist" trade, it is important for the performer to be observant at all times. A quick glance at any printed matter of any kind can provide prime material for the act. On one of Grant's programs, I spotted a very clever use of this resource. A man wearing a white shirt stood beside the healer. Grant told him that he was "smoking too much." The man agreed. Grant said that he had an impression of the letters "P" and "M." The man answered that he smoked Pall Mall cigarettes. Quickly Grant asked: "Where are they? Are they in your car or in your back pocket?" The man reached for his breast pocket and pulled out a pack of Pall Malls, which Grant crushed and threw away, to the cheers of the audience.

Close observation of the videotape of that show reveals that the Pall Mall package was visible through the white fabric of the man's pocket. Grant had spotted this and used the information to his advantage.

The Wheelchair Trick

One of Grant's most impressive gimmicks is to "heal" someone in a wheelchair and then have him jump out of that chair and push Grant down the aisle in it. It is an attraction that he is very proud of, and one that he advertises prominently. I have heard Grant begin a meeting by telling his audience how many people "jumped out of wheelchairs" at his last meeting, only to give a different number half an hour later when he repeated the claim.

Many of these people end up pushing Grant himself up the aisle in the very same wheelchair they've just abandoned. That's a real crowd-pleaser, and never fails to bring cheers.

(This stunt appears to have been invented for the trade by Kathryn Kuhlman, a healer/evangelist discussed in Chapter 14.)

When I looked into this trick, I was immediately struck by two facts: First, disabled persons who spend much of their lives in a wheelchair naturally equip it for their specific needs, and Grant *never* summoned from a wheelchair any person who had personalized the device. Second, almost all of those who rose up "healed" did so from one color, model, and make of wheelchair; even Grant's slick, expensive four-color magazine, *Dawn of a New Day*, showed those same wheelchairs in the illustrations, every issue.

I'd already solved the wheelchair gimmick when Professor Barnhart and I interviewed an elderly man who declared he'd been healed by Grant of cancer earlier that day. He'd been told by the evangelist, "Get up out of that wheelchair and walk!" and he'd done so, vigorously. Questioning revealed that his cancer was no impediment to his walking ability. In fact, we interviewed him at his home, where he lived in a fourth-floor walk-up whose stairs he had to negotiate several times a day! Why had he been in the wheelchair? Because, he said, his pastor had told him to sit in it when he arrived at the auditorium. The chair was supplied by an usher. He'd never been in a wheelchair before in his life.

Replying in his periodical to the exposé of his wheelchair trick, W. V. Grant said:

> [Secular humanists] said we carried 30 empty
> wheelchairs on our revival trucks and stuck
> people in them—then later in the service pre-
> tended that they were crippled and had them
> get up and walk.

Yes, that is precisely what was said. For once, Grant has his facts right. And it is 100 percent true. But note that *Grant does not deny that this statement is true!* By quoting it in this fashion, he allows readers to assume that he is denying the accusation.

I will not deal with the rest of the nonsense in that periodical, other than to say that it shows a drawing of a magician with the number "666" on his forehead, pulling a rabbit from a hat. This pathetic attempt to obfuscate the findings of this investigation suggests that Grant was desperate. His audience for such juvenile mud-slinging apparently accepts this sort of material.

And every spirit that confesseth not that Jesus Christ is come in the flesh is not of God: and this is that spirit of antichrist, wherof ye have heard that it should come: and even now already is it in the world.

(I John 4:3)

Grant's illustration of the dreaded beast.

When Grant was in Fort Lauderdale for a three-day stay in January 1987, I put his operation under intensive surveillance. I saw his unmarked truck arrive behind the War Memorial Auditorium where the show was to take place, and I saw some 30 of those familiar wheelchairs being unloaded and taken into a staging area in the front lobby. Later, when my team and I attended the show, we saw early arrivals walking in, some using canes. A few were taken to those same wheelchairs and wheeled up front by Grant's assistants. Asked why they did not think it strange that they were asked to rise and walk when they were already able to do so, they either replied that they thought Grant had misunderstood their malady and they had not wanted to embarrass him, or they refused to discuss it and turned away from us.

That last attitude deserves close attention. Many people who attend these services are well aware that they or others around them have been questioned by the evangelist or his assistants in preparation for the "calling out" trick. Some of them have gone to Grant and have volunteered information. They know about the wheelchair fakery. Many are fully conscious of the fact that they are *not* healed when they stand and declare that they *are* healed. Perhaps Professor Barnhart is correct in his theory that they are "play-acting." I prefer to believe this than to believe that they are simply not very bright.

A Theologian's Opinion

Professor Harvey G. Cox, a theologian at Harvard University, had a similar view of the faith-healing notion. In 1976, he wrote:

> What happens in the mass healing rally is a primal wrestling match. Its roots go back to a ritual that substantially antedates Christianity: the cosmic battle between the godly hero and the seething forces of chaos. For modern people irrational chaos expresses itself through the terrible mystery of disease—so resistant to rational planning, so fearful in its power. . . . The healing evangelists appeal to so many because they are enacting an ancient struggle. . . . [The evangelists] represent the desperate hopes and cries issuing from millions of people who feel lost, sick and hopeless but who have not given up. . . . [Their] spirit is still expressed in the hymn they often sing as they surge down the aisles reaching out for health, salvation and dignity, "Only believe, only believe. All things are possible. Only believe."

Behind the Scenes

Belief in faith-healers is not easily obtained from those who get a backstage view of the operations. John LeBlanc, a stagehand at the West Palm Beach (Florida) Auditorium, where W. V. Grant plays regularly, told me after Grant's 1986 appearance there that the crew resented such healers and knew they were fakes. Though LeBlanc believes that some of the evangelists who play there are genuine, Grant "didn't seem like it at all. He didn't appear to be honest." LeBlanc said that, following the services, the first-aid people at the coliseum helped the "healed" to find their canes and assisted them to their cars because they just couldn't make it on their own. Said LeBlanc:

> The whole thing is money. Some people just
> want to be taken. It seems like they *like* to be
> taken.

When Grant offered the afflicted sheets of paper with foot outlines on them that were to be cut out and placed into the victim's shoe to bring a blessing, and the faithful snapped them up—at $20 a shot—"all the people who work here were appalled," LeBlanc told me.

Former Grant TV cameraman Gary Clarke is similarly aware of the hopelessness of the situation. He was with the Grant crusade in Philadelphia when it all dawned on him.

> When I saw all these people doing all these
> crazy things, it just hit me. These people—they
> just don't care! They're looking for something.
> They're looking for someone to guide them, to
> show them the way. *I* don't know what they're
> looking for. *They* don't know what they're
> looking for. And you just can't talk to them!

Clarke once saw a very elderly woman and her two daughters marooned at the top of a staircase following one of Grant's meetings. The mother's two canes had been taken away from her and broken by Grant when he pronounced her healed. Now the three women were helpless, unable to move from where they were trapped. Yet they persisted in believing that the mother had been healed.

"What do you think of this guy?" he asked one of the daughters. She replied eagerly: "I think he's *great!* He's wonderful! We're glad we came!" Clarke's response was perhaps less than kind, but he was angered by the naiveté and blind belief of the women: "Your mother's afraid to go down the steps and you're telling me *this*? You're going to have to help yourselves!" And he walked away from them.

One must actually experience a similar situation in order to understand Gary Clarke's reaction. You are facing people who refuse to recognize their own foolishness. They pet a dog. They get bitten. Nursing the wound, they again stretch out a hand to the dog. The rage one feels at such times is generated as much by the obstinacy of the victims as by the perfidy of the one who cheated them.

Adding to Clarke's anger was the feeling that he, too, could be as fat and rich as W. V. Grant if only he had the nerve and no integrity. He told me: "I got to thinking, I'll just never get anywhere in life because I don't think like these people. To get ahead, you've *got* to be one of these people!" It is a thought that has occurred to more than one employee of a faith-healer, and has been acted upon often, as we shall see.

But what happens to the victims when the spell *is* broken, as it eventually must be when they get home, the euphoria passes, and they find that they are no better off, if not worse, than before? My team followed up on as many people as we could find after six Grant performances. We found a lot of unhappy, angry, and bitter people, some of whom had traveled hundreds of miles seeking cures. They complained that Grant had misstated and exaggerated their ailments. Some had been told that they had heart trouble that they hadn't even suspected and didn't really have—an ailment that Grant had thrown in as a bonus. Many had to buy new canes to replace those dramatically broken across Grant's knee and tossed up onto the stage.

Does Grant Ever Heal Anyone?

Let us examine whether evangelist W. V. Grant is actually able to heal the afflicted as he says he can. It would seem that checking out his healing record would not be difficult. It's a simple matter of following up on as many "healees" as we can find. But that can be a lengthy, harrowing, and often unsuccessful task. For instance, from a videotape of one of Grant's revival meetings in Atlanta, Georgia, we were able to transcribe—from one healing ritual—the full name of a patient, the names of his six doctors, the name of his hospital, the date of a specific planned coronary operation for that patient, the birthday of the patient, and the name of the church that he attended. Grant, it seemed, had even correctly divined a comment made to the patient by one of those six doctors. Because the tape had been made less than four weeks before the broadcast, I decided to visit Atlanta and determine whether the patient had undergone the operation, and what his present condition might be.

In his healing hocus-pocus on the videotape, Grant had told this man that "Dr. Jesus" had "put a new heart" in his body by means of "closed-heart surgery" and that he no longer needed orthodox open-heart surgery, an operation that the man agreed was planned to take place shortly. The patient, toothless and advanced in years, had trotted up the aisle and back to demonstrate the "new heart" in response to Grant's command.

I felt that this was an ideal prospect for checking because so much data had been given. I arrived in Atlanta and enlisted the help of an associate at a medical school there, who agreed to try contacting the doctors named in the videotape. We were both in for a surprise.

Not one of the six doctors named by Grant appeared in the current list of the Medical Association of Georgia (MAG), which lists all of the state's more than 8,000 physicians, MAG members or not. Nor were any of the six listed as chiropractors. The hospital named by Grant had no such patient and no such operation planned for that date. In fact, it reported that it *never* performed cardiac surgery *of any kind*. Furthermore, the pastor of the church named could not identify this person as a church member, by name or by description. We had apparently discovered an absolute "ringer," a person who, for one reason or another, had fabricated the entire situation. And W. V. Grant and Dr. Jesus had looked pretty good in that videotape.

An Unhappy Customer

But one victim of Grant in St. Louis, J. Elmo Clark, was a different story. When we located him, he was eager to talk to us about what Grant had done to him. He'd gone to Grant's service after having sent him "a lot of money" by mail over a period of years. Clark is blind in one eye, and he firmly believed that this preacher he had seen heal so many others on television could heal him, too.

When I spoke to him two days after his encounter with Grant, he was angry and upset. Grant had "called him out" of the audience, announcing his name, his doctor, and his ailment. But Elmo Clark is still blind in that eye, although witnesses believed he was able to see with it following some mumbo jumbo by Grant. How this came about, we will learn later. Though Grant led his audience to believe that he had restored Clark's vision, that claim was not true, and Clark recalled that the information Grant "called out" had been obtained from him in a pre-show interview. He was not at all deceived by that procedure, but had been given no opportunity—until he talked with us—to tell his story.

The Pretending Game

Looking through the evangelist's glossy periodical, *Dawn of a New Day*, we found names of many people testifying to their healings. One was a man from Erie, Pennsylvania, who stated, concerning his encounter with Grant 18 months before, that his healing was still in effect. He testified:

> For 20 years, I had sugar diabetes, and thank
> God I am healed.

(Grant often refers to diabetes as just "sugar," as in his expression, "You've got the sugar, haven't you?") When I contacted this man by telephone, he was wary. He wanted to be assured that we weren't trying to disprove Grant's work. All I could tell him was that we were investigating the whole matter, with no prejudice at all. Reassured, he agreed to give me the name of his physician, adding that he was sure the doctor would disagree with him, but that *he knew* he no longer had diabetes. He admitted that he was still taking insulin (the standard treatment for this ailment), but the dose was smaller, he said. The impression I got was that he could not contemplate discrediting faith-healing and that he was clinging to his preferred—and comforting—belief. The fact remains that this man, despite his wishes, his faith, and Grant's claimed intercession with supernatural forces, was not and is not healed.

Others whose testimony appeared in that publication could not be found, even though some of the names were quite unusual. Whether they were legitimate, we do not know.

Not Blind Enough to Be Deceived

Back in 1982, Pearl Kidd of Racine, Wisconsin, had been angry enough with one of Grant's deceptions to tell a reporter the whole story. A color photo of her husband, Morris, had been published in *Dawn of a New Day* with the statement that he had had his sight miraculously restored by Reverend Grant. The caption of that photo described the miracle:

> This Milwaukee man was blind all his life. After
> Rev. Grant prayed, he saw for the first time.

Fumed Mrs. Kidd: "What miracle?" Her spouse, she said, was still almost totally blind and she resented this lie being told in print.

First of all, Mr. Kidd had not been "blind all his life." His sight
had been deteriorating for only a few years. The photo and caption were misleading. "It was just a hoax," said Mrs. Kidd, and
she suggested that Grant should be "put out of business for lying
to people."

Mr. Kidd had been carrying a white stick when he attended
Grant's service. Suffering from an incurable, degenerative eye
disease, he could see, but poorly. Grant had declared him healed
and had thrown his stick up on the stage in a dramatic gesture.
At the close of the meeting, Kidd had to ask for his stick to be
returned to him so that he could find his way out of the auditorium. "[Grant] claimed to have healed him," said Mrs. Kidd,
"but he lied!"

The Media Attitude

The unhappy and injured victims of faith-healers are seldom in a
position to be heard. Few media sources care about them, and
most dare not take on any religious group. There are exceptions.
The *Cincinnati Enquirer*, the *Dallas Morning News*, and the *Oakland Press*, among other newspapers, have run scathing articles
about Grant's chicanery. And at Grant's 1986 Fort Lauderdale
meetings that I attended, I was accompanied by a film crew from
the CBS-TV news program "West 57th." Grant, not knowing that I
was with them, allowed them to film the service. When he later
discovered that they were also filming and interviewing unhealed
people who were leaving the meeting in the same state as when
they had entered, he sent out his flunkies to warn the crowd by
chanting loudly, "These people are not Christians! Pass them by!"

The "West 57th" piece should have been devastating to Grant.
CBS-TV aired it twice. On the screen, he was represented as a
pretentious faker bringing in fabulous amounts of money with a
strange, manipulated theology twisted to serve his purposes. And a
new slant was given to the wheelchair trick when the interviewer
questioned an elderly woman with a heavy European accent as she
left the War Memorial Auditorium, walking under her own power
and quite unassisted. She had risen from a wheelchair at Grant's
command, and the audience had applauded wildly as she walked.
But we had seen her walk in and we'd seen Grant talking with
her. The television interview went like this:

> Host: Now, I saw you get up out of a
> wheel chair. Was that a miracle?

Woman: Not exactly, because I wasn't crippled—I wasn't completely crippled, but
I—I only got difficulty to walk and so
far I think I feel much better.

Host: You mean—whose wheelchair was that,
that you got out of?

Woman: That was from here. I didn't come
here with—no.

Host: Do you own a wheelchair?

Woman: No.

Host: That's not your wheelchair?

Woman: No.

Host: Don't you think it's kind of funny
that you come here, sit in a wheelchair, and then he makes a big deal
of getting you out of a wheelchair
that you don't even own?

Woman: I—I can't tell you. I believe in miracle anyway. Now I pray for this and
I believe.

As might be expected, Grant responded to this television
exposé by spouting scripture during a subsequent interview and
warning the faithful against the danger of asking too many such
questions:

Let God fight your battles. "Vengeance is mine,
saith the Lord." You just spend your time
witnessing to your neighbors and your friends
about the power of God and don't try to
answer agnostics and atheists!

Beginning in April 1986, shortly after the wheelchair trick was
exposed on "West 57th" and in *Free Inquiry* magazine, W. V.
Grant stopped placing people in his wheelchairs. He now asks
occupants of wheelchairs to verify that their chairs actually belong to them. He gives a brief and incorrect account of the
accusation made against him and claims he has never done such a
thing and would never stoop to such a pretense. He accuses
secular humanists of spreading those lies. The truth is simply that
one of his favorite deceptions has bitten the dust.

A Devastating Exposé in Rochester

That CBS-TV program was nothing compared to the job that newsman Al White, now with WWOR-TV in New York City, did on Grant when White was with WOKR-TV in Rochester, New York. In a six-part series featured on the WOKR newscasts, Grant's ministry was taken apart piece by piece, and the question was asked, "W. V. Grant: Who is he healing?" The answer: No one. WOKR showed viewers an evangelist who licked his lips, stuttered, blinked, and faltered as he was faced with penetrating questions that he could not answer. Al White said that, in examining Grant's claims, he had found "shocking examples of trickery, magic and deception used in his ministry to bring in those big bucks."

At Grant's April 8, 1986, crusade in Rochester, at the Dome Arena, White was shocked to see Grant "mass-heal" 114 cases of "sugar diabetes," 132 high blood pressure problems, and 800 arthritics, merely by saying that God had told him these were now healed. Then, three weeks later, WOKR looked at some individual cases in detail. White interviewed Evelyn Green, a woman whose leg had apparently been lengthened three inches by the Grant leg-stretching trick, in which the subject is seated and a leg which has been declared "short" appears to grow out visibly.

(This is the same trick that fooled Cheryl Prewitt, Miss America 1980. She told the press that 11 years previously, when she was 10 years old, she had been in an automobile accident and had been confined in a body cast and a wheelchair for eight months while she was receiving treatment for her left leg, which had been "crushed" in that accident. She said that in 1975, at a Jackson, Mississippi, revival meeting she had been told by a faith-healer that she had one short leg. He promised to lengthen her leg. She said that she "was sitting there very calmly. We prayed and we asked. I sat and watched my leg grow out instantaneously two inches." I will describe later how this trick is performed.)

An Odd Coincidence

Concerning Evelyn Green's leg-growing miracle, White said:

> Reverend Grant claims God was revealing to him that she had a back problem that made her leg short and caused her to walk sideways, although it wasn't obvious to our camera or to Mrs. Green.

But Green was less than willing to accept this miracle. She was understandably puzzled, because she had visited Grant during a previous crusade two years earlier, and at that time, too, she had been "called out" and then *Grant had seemed to lengthen that same leg* by three inches! He had the bad luck to choose the same victim twice for the same stunt! As White pointed out, if both miracles had been true, Evelyn would have had to walk with one foot in a ditch in order to walk straight.

Barney Medwin, who suffered from two ailments—arthritis in his legs and a deformed left arm—was "healed" by Grant of the arthritis but was warned not to expect a healing of his arm. To the TV cameras, he appeared to walk with just as much difficulty both before and after the "healing."

Elmer Barber, a victim of polio and arthritis, was another Grant "healee." He was asked by Grant to leave a wheelchair and walk, which he did. This had pleased the enthusiastic crowd that saw the miracle performed. Al White questioned Barber afterward:

> White: Were you surprised that you could do
>   that?
> Barber: No, no. I could do that before!

Not only could Barber walk, he could drive his car as well! White questioned him further:

> White: What did W. V. Grant do for you?
> Barber: To be honest about it, I feel just as
>   I did before I went there.

Al White commented at that point that the wheelchair stunt was, in his opinion, "nothing more than a cruel hoax." But Grant's audience had gone away believing they had seen a miracle.

White also covered an episode in which a woman in a wheelchair, accompanied by her daughter-in-law, was "healed" to the cheers of the enthusiastic crowd, who never got to know the outcome unless they watched the WOKR program. White told viewers:

> There were sad consequences from the phony
> healing of this Rochester woman. While at the
> Rochester Dome Arena, Reverend Grant claimed
> that, in the name of Jesus, this woman should
> get out of her wheelchair, too, and he said she
> was healed of terminal cancer.

But when White spoke to the daughter-in-law a few days later, she was furious with Grant. Asked what condition the cancer victim was now in, she sighed and said simply, "She died." When asked why this woman he had "healed" of cancer had died of the disease 48 hours afterward, Grant just smirked and said, "Everyone Jesus ever prayed for, died!"

The Story Starts Falling Apart

During his investigation, White showed that places Grant named as those where he'd had major successes didn't even exist. Grant claimed to have had a holy vision in a specific motel in California. White showed him that such a motel had never existed. His published personal history was false. Grant had also claimed he received an in-person visit from Reverend William Branham, one of the earliest of the evangelist healers, in 1962, while at school. Grant said that he had just responded to a football scholarship offer from UCLA. Branham, he said, had walked into his room, looked him in the eye strangely, and declared:

> W. V., even as Elijah's mantle fell upon Elishah,
> soon my mantle will fall upon you.

Grant claims that he gave up a promising football career and dedicated himself to God and that "just a few days later, Brother William Branham was killed in a car accident." Not so. The Reverend Branham was alive and well at that time. He met his demise a full three years after the date claimed by Grant. What's more, UCLA denies that Grant was ever enrolled there, though Grant advertises that he attended the university.

Finally, when Grant was asked about an incident in which he'd been captured on videotape by the WOKR cameras tip-toeing from a former showgirl's motel room at 1:00 a.m. with his shoes in his hand, he told a justifiably skeptical Al White that he had been "ministering" to the young lady. He had made *four visits* in one night! As he ran off to his car and to the faithful worshipers awaiting his wisdom at the auditorium, Grant said to White, "Pray for me, brother!" White answered dryly, "I sure will."

A Syracuse University student, Beth Zanowick, was present at the WOKR filming. She wanted to know why some persons who had been "called out" by Grant were willing to ignore the truth and allow the facts to be misrepresented in Grant's favor. She observed:

> I think because they just want to be healed so
> much, they have so much faith in this man,
> that they're willing to say anything to have
> healing come to them.

Concerning a specific woman who was "called out" and whom she questioned afterward, Zanowick said:

> [Grant] said, "Did anyone else in this room talk
> with you?" And she said, "No!" And, in fact,
> she had talked with *me*, and *I* knew her name
> and what was wrong with her!

(Note that question: "Did anyone *else* in this room talk with you?" Grant is implying that the woman spoke to *no one*, but he is really asking if "anyone else *but Grant*" spoke with her!)

The Haitian Orphanages

Grant's claims about his good works in Haiti interested investigator White. Grant had claimed, during the Rochester meeting, that he was feeding 4,000 to 5,000 orphans there every month. White was able to find a group of only 30 or 40 who had ever been fed by Grant. But he gave Grant an opportunity to prove the rest of them. He asked Grant if all those orphans were really benefiting from the Grant ministry. Replied Grant, obviously uncomfortable with the question:

> Yes. Oh, yes. In fact, I can show you—uh—can-
> celled—uh—checks where we send—uh—prob-
> ably—I'm now—uh—I would say an average of
> between $3,500 and $4,500 hundred down there
> each month.

Though WOKR sent Grant mailgrams following up its requests to see those checks, it never received proof that Grant ever sent *any* money to Haiti for any purpose.

What is even more interesting—and gratifying—about the WOKR episode is that Vince De Luca, general manager of the TV station, announced that for ethical reasons it was dropping the Grant broadcast immediately at the close of its series of reports. Unfortunately, WOKR replaced his show with that of David Epley, a Florida-based faith-healer using essentially the same methods!

W. V. Grant Replies to WOKR-TV

In the *Dawn of a New Day* periodical Grant sends to the faithful, now renamed *Where Eagles Fly*, he displayed his panic at what WOKR had aired. And his mendacity was suddenly very evident in print. What follows is a series of outright lies manufactured by Grant to deceive the believers even further. On page 12, volume 22, number 3, of the Summer 1987 issue of his publication, Grant wrote (the numbers refer to the notes that follow the quotation):

> In the Rochester/Syracuse area Al Waite,[1] a self-described troubleshooter,[2] followed our evangelistic party around, hiding with T.V. cameras in the halls of our motels, until we had almost no privacy at all.[3]
>
> Inspired by the Secular Humanists'[4] wicked and slanderous[5] accusations that the healings were not real, he went to several homes of those who had testified[6] to undeniable healings,[7] attempting to talk them out of the healings,[8] and saying "Grant must be exposed."[9]
>
> This reporter, claiming to be a "fellow Christian"[10] as he rang their doorbells offered people money,[11] and "Christian advice," in apparent underhanded tactics. We have letters in our files,[12] handwritten from supporters in the Rochester area, telling us how he came to their homes, trying to talk them "out of" their healings, giving them "offerings" of $50.[13] In some cases he tried to talk one elderly couple into discontinuing our Bible Correspondence Course they were actively taking.[14] He said he would get them "in touch with another *reputable* course."
>
> Mr. Waite, inspired by these same humanists[15] who are out to destroy our children, ran a 5-part series[16] in his area on television, downgrading our ministry, claiming it was an "exposé."[17] In this same crusade, someone tried to "set us up"[18] with a young woman by having her write to us inviting us to call her.[19] God watched over us and protected us.[20]

1. It's Al *White*, not Waite.

2. Al is *not* "self-described." Now with WWOR-TV in New York, he was at that time a recognized, responsible investigative reporter for WOKR-TV, Channel 13, in Rochester. His program was a regular feature on WOKR, and his highly regarded work has appeared on network television as well.

3. True. The cameras found the Grant crew in the hotel bar after midnight, and Grant himself was wandering around the Holiday Inn in bare feet.

4. Not so. Al White was *not* thus inspired. He did his investigation because he, like so many of us, is angry and dismayed by the shameless flimflam being perpetrated by W. V. Grant.

5. "Slander: A false tale or report . . ." (according to *Webster's*). The statements were *not* "accusations"; they were true. Note that Grant does not deny the truth of White's revelations.

6. True.

7. Not true. White found no healings. He says: "Undeniable healings? Well, *they* denied 'em!"

8. Not true. White says, in response: "I went to them as an investigative reporter, and asked them to describe their healings, and how they were healed. They weren't!"

9. If White said that, I heartily agree. That is one purpose of this book.

10. Al White *is* a devout, church-going Christian.

11. Not true. The *only* person to whom Al White offered *any* money was Evelyn Green. Says White: "Evelyn Green was not a lady of means. She said she was going to send for Grant's Bible course, and out of compassion, I said, 'Look, I'll pay for a course and I'll give you the name of a reputable Bible company.' That part is true. It wasn't as if I was offering her money for her story. That's clear, and I have a witness to that. And I didn't try to talk her out of her healing. I asked her to explain how come she was healed twice of the same thing!" Did White pay people for their stories, or to reverse their testimonies, and did he offer anyone $50? His answer is simple: "No! Actually, I did give [Evelyn Green] money for the Bible course, but not for the interview, and not to say anything."

12. May we see them?

13. Not true.

14. A wise suggestion, if Al White made it.

15. See No. 4, above.

16. It was a six-part series.

17. It certainly was!

18. Grant is using "us" to mean "me." This usage is reserved for royalty and the Deity, but Grant finds it appropriate for his use. And he didn't need any "setting up" at all. The young lady, Lynda Oxley, was a former Grant worker and ex-Playboy bunny who left the ministry because Grant was "putting the make on her" and she had discovered his tricks. She fought him off when he made advances, and he left, being filmed in the process by the WOKR crew. Says White, in response to this accusation: "[Grant] is entitled to his interpretation of whether it was a set-up. This lady volunteered to come here to expose him—at her own expense—because of some alleged prior contact with her that was, ummm, *less* than Christian."

19. Not so. Grant met her in the Holiday Inn, recognized her, and got her room number. He didn't need an invitation.

20. If so, why did He allow WOKR to uncover and broadcast all the damning evidence it gathered on Grant and his ministry?

The truth has hurt W. V. Grant, and his only defense, it seems, is to try to cover up with another set of lies. I am enraged that he has attacked a well-informed and careful investigator like Al White by trying to perpetrate misinformation about both his work and his reputation. I'll let Al have the last word on this matter. He exhibits a far more charitable attitude than I would be able to summon up: "My overall reaction to what [Grant] says? I stand behind my story. It is absolutely correct, and it is a very different, inaccurate picture he is portraying of our investigation."

A Brother in Trouble

I must mention one more item used by W. V. Grant in his *Dawn of a New Day* tirade against secular humanism. A thinly-veiled accusation read like this:

> In some areas, after the "Amazing Athiest" [*sic*] magician had had free media time to lie and downgrade the Power of the Holy Spirit in our ministry, we have had death threats against our lives. These threats were probably not by criminal types, but by well-meaning pseudo-Christians he had incited. . . . Just today, (April 23, 1987), as I write this, a prominent local pastor's wife was strangled nearly to

> death, after a series of threats. At this writing,
> she is still in a coma. Secular humanists, and
> people they incite, mean business!

As of *this* writing, four months later, much more has been discovered about that case. The preacher Grant writes about is the Reverend Walker Railey, of Dallas. He is known to have a lady friend who is not his wife. The threatening letters he said he received from the secular humanists turned out to have been written with his own office typewriter. He is the only suspect in the crime. His wife is still in a coma and is not expected to survive. A trial is pending.

Another Well-Informed Reporter

In May of 1987, the *Oakland* (California) *Tribune* teamed up with Don Henvick, a mover and shaker with the Bay Area Skeptics who has been on Grant's trail for several years. Reporter Don De Main was carefully prepared by Henvick and his associates to attend a "crusade" at Oakland's Calvin Simmons Theater. He knew what to look for, and he found it. In the May 22 issue of the *Tribune* a story appeared describing De Main's experience at the Grant vaudeville show that said, in part:

> Victoria, wearing dark glasses, is called up from
> the front row. "How many think God can heal
> this blind sister? Everybody say, 'Praise the
> Lord.' " Everybody does.
> Grant says Victoria is totally blind. "I'm
> just crazy enough to believe God can heal a
> blind eye. I'm going to start praying. Victoria,
> I'm going to take my hand off your eyes. Say,
> 'Jesus, you healed blind Bartimaeus.' "
> Grant places his hands in front of her
> face. She says she can see his ears, his nose, and
> the number of fingers he is holding out.

Now, De Main knew something more about this case than the rest of that audience did. He knew that Grant, during his dramatic "healing" of Victoria, had hyperbolized her claim of "limited sight" to "total blindness." De Main also knew that Grant had approached John Taube, another Bay Area Skeptics member, in the auditorium lobby before the program and had asked about the young lady accompanying him. John had told Grant that it was his "niece" Victoria who was having sight problems. Taube had been at Grant's meeting the week before and had been "healed." Taube felt that Grant would recognize him, but he didn't. The mnemonic system he uses is short-term, of necessity.

What De Main missed was a statement by Grant that shows his careful and clever use of implications. He had said:

> It's not God's will for her to have a white cane
> and walk around with dark glasses.

The truth is that "Victoria" did not carry a cane. Grant's statement is designed to allow listeners to assume that she did. This semantic trick is commonly used by conjurors, too. The conversation between Grant and Taube had gone like this:

Grant: Have you been in an accident?

Taube: No, Reverend Grant. Don't you remember me? I think you're the most wonderful man in the world.

Grant: No, Jesus is.

Taube: . . . The reason that I'm here tonight is because I'm concerned about my niece, who is blind.

Grant: Is she completely blind?

Taube: Oh no. She sees a little.

Grant: We're going to have a "laying on of hands," so we'll pray for her. What's your name?

Taube: I guess you forgot from last week. My name is John.

Grant: What's your niece's name?

Taube: Victoria.

Grant: Her doctor is who?

Taube: Dr. Rice. In San Francisco.

Grant: Well, we're gonna have a "laying on of hands." We'll be praying for her.

Thus prepared, the Reverend Grant launched into the public part of his meeting. Reporter De Main had watched as Grant got the information from John Taube and witnessed the performance as "Victoria" was "healed." He wrote in his story:

But in Victoria's case, Grant had gotten the wrong message from God. "Victoria" is really Genie Scott, an anthropologist from San Francisco, accompanied by John Taube, who had been called out two days earlier and "healed" of crippling arthritis. They are both supporters of the [Bay Area Skeptics] who went through Grant's "miracles" for the society's efforts to uncover the chicanery of faith healers. Both are healthy. . . .

Grant got his information about Genie from chatting with [John] before the faith healing session. But [he] told him she was not totally blind, and could make out lights and shadows and contrasting objects, like Grant's ears, nose and fingers.

Where Grant gets his information on his healing subjects is more mundane than from God. It comes from carefully phrased, casual chats early in the four-hour sessions by Grant's associates, notably his chief aide, the Rev. Glen Cole, who talks to companions of the would-be subjects and passes on the information.

In this case, De Main told the whole story, based on personal experience and observation in the field, assisted by experts who had the ability to prepare him for the experience. He had to suppose nothing. It was all there for him to see, and he made a complete revelation of Grant's deception to *Tribune* readers. One of his sentences sums up the entire faith-healing phenomenon:

The real miracle of Grant's performances, and others like him, is not in their healing, but in charismatic convincing of those who want to be convinced.

The Trash Detail

At the 1986 Fort Lauderdale meeting, I watched W. V. Grant at work with his expensively coiffed and costumed wife, Shirley, various assistants busily scurrying about, and ushers trotting baskets of cash and checks backstage. I got the impression of a somewhat rushed and desperate gang of cattle rustlers at work, wearing the wrong costumes. They threw fixed smiles in every direction, handling each person with assembly-line precision and galloping toward the final moment of mass testimony that would terminate the magical ceremony.

I wanted to get hold of those crib sheets that Grant carried for the "calling out" stunt. I'd stood close to the edge of the stage as he worked at memorizing one, the writing on it plainly visible through the paper as it rested on a transparent lucite podium in front of him. At that moment, as I saw this careless procedure, it seemed to me that Grant might not be quite as smart as I'd thought. It occurred to me that there might be another weak spot we should investigate.

When the meeting broke up, I approached my colleague Chuck Saje and suggested that we monitor the trash thrown out by the Grant group each night. It was just possible that Grant might fail to destroy some evidence. Chuck felt that we would find nothing. After all, he opined, a counterfeiter would be insane to throw his rejects in the trash, instead of burning them. I was grasping at straws to hope that Reverend Grant would be that careless. But we went ahead with the plan.

The first night yielded nothing. Two large dumpsters beside the Grant truck remained empty but for a few food wrappers. The second and third nights were the same, and even the food wrappers were gone by Saturday, when the Grant caravan had departed. I felt as if I should abandon the surveillance, but made one more forage on Sunday. Eureka! Two plastic trash bags had appeared atop some tree cuttings, and, to the amusement of several early-morning joggers, I made off with them. It was a bonanza.

Chuck and I picked among the coffee grounds, cigarette butts, and fried potatoes, and the first thing we came up with was a note from Shirley Grant to her husband. What made this note even more interesting was the form on the other side. It shows how careful Grant is—at least with money.

We knew that we'd really arrived "behind the scenes" at the Grant show when we found a trash bag with letters, envelopes, bank money wrappers, and deposit slips. Grant had shown his audience a bundle of bright red envelopes. He'd explained that there were 120 of them, numbered consecutively from 1 to 120, and that anyone who agreed to take an envelope "at random" was expected to place within it a check made out in the amount represented by the number on that envelope. If the numbering had been as represented, and there were only 120 envelopes, Grant stood to collect $7,260 from that offering alone.

Shirley Grant's note to her husband at Fort Lauderdale, Florida.

But my colleagues and I managed to get 11 of those envelopes as they were given out, and more from sifting through Grant's garbage. The numbers they bore were mostly in the upper half of the scale, from 70 to 120, and several large numbers were duplicated. Mathematically, the chances of our happening upon such a selection at random are slightly more than 1 in 5,000. (Actually, probably less, because some recipients might have failed to return envelopes with large numbers on them, and those with smaller numbers might be more likely to show up.) In other words, it is highly likely that those 120 (or more!) envelopes had been numbered so that many more high numbers were available than low ones. This would bring Grant considerably more than $7,260.

It seems that W. V. Grant's operation has little that is not in some way slanted to provide an altered version of reality and increase his income.

A Sad Record of Problems with No Solutions

A total of 97 letters and envelopes, torn in half, showed up in the garbage. Some were the bright red numbered ones, but there were also blue, orange, pink, white, yellow, and beige envelopes—all, we discovered, for different purposes. One envelope contained a letter from a Mary Birchman, a subject who later had been "called out" and "healed" of colon cancer and a swollen leg at the first Fort Lauderdale meeting we attended. This woman was *not* healed, and her letter, which she had personally given to Grant, contained every detail he later revealed to her during the service. A score or so more letters were similar, revealing specific details that Grant had purportedly been divinely inspired to announce.

The Written Evidence

The big prize from that garbage search was a crib sheet. Grant had met certain people as they gave him the beige envelopes, each containing $20 and a letter. These had been sent out in advance of his arrival in Florida, with instructions to hand them to Grant in person at the auditorium with a "$20 love offering" inside. As Grant met these people, he associated their faces with their first names (on the outside of the envelopes). He had about ten envelopes at a time taken backstage and received in return a 4-by-6-inch data sheet some time later from an assistant. He studied the sheet, adding the new data to his memory or putting it in his pocket for later use. This is the crib sheet we found:

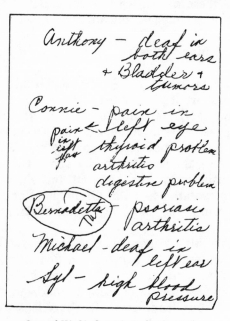

One of W. V. Grant's "crib sheets."

Almost all of the beige-colored envelopes we found contained
letters to Grant. These had probably been thrown out because the
people who received that color envelope were already entered on
the computer mailing list. Most other colored envelopes had no
letters thrown out with them, except where no donation had been
enclosed. Two contained $5.00 checks that Grant either had missed
or discarded because of the low value.

In his personal ministry and on television, the Reverend Grant
had encouraged his congregation to enclose letters expressing their
prayer needs along with their money. He had promised:

> I will take each letter and anoint it with this
> holy oil from Israel, and I will pray over your
> letter back in my church in Dallas.

The callous fact we discovered was that those letters, some several pages long and filled with heart-rending pleas for the minister's prayers and intercession with God, had been torn up,
crumpled, and tossed in with the garbage. They never reached the
hands of Grant at all, and they certainly never made it to Dallas.
The only oil that got on those letters was snake oil, and possibly
some cooking oil from french fries. By piecing together these
scraps of the congregation's hopes, bit by bit, and learning how
Grant handled these needs, we were gradually beginning to see the
true attitude this pastor held toward his flock.

The "Leg-Stretching" Miracle

At every crusade meeting, Reverend Grant announces that a
subject has "a short leg" that needs to be adjusted. He brings the
person on stage, and seats him on a chair facing across the stage
but slightly turned to the audience. He lifts both legs up, parallel
to the floor. At this point, the spectators see that one leg (the
one nearest them) appears shorter by about two inches, judged by
the relative positions of the heels of the shoes or boots. During
some heavy incantations, with Grant holding both feet resting
upon his one hand, the short leg seems to lengthen to match the
other one.

(Grant does this no more than once a show. But back in 1970,
Brother Ted Whitesell did a marathon demonstration in Australia,
when he claimed that he not only gave sight to a young boy,
cleared up several arthritic conditions, and cured astigmatism and
stuttering cases, but lengthened *16* short legs as an encore! Fur-

thermore, he said he often raised the dead. Whitesell himself is now dead.)

The stunt is similar to one that is still a carnival mainstay. "The Man Who Grows" is the name of the act. In this performance, a man is revealed onstage who seems to fit his clothes well enough. He is seen to go into a "trance" and appears to grow by seven or eight inches, by which time his sleeves are far too short and his pants go to half-mast as well. The gimmick is simple: The man is dressed in a too-small suit, and only has to "scrunch down" while in a standing position. The suit appears to fit him at this point, but as he straightens up and swells out his chest, the bad fit becomes apparent. It is a striking illusion, often enhanced by a popping belt buckle and falling shirt buttons thrown in for further effect.

Grant's trick is even simpler. His subject must be wearing loose shoes; cowboy boots are far better. As the subject sits, Grant merely places his hand beneath the feet, twisting his hand so that one shoe is pulled slightly off the foot (the farther one) and the other shoe is pressed tightly against the sole (the nearer one). By reversing the twist, the farther shoe is pushed on against that sole and the two shoes—as well as the two feet!—are now seen to be the same length.

Refer to the photograph section of this book. I have reproduced two leg-stretching pictures from Grant's own publication. In the upper photo, the far (right) leg appears to be longer than the left one, judging from the position of the woman's shoes relative to one another. In the lower photo, Grant is praising Jesus for having lengthened the left leg. Simple observation shows that it is not the left leg that has grown, but the right leg that has *shortened*! Look at the photos carefully, and you will see that the left shoe did not move at all. The right shoe, pulled away from the foot, has simply been pressed back on again. This is further proved by the fact that the woman's slacks have *stayed in exactly the same position* relative to her left foot! If Grant caused her left leg to grow, he also caused her pant leg to grow along with it. Polyester seems to be subject to faith as much as are flesh and bone.

There is another trick used here as well. The illusion can also depend upon the fact that Grant swings the two legs away from the audience so that they are not truly at right angles to the audience, while the chair (and the person's body) remains slightly turned toward the audience. This displaces the feet relative to one another, and they do not meet, the legs thus seeming to be of differing lengths. To cause the "growth" of the nearer leg, Grant simultaneously presses the loose shoe into place and swings the legs into line with the subject's body.

Accurate measurements of photographs of this trick prove that these are the methods used to produce the illusion of the growing leg. As mentioned earlier, cowboy boots are an advantage to the trick. The very fit of such a boot allows it to be pulled away from the foot for some distance.

(It appears that Grant's subjects get the notion about a too-short leg from their chiropractors, who frequently tell them that this discrepancy exists and prescribe a custom-made "lift" for the shoe. In my visits to chiropractors to examine their claims, I've had several such devices prescribed, some for one shoe, some for the other.)

Celebrities at His Feet

Grant's fans include musician Billy Preston and former football player Rosie Greer, who shows up at many religious functions and on television evangelists' programs. Preston, having worked with a very hard-nosed faith-healer who calls herself "Amazing Grace," is quite accustomed to the shenanigans that take place at these meetings. But Greer, says cameraman Gary Clarke, was astonished:

> The first time we did a show with Rosie, he didn't expect that healing stuff. It was kinda funny, watching his face. He's standing there, and W. V.'s doing this healing act, and Rosie is thinking, "What's going on here? What am I doing here? Someone's going to catch me sitting here!"

Clarke, besides being the lead cameraman, was supervisor of remote operations for All-American Video, the production company owned by W. V. Grant. While head man Rod Sherrill flew from location to location in style, Clarke loaded and unloaded the trucks and drove between locations.

In the opinion of Clarke, who videotaped some 200 of Grant's shows, "He sure knows how to grab an audience." Clarke would marvel to see Grant, sensing that an audience was not yet quite ripe for the offering baskets to be passed around, launch into a back-home story about his childhood that the people could relate to, and thus rescue the situation.

Clarke easily solved some of Grant's tricks:

> It was such a phony operation. At first, when
> people would give in checks, [the checks would]
> all come backstage and he'd memorize the
> names and addresses on them. A lot of people
> were so excited to talk to him, that if he told
> them they'd had indigestion problems, for
> example, they'd just agree.

Another Grant cameraman was Danny Jenkins, son of faith-healer Leroy Jenkins. Grant told him with great confidence that he could never be "set up" by skeptics supplying him with a phony identity during his pre-show interviews—which is exactly what we succeeded in doing. Grant told Danny that he was always suspicious when someone came up to him and voluntarily told him his name, ailment, the name of his doctor, and other details. But he was too smart for his own good. When we set him up, one of my first instructions was for my colleagues not to approach Grant, but to let *him* find *them*. He did, and we got all the evidence we needed.

Shortly after I first began my investigation of the faith-healing business, I'd received a letter from Danny Jenkins, offering to "rat" on W. V. Grant and Peter Popoff, but insisting that his father, unlike them, was the real thing. He exhibited a knowledge of Grant's methods in that letter, but seemed to have genuinely been deceived by his father, and he said that he believed he could supply me with evidence of healings. He never did.

Danny had become so familiar with Grant's trick of questioning his audience in advance and memorizing the data in order to "call them out" that he was even able to focus in on the next victim that Grant would approach, because he'd seen that person being interviewed and knew that Grant would be approaching his subjects in the same sequence he had memorized them. Once, when he confronted Grant with this observation, the answer was typical. Said Grant, quoting from scripture, "The Holy Ghost will bring all things to your remembrance." Well, that satisfies me!

A Disillusioned Employee

In the summer of 1984, Clarke witnessed—and videotaped—an episode in Tampa, Florida, in which a woman with a heart condition was "healed" by Grant and then instructed to run up the aisle. As she returned to Grant, Clarke could see her turning bright red, and he knew she was having a heart attack. She suddenly collapsed at the feet of the healer, who turned to the crowd and declared that she was drunk. The woman was carried away by her friends. Whether she lived, we do not know.

Clarke's tour with W. V. Grant was not without humor. A few days after the heart attack episode, at the end of the Tampa stay, Clarke was leaving the meeting when a young man in his early twenties came running up to him. "I've *got* to see Reverend Grant!" he exclaimed to the cameraman. Clarke told him that Grant had left the auditorium, and the distraught young man explained that he had given Grant his last $10 bill and now had no money to get his car out of the parking lot. "He asked for it, and I gave it to him," he said to Clarke. "I was caught up in the moment, and I gave it *all* to him!" Clarke doesn't know if the man ever got his car back.

As a cameraman, Gary was in a particularly good position to observe certain aspects of the Grant ministry. For example, he was once on a tour of Charlotte, North Carolina; Richmond and Norfolk, Virginia; and New York City; looking through his TV viewfinder, he noted a startling fact. Either Grant had many of his flock devotedly following him around on that tour or he had a small repertory company working for him. There were a number of faces there that showed up *at all the services!*

How could Gary Clarke, a practicing Christian, stay with the Grant operation as long as he did? He told me that he was bothered by what he had seen and what he knew about the fakery. He said:

> It upset me. I never thought anything was being accomplished . . . I just got caught up in the position in the first place, and the status that was given me, and the opportunity. The big joke—well, not so much of a joke, I guess—was that we were all going to Hell. When we'd do a good job, we'd say, "Boy, we're really going to Hell for this one!" I hired a friend of mine, a Catholic, who only lasted a week. With W. V., there was a kind of fascination. The guy was so quick. He was the kind of guy you love to hate. You knew he was a fiend, but you wanted to see what he was going to do next. I used to think, you can't admire a guy like that at all,

because of the cruelty he's doing to people,
forgetting any religious convictions, just being
a human being. I mean, what is this person
doing to this other human being? It's intoler-
able! That's the thing that got me—how can this
guy, because he's so good at lying, hurt this
other person? You want to just take the guy
and punch him out, or something. He's so
despicable.

When it got to be too much for Clarke, he announced his
resignation to Grant. He promptly received a letter several pages
long that threatened a lawsuit if Clarke told what he knew and
had witnessed of the internal operations of the W. V. Grant
operation. Michael Beck, hired off the street by Grant at $70,000
a year, was at that time the head of Grant's TV production company. Beck told Clarke when he left, in very plain language: "[If
you talk,] we're going to get you. We have the dollars to do it."
There was good reason for Grant's organization to fear Gary
Clarke. He had been in on so much of the behind-the-scenes
operation and had stayed with it for so long that Grant believed
he would just continue on without allowing his conscience to
bother him; therefore, little had been concealed from him.

A Brooklyn Encounter with Grant

Rochester TV reporter Al White accompanied Dr. Paul Kurtz and
me to Grant's April 15, 1986, healing crusade in Brooklyn. White
and I adopted disguises. Willy Rodriguez, a long-time colleague of
mine, showed up to infiltrate the Grant camp. He dressed in a
maintenance uniform and waited outside for the Reverend's arrival.
As Grant's car pulled up, Willy jumped for the door and grabbed
Grant's briefcase, literally pulling it from his hand. Grant did not
seem to want to let go of it, but Rodriguez was very persuasive.
He simply cleared the crowd away, walked down the aisle of the
Brooklyn Academy of Music, and went up the stage stairs with
Grant puffing along behind. He authoritatively asked where the
dressing-rooms were, thus eliciting curious stares from the stage-
hands, who must have assumed he was working personally for
Grant. Grant, in turn, probably assumed he was working for the
Academy. Watching from the balcony, Kurtz was astonished to see
Willy walking around freely with Grant, but I was not at all
surprised. He and I have been through far more than that to-

gether, and he has always managed to do the impossible. He came back to us with interesting details about what was going on backstage.

Later, when Grant came onstage to do his bit, I decided to do some reconnaissance myself. That section of the Academy, I discovered, is divided into two theaters. Grant was using one, and the other was empty. However, the backstage areas are connected. I groped down a dark aisle in the empty section, mounted the stage stairs, and carefully inched into the backstage corridor. Voices were coming from several rooms, and I intended to listen in wherever I could. Just as I passed a water fountain, two coveralled workers rounded a corner and I barely had time to bury my face in the stream of water, to appear busy. As I straightened up, they were looking at me strangely. I said to them: "We'll be out of here by ten-thirty, guys." One of them snorted: "We don't care. We have to be here all night anyway." I wished them goodnight, and stepped into the nearest room.

I paused, hearing Reverend W. V. Grant in full evangelical fervor out in the theater singing and screeching about hell and damnation in the first part of his evening tirade. I was suddenly aware of someone's breathing near me, and as my eyes adjusted to the darkness I saw a woman festooned in several gold chains and bracelets, curled up asleep on a couch right beside where I was standing. I quickly stepped out into the hall and headed back into the theater, into the blackness. Stumbling around in the dark, I was almost at the exit when two rented cops burst in, waving walkie-talkies. Flashlights were aimed everywhere, and I ducked down just in time.

The two decided that this was a good time and place for a short break, and they plopped down into seats *one row behind me.* From the conversation I overheard, it seemed they had been told that a strange man had been seen entering the unused portion of the Academy, and they were checking it out. Judging from their lack of success, I felt that they'd have been hard put to find a bowling ball in a bathtub. Finally, they decided to move on, and I was once again able to rejoin my colleagues in the balcony, where I saw the woman whose nap I'd almost ruined with W. V. Grant on stage! It was his wife, Shirley Grant.

An On-the-Scene Report

Elinor Brecher, a reporter for the *Courier-Journal* in Louisville, Kentucky, paid a visit to Haiti in December 1986. The result was a blockbuster feature article that laid bare the heartless exploitation of children in that country. She discovered that Grant was staying at the El Rancho Hotel, in a suite (214/215) draped in red velvet and gold trim, at $110 a night. He was there to film at a nearby orphanage he claims to support and was shown by his TV crew giving what was supposed to be the annual Christmas dinner for the kids. Dressed up in a monogrammed designer safari outfit, pith helmet and all, the reverend posed with emaciated children on his knee and pleaded to the cameras for donations to cover the cost of the sumptuous meal being served to them. Brecher discovered that the entire meal consisted of half a paper cup of Kool-Aid and a wrapped candy. In her very powerful and devastating March 29, 1987, article describing the incredible conditions she found in the orphanages there, she reported:

> In one, a home for about 30 young girls and one boy supported at the time by Dallas faith-healer W. V. Grant, West Virginian James McClelland allegedly raped a young child in his care. Arrested and jailed in December, he was allowed to leave Haiti three weeks later.

And, according to Rod Sherrill, a TV director for Grant who twice visited Haiti to film for his program, Grant would choose an orphanage there and simply use whatever preacher happened to be handy. The preacher whom Rod encountered on his last trip there, he says, was very "touchy-feely" with the children. Rod left after the filming and left Grant behind in Haiti.

The Interior Decorator Tells All

It is said that psychiatrists, hairdressers, and bartenders may become repositories of their clients' innermost secrets. We may add to that short list the profession of interior decorator. When the Grants moved into their Fort Wright, Kentucky, mansion in 1979, they summoned several local artisans to do alterations and general fixing-up for them. One of those called upon was a worker we shall call Raul Mitchky, for reasons he will best understand.

He was amazed at the behavior of Shirley Grant. Willy-nilly, he found her confiding in him about all manner of things that she would certainly not wish to share with those who were contributing to her lavish lifestyle. Raul told me:

It was funny, because she was very candid. She
made this one comment. There was a photo [of
her] in one of their [*Dawn of a New Day*]
magazines. "That God-damned photographer!"
she said. It was at Las Vegas. She was holding
a drink, and they cropped the picture, but the
top of the swizzle-stick was still showing!

But that was nothing. Shirley apparently didn't care what Mitchky
knew. Camilla Warrick, of the *Cincinnati Enquirer*, had directed me
to Mitchky because he said he had become aware of a large
quantity of pornography present in the Grant home. He told me
how he discovered it:

What totally flabbergasted me was, I was doing
the master bedroom and they had this big
dresser in there and [Shirley Grant] said to me,
"Would you just take everything out of it and
put it on the bed and cover it up because the
people from the church are coming to pick [the
dresser] up." It didn't dawn on me at first,
because a lot of people ask me to move stuff. I
opened up these drawers and started taking
[pornographic material] out, and it wasn't
simple little stuff, you know, like *Hustler* or
Playboy. It was all *really*, real filth porno.
Action porno, everything. And the [dresser] was
just full of it. I mean, I couldn't believe—you'd
think that someone might have a *few*, but this
was *drawers* full of it.

I asked Mitchky, "Shirley didn't seem to mind you going into
those drawers and removing those drawers?" He replied:

She *told* me to do it. She's the one who told
me. I'd touch nothing, you know, without
permission. . . . It's amazing. How can someone
like that repeatedly and continually fool so
many people? . . . He's screwed so many people,
and the way [Shirley Grant] would be so candid
about it: "I have to go to the church and
collect the envelopes today and get some cash
in the bank."

Mitchky's dismay is shared by many of us.

While working at the Grant home, he got to talk to Misty, the Grants' daughter. He had noticed that there were no religious artifacts at all around the house. He himself is a deacon in a Baptist church, and he found it strange that the Grants, so devoted to religion, had no signs of it around the house. He told me:

> It was funny. . . . I asked [Misty] if she went to Sunday school. She said she'd never been to church, 'cause they don't let her come to church. . . . And I've seen this publicity that he puts out [*Dawn of a New Day*] and they'd have pictures of [Misty], like on the seashore with a halo around her head, picking up seashells. I thought it was awfully strange.

Mitchky also got in behind the scenes with the Grant mailing campaigns:

> I had to get water to clean my tools up, and [Mrs. Grant] told me I could use this laundry room down in the basement. It was their supply room for holy oils and prayer shawls and mother-of-pearl praying hands [all the "gifts" they mailed out].

For the job he did at the Grant mansion, Raul Mitchky was paid in cash—in bundles of $5 bills. He was aware that these bills represented the love offerings of many hundreds of poor folks who had mailed in what they could to assist in God's work.

W. V. Grant is seen on television in a number of United States markets. His penetration of Canada has been minimal.

9
Peter Popoff and His Wonderful Machine

Enter Peter Popoff, Anointed Minister of God, possessing the Nine Gifts of the Spirit, smuggler of Bibles behind the European Iron Curtain and into Cuba, TV star across the United States and Canada. According to his autobiography, the Reverend Popoff is no stranger to miraculous events. Peter says that as a child he saw his father change water into wine for one of his communion services in war-torn Berlin, and tells of his mother slicing up a small heel of bread into two full plates of bread to feed ten people. Traveling for his own ministry many years later in the United States, he says that he and his wife, "Liz," drove their car to a service more than 50 miles away on a nickel's worth of gasoline because God revealed to them how to do it.

Squeaky-voiced Popoff directed his religious empire from Upland, California, sending out more than 100,000 computer-generated begging letters from coast to coast every two weeks. In 1986, he *admitted* to an operating cost of $550,000 a month; his actual gross income can only be guessed at. Since most of that income entered the collection plates—which are four-gallon plastic wastebaskets—in the form of cash, we suspected that the official figure *might* be somewhat smaller than Popoff's declaration. Because Popoff—like all the evangelists—is not required by any government agency to account to anyone for any of the money that is taken in, except whatever he decides to pay himself as personal income, it is difficult to know just how much is collected.

A Religious Entrepreneur

Popoff always depended upon his valuable mailing list for most of his income. The crusades were really only methods of obtaining new names for that list, and his television and radio shows added to that number, of course. After the first few years of his electronic preaching, Popoff expanded his mailing list by contacting "Reverend" Gene Ewing, the owner of Twentieth Century Advertising, in California, who had many such valuable names for sale. Ewing had already been working for Popoff, writing emotional and highly effective promotional pieces for him and inventing clever sales stunts for the mailings. The mentality of Popoff's contributors was demonstrated when Ewing had "business reply" (prepaid postage) envelopes printed up for Popoff to include in his mailings as a convenience for donors. The gesture backfired. The faithful wrote in complaining that it looked too businesslike, and from then on they had to pay their own postage.

Former Popoff aide Mike Delaney described Ewing's product:

> He sold letters and mail-order gimmicks to Popoff. Guaranteed, copyrighted money-making letters.

Though he paid full price for those letters, they may not have been as exclusive and original as Popoff thought. Lawyer Henry Eckhart—who has looked into Popoff's business methods—claims that in some cases Ewing merely copied old letters designed for other clients, such as Leroy Jenkins, and resold them to Popoff. Popoff purchased from several sources a group of 80,000 names, bringing his total list to 130,000 potentially generous persons, though Popoff's former controller, Ira McCorriston, says that only about 30,000 to 40,000 of the new list were really "big money" ("Code Seven") names.

McCorriston told me, "The trash [Ewing] put out was just unbelievable." One such piece was a "Holy Shower Cap." This was a cheap plastic affair that was to be worn by the recipient and then wrapped around some cash or a check and mailed back to Popoff. As such things go, it was a relative failure; it brought in only $100,000 from a single mailing. Some other gimmicks were: holy gloves (throw-away vinyl work gloves), golden prosperity envelopes, special red faith strings, mustard seeds, gold and silver lamé patches, holy ribbons, blessed shoe liners, sanctified handprints, Russian rubles, and red felt hearts. There were also sacred handkerchiefs imbued with the preacher's sweat. Popoff bought 36,000 of these from Synanon, another religious organization, at 25¢ apiece. He tore each into three pieces and represented to the faithful that he had mopped his brow with each scrap he mailed out. I have a large collection of such gimcrackery.

Since Reverend Ewing needed time to compose each letter and it had to describe some dire crisis for which money was required "immediately," and since Popoff's staff needed time to actually print the 100,000 begging letters and mail them out, Popoff had to invent his monthly crises many months in advance and get the information to the advertising agency. It's obvious that a lot of hard labor, thought, and planning goes into this kind of work.

Ewing first began working for Popoff on a percentage basis, about 20 to 25 percent of the "take." But when Popoff had to write him a check for $96,000, immediately followed by another for $100,000 each as his share of *one month's* results, the arrangement was changed to a flat $20,000 per letter, produced six at a time. Ewing managed to survive on that. Former Popoff assistant Mike Delaney remembers that he hand-delivered several $120,000 checks to Ewing, who is still active in that trade, writing the same valuable junk and inventing crisis situations for evangelists like Oral Roberts and Rex Humbard, under the trade name Twentieth Century Advertising.

A Major Exposure

Popoff was featured on the NBC-TV "Tonight Show" (popularly known as the "Johnny Carson Show") in February 1986 (repeated in June 1987)—but not in quite the manner he might have chosen.

Having obtained strong evidence that proved he was lying to his congregation and presenting faked miracles, my teammates and I went to several federal and local officials in California and asked that they take action against him. They clucked a great deal, promised to "look into" the matter, and then apparently forgot all about it. One U.S. Attorney wrote me that in March 1986 he had "referred the matter to the FBI with a request for input from the Postal Inspectors and Internal Revenue Service." He said that he expected to hear from them "within a few days" and that he should have "a better fix on what action might be appropriate" within a week. As this book goes to press, it is 16 months later. Nothing has been done.

Finding that the government (both state and federal) was uninterested in what had been uncovered, I was forced to present the case to the American public via television, on one of the most popular network programs.

The major item in the Popoff exposure had been the revelation of his rather advanced technique for "calling out" audience members. Armed with the broadcast videotape of a portion of the Popoff show recorded in Anaheim, California, I approached the producers of the "Tonight Show"—a show I'd been on many times before—and shortly thereafter I appeared there and played two tape segments. First was a 60-second segment of a "healing" by Popoff exactly as Popoff had presented it on his own telecast. He had called out names and addresses of people he had not spoken to, and then he had "healed" them. I informed Carson that we'd discovered that Popoff had a tiny hearing aid in his left ear, connected to a high-frequency receiver, and we showed that same tape segment again, this time *with the added audio track of Mrs. Popoff's voice, broadcast to Peter from backstage*, giving the needed information to Popoff and directing him to the right people. The audience was amazed at this blatant deception, and Johnny himself made his dismay quite clear in his comments.

I explained how Popoff had sent Reeford Sherrill (his "front man"), Volmer Thrane, and his wife, Elizabeth, into the audience in advance, equipped with transmitters to gather and broadcast the needed data backstage to the reverend.

I cannot resist the temptation to demonstrate that Popoff's gimmick had been prophesied in Matthew 10:26-27:

> For nothing is covered that shall not be revealed: nor hid, that shall not be known. That which I tell you in the dark, speak ye in the light: and that which you hear in the ear, preach ye upon the housetops.

Following this national exposure, everything hit the fan. Carson, long known as opposing such flummery, had given my campaign exactly the impetus it needed. Consternation took over at the Upland camp. Only a few there had known anything about the electronic device, because it had been secretly obtained for Popoff by Volmer Thrane, through another employee, Tisha Sousa. Volmer is the brother of Nancy Thrane, Popoff's general manager, who is in complete control of the computer records. She is also the employee who has been with the organization longest—eight years. Early the following morning, an emergency meeting was held. Popoff was bewildered, never having had to answer the kind of serious questions the media were now asking him. He floundered, and he made the wrong decisions.

At that crisis meeting, the public relations person was instructed to answer all inquiries by saying, "Everything Amazing Randi says is not true." Callers were asked to "pray for the ministry." Popoff also averred that he was going to sue me, though for exactly what we never learned. David Alexander offered to immediately produce me, live, at the Upland office of the Peter Popoff Evangelical Association to be served with papers by the Popoff lawyers. The offer was not seized upon.

The phone message was the total official response at that time. The Reverend Popoff tried to explain himself to those of the staff who had not known about the electronic assistance that he had been giving to God. There were some resignations by longtime associates of the ministry. Among those resigning were a few who then promptly contacted my group with some very important inside information about further chicanery within the camp.

But one of the principal officers, Garry McColman, president of marketing for the Peter Popoff Evangelical Association, remained faithful. As he later confided to a television producer, he gave Popoff some excellent advice. In answer to the question of the day, "What shall we do?" he simply said to Popoff:

> Peter, cover your ass! If the government people
> come poking about here, make sure your ass is
> covered *before* they get here!

On Day Two following Armageddon, the Upland office was claiming that NBC had hired an actress to impersonate Mrs. Popoff on a "doctored" videotape. That explanation didn't sell too well, and the media continued to press for the truth.

Finally, on Day Three, Reverend Popoff admitted the existence of the radio device, claiming, incredibly, that "almost everybody" knew about the "communicator." And, he added, "My wife *occasionally* gives me the name of a person who needs special prayers."

Since that time, in response to further pointed questions, Reverend Popoff has also stated that he never tried to imply that he was using his Gift of Knowledge for the "calling out." He said that he uses the "communicator" for two reasons: one, "to keep in touch with the television crew," and, two, as a convenience, so that he does not have to carry the "healing cards" around with him. And he promised to insert a disclaimer at the beginning of his TV broadcasts. More on that shortly.

This claimed use of the device to talk to the TV crew, we knew just wasn't so. In all of the many hours of recording we have of Mrs. Popoff speaking to Peter on the "communicator," *not once* is the television operation referred to. And the channel used by the TV crew *never* attempted to get information to him. As for the "occasional" name given him by Elizabeth, we found that *all* the names of the people he "called out" were given him via the secret transmitter and that *no* names were given to him that he did *not* call out.

Volmer Thrane, former Popoff confidant and vice-president of the ministry, informed us that the reverend did not obtain and start using the secret radio device until March 1985. Before that, he said, Mrs. Popoff would do audience interviews, then just take the data backstage to Peter, who would memorize it as best he could. Thrane had noticed early on that the people Elizabeth and Reeford talked to before the service were the ones Peter eventually "called out." Thrane was not allowed to be backstage before the action started, but Rod Sherrill was. Thrane told us that, at one point, Rod told him, "You're going to have to know." In January 1985, he said, he was told about the interview angle, but not about the radio device. Then, in March, Thrane was invited to get involved in the information-gathering process, and, of necessity, he was told the whole story.

It is just not true that, as Popoff claimed, "almost everybody" already knew about the device he was using to fake the Word of Knowledge. To examine this claim, members of the Bay Area Skeptics, the Southern California Skeptics, the Houston Society to Oppose Pseudoscience, and the San Diego Skeptics (in particular, Don Henvick, David Alexander, Bob Steiner, Steven Schafersman, and Ronn Nadeau) tracked down a good number of Popoff's victims. *All but one* of them, a woman who mistakenly believed that Popoff had her healing card in his hand when he called her out of the audience, asserted that they believed Popoff knew their names and addresses by the Gift of Knowledge. That, in itself, should show that Popoff's excuse has failed. But there is much stronger evidence available.

The Leaflet Campaign

Exactly as they did with W. V. Grant, local skeptics groups prepared leaflets that were handed out to all those who entered the Popoff meetings. In Chicago, details of the Johnny Carson show exposure were given and readers were asked to think about whether they should support Popoff. On each sheet was printed:

> You will be told to tear up this notice. If you
> do so, you will be responding to the Popoff
> organization, which takes in $10 to $20 million
> a year, tax-free, and has every reason to fear
> your receiving this information. This notice has
> been prepared, not by "atheists, secular human-
> ists, communists and Satan-worshipers," as
> Popoff would have you believe, but by rational,
> decent people who think you should know the
> truth. Whether you choose to accept the truth
> is, of course, another matter. And, be advised
> of this: Popoff has *refused* a simple challenge
> to provide us with just *five* persons to whom
> he has brought divine healing through God's
> power, persons who will submit to the examin-
> ation of *independent medical doctors*. Though he
> will tell you of miracles he has brought to pass,
> you should know that those miracles have been
> examined and found to be without merit. This is
> Popoff's show, in which he cannot be challeng-
> ed about his statements. There is another side
> that you do not know, and we invite you to
> investigate it, in the spirit of truth and justice.

Popoff had instructed Reeford Sherrill how to handle this
problem of the leaflets. In his warm-up talk before the Reverend
Popoff made his entrance, Sherrill told the audience:

> I'm gonna tell you, that ol' Devil sure don't
> like what we're gonna do here this afternoon.
> He's not gonna come against something that's
> not doin' anything. The Devil's gonna come
> against somebody that's doing something for
> Jesus Christ. Amen? Amen. And you know
> (showing the leaflet) they talk about Johnny
> Carson here. I'm gonna tell you something for
> everyone to hear. Johnny Carson is embarrassed
> by this whole situation. He even says he wat-
> ches our show! Amen? I think that's beautiful,
> don't you? Praise God! So, what I want you to
> do, everyone here—if you do, I want you to

hold it up real high. Everyone that's got one, I
want you to wad that paper up. Let that Devil
know you're not gonna listen to anything he
has to say. Praise God! I want you to join
hands right now and we're gonna pray for all
these people that's come against this ministry.
We're not gonna pray that God puts a big ol'
fire under their nose! We're gonna pray they
get saved.

The appeal to discard the leaflets was not very effective.
Perhaps those Chicago folks were curious to see just what they were
being asked to ignore, because my colleagues reported that not many
hands went up at that meeting with leaflets in them.

Revelations

It would be well to go into some detail on how the Popoff trick-
ery-by-technology was uncovered. When I attended my first Popoff
meeting in Houston, Texas, I was assisted by the Houston Society
to Oppose Pseudoscience, a dedicated group of people who distributed themselves through the audience to test Popoff's system.
I instructed them to allow themselves to be approached, and to
give out incorrect names and other data whether they were
"pumped" by questioners, asked to fill out healing cards, or both.
They were told to supply slightly different sets of information to
the two data inputs, so that if any of them were "called out" we
could tell from the incorrect information just which method had
been used.

Now, critics have objected to this plan, saying that it appears
we were only out to cause trouble with the faith-healers' methods,
but that is not so. The intent of our system was to show beyond
any doubt that the faith-healers were not getting their information from heaven, but from audience surveys. If they actually had
been getting that data by supernatural means, God would have
warned them when it was spurious.

In Houston, as in most other cities, we got very lucky indeed.
Several of our people were questioned—by Elizabeth Popoff—and
were asked to fill out cards. Three of them were "called out" by
Popoff almost immediately.

At this meeting, I was personally assisted by Steve Shaw, a
young mentalist who is making a big impact in the conjuring
business. Steve had been half of the Project Alpha team. (See

Skeptical Inquirer, 7, no. 4, and 8, no. 1.) For the Houston encounter with Popoff, Steve had volunteered to assist me, and I
knew I had a good man on my side.

When Steve and I saw Popoff dashing up and down the aisles
calling out as many as 20 names, illnesses, and other data, one
after the other, we knew something more than a mnemonic system
was at work. I said to Steve, "You know what to do?" He replied:
"Yep. I'll go look in his ears." And he did, almost bowling the
evangelist over as he bumped up against him to get a good look.
Steve saw the electronic device in Popoff's left ear. When he
reported this to me, I knew what my next step would be. Popoff
was using a receiver to get information from somewhere backstage, information gathered in advance by his wife and others.

Popoff was due the following week in San Francisco, and I
had excellent allies there among the Bay Area Skeptics. They
jumped at the chance to help, and I had as many bodies as I
needed to test the Popoff methods. One additional person was
enlisted, without whom we probably could not have cracked the
Popoff case. He was Alec Jason, an electronics specialist who
gladly volunteered his talents to us. He had access to a sophisti-
cated radio scanner that could pick up any transmission from or
to Popoff. But the problem was that we didn't know the frequency
being used, and with a radiation-rich civilization surrounding us,
we might have to scan for days to get the correct setting.

Sophisticated Technology at Work

But Alec's apparatus was rather specialized. It had been designed
for just such a situation. The night *before* the Popoff meeting at
the San Francisco Civic Auditorium, our sleuth had donned work-
man's clothing and wandered about the place with his scanner
switched on while the built-in computer plotted all the many
frequencies being used during another event being held there.
These broadcasts came from intercoms, communicators, and other
electronic machinery. The following night, Alec was back, carrying
the scanner connected to a tape recorder, and accompanied by
magician Robert Steiner, who has a history of detecting and
exposing fraud and was an excellent choice for this job, too. Alec
Jason set his scanner to again track down frequencies in use, but
he told it via the computer *to ignore those frequencies detected
the previous night.* This way, it would lock in on only those
frequencies peculiar to the Popoff operation. Almost immediately,
the device locked onto 39.170 megahertz, and Jason gave Steiner

the "thumbs-up" sign as he heard—and recorded—the voice of Elizabeth Popoff as she began the evening's business by saying:

> Hello, Petey. I love you. I'm talking to you. Can
> you hear me? If you can't, you're in trouble,
> 'cause I'm talking. As well as I can talk. I'm
> looking up names, right now. I forgot to ask.
> Are you going to preach first, or are you going
> to minister first? Helloooo! I love you!

(On September 5, 1985, Popoff's office assistant, Tisha Sousa, had ordered the secret radio equipment by telephone from Audio Specialties, in Los Angeles. Popoff, in person, picked up the equipment, using his platinum American Express card to pay for it, and drove away in his gold Mercedes. He was already using two of the Audio Specialties wireless microphone units, purchased earlier, but these were for regular voice-amplification use. The new technology, consisting of an induction neck loop, a tiny, nearly invisible earpiece, and the sensitive receiver, used to pick up a clandestine voice from the very high-quality transmitter operated by Elizabeth Popoff, provided the team with the means to flimflam their audiences into believing Peter had supernatural connections.)

What followed the "Hello, Petey" greeting was a recitation of the names and other data that had been so carefully gathered by Elizabeth and written down by Peter Popoff on sheets of paper from which Elizabeth was now reading, while watching her husband on the TV monitors outside at the transmitter. We have some of those sheets, and we found that there were standard abbreviations used. "Del." stood for "deliverance," "Sal." for "salvation." A sample sheet, which was used when Peter had to visit tables at the Inner Circle Club in San Francisco, read as follows:

> A-1 Table 5. White dress with flowers. Dorothy
> Brownlee. Thyroid problem—needs a better job!
> Sal. of loved ones. Janet Perdue. Sal. of family.
> 4. Gives. Mae Eusz Del. from worry. Ruth's
> emotional healing. Girl friend just had stroke
> on left side. (proxy) had to leave at 12:15 P.M.
> B. Table 2. Katherine Atchinson. Open doors
> that have increase in faith. Financial break-
> through.
> 3. Ruth Boyd. Legs, veins, feet swell, back,
> memory.

3. Table 8. Esther Dallas. High blood pressure. Dizziness. Hus. and grandma have asthma. Had stroke 6 yrs. ago.

And so on, for several pages. (The original is reproduced in Appendix III of this book.)

An Intended Deception

Before the Carson show was aired, I appeared on Cable News Network (CNN) and revealed that Popoff was being supplied with the information obtained from the in-audience interviews. But I did not mention that we had detected the secret transmitter and receiver, expecting that Popoff would assume that what I said on CNN was all I knew. He fell for it. The next week, he broadcast a series of testimonials which he felt would validate his ministry. Thus there exists a videotape segment *from his own broadcast, edited and chosen personally by Peter Popoff himself* demonstrating his deception. I quote here, word for word, the testimonial from an unnamed woman in Pennsylvania, who said:

> As of approximately six weeks ago, I never knew of you. And I ran—happened by your—your telecast. I won't say "by accident" because it was the work of the Lord. Ahh, oh—about four weeks ago, five weeks ago. And I says, can this be? Can this be, that this man is calling out names and addresses? Amen. And, ahh, so as I said, I watched about three, four programs and then—I found that you were coming to Pittsburgh. I says, well, I—I—I *really* didn't believe it. I said—I have to—I just *have* to go and see. And today, when you called my name—first name *and* last, street address—uh, *number* and address —I mean, believe me, people, God is *real!* Ooooh —God is *real!* Hallelujah!

There it is, positive proof that *Peter Popoff did indeed want to give, and did give, the impression that he was speaking to God—and hearing from Him personally.* That was the gimmick that sold all the rest of the act. But remember Popoff's announced intention to put a disclaimer at the beginning of every performance? Well, he did just that. But did he tell people in this dis-

claimer that he was using a "communicator"? Did he admit that
his wife had been gathering data for him from the audience? Did
he deny hearing from God through the Gift of Knowledge? No, all
the Reverend Popoff said by way of a disclaimer was a brief
voice-over statement *on one program only*: "People at the Peter
Popoff services are prayed for by request." If it were not tragic,
we would laugh.

Case for the Defense

My exposé of W. V. Grant had by now appeared in *Free Inquiry*
magazine. In that article, I had revealed his gimmick of supplying
wheelchairs to selected people who were able to walk, and then
seeming to have healed them when they responded to his command
to get up out of the wheelchairs. When Garry McColman, representing the Popoff camp, appeared on television with me in St.
Louis to debate the matter, he arrived rather poorly informed by
his master. Though he frequently invoked "Blessed Jesus" and
used other similarly powerful phrases whenever my comments
seemed too trouble him, he blew it all by insisting that, unlike the
Reverend Grant, the Reverend Popoff did not use rented wheelchairs for the old wheelchair trick.

After getting him to twice firmly assert that fact, I played
for him and the television audience an audio tape prepared during
the Popoff Detroit crusade, in which Mrs. Popoff, by way of the
secret transmitter, assured her husband that the woman he was
about to "heal" in the wheelchair *could* really walk, and then she
added, "That's one of our rentals." Popoff was then heard to
command the woman to "Get up and walk!" The on-camera reaction of the Popoff flunky to this unexpected evidence was rather
colorful, and the show's host and audience were shocked. What
they did not know was that the "woman" in that chair, placed
there by Reeford Sherrill, was not only someone we had planted in
the audience, but was in actuality Donald Henvick, a San Francisco post*man*! He had just been "healed" by Popoff of uterine
cancer.

During the Popoff Detroit crusade, I had placed my eaves-
dropping equipment in a trash bag in the bushes outside the
window near where Elizabeth Popoff was seated with the secret
transmitter relaying information to her husband inside the auditorium. My scanner, tuned to 39.170 megahertz, was feeding its signal
into a tape recorder. When I later played back that tape, I heard
Mrs. Popoff's voice directing the reverend to the front of the

auditorium, where Scot Morris, covering the event for *Penthouse* magazine, was posing as the son of "Bernice" (Henvick), pushing "her" around in a wheelchair. Elizabeth Popoff said:

> Peter, there's one there that has a beard. Looks like she has a beard. Her name is Bernice—Meticall. She can't walk. She gets real tired and the doctors think she has—doctors think she might have cancer of the uterus. She can walk. She can walk. That's one of our rentals.

At this point, Popoff asked "Bernice" to get up and walk. "She" did, but in so doing, revealed the masquerade.

Henvick had developed a peculiar gesture of "ecstasy" that had impressed the Popoffs *back in Anaheim*. This encounter in Detroit was the third time that Popoff had "healed" Henvick, and as Henvick waved his hands about in calculated jubilation, the backstage people finally penetrated the disguise. The tape recording reveals that moment of truth as Elizabeth, recognizing that gesture, reacted. All heaven broke loose in the "control tower":

> That's a woman? *That's not a woman!* Hey! Is that the—isn't that the guy who was in Anaheim? Pete! That's the man who was in Anaheim that you said—that had arthritis. Do you remember that man? The way he was—Let's go on to the next! Get rid of him! . . . Remember the guy who was on the news the other day? Remember that guy? When he went out—That was it! That's the same guy that was in Anaheim! . . . We're gonna move to the other side. We don't like this. There's some funny bunnies out there.

At that point, a man sent by Elizabeth from backstage came running out to confer with Reeford Sherrill, who was accompanying Popoff in the audience. It seems that observers of the TV monitors had noticed that Scot Morris taking photos, and because he was in the company of the now-exposed Henvick, Morris had to be stopped. Sherrill hastened backstage, and as he burst in on Elizabeth in the trailer, she broke away from her communication with Peter and this is heard on the tape:

(Elizabeth Popoff, aside:) The guy's taking pictures. . . . (Reeford Sherrill, aside:) A camera guy. Taking pictures . . . His flashbulb's popping. Oh-oh! Oh-oh!

Emerging rapidly from backstage into the auditorium, Reeford trotted over to Scot, who was busily snapping photos of Popoff, and snatched Scot's camera away from him. "I can get a better shot for you from here," he assured Scot. He stepped up onto the stairs leading to the stage, popped the back of the camera open, pulled the film out, and tossed the camera back to Scot with the film dangling.

A Valuable Colleague

Before the end of our investigation, Don Henvick would be healed by four different healers, in six different cities, of six different diseases, under four different names and two different sexes. Believe me, as "Bernice," Henvick is not a beauty. During his campaign, he went through an astonishing set of changes. He shaved off his beard, then most of his hair, dyed a fringe of hair gray, wore thick glasses, walked on crutches, dieted and lost 40 pounds, wore wigs and funny costumes—all for the cause. By these means, he proved beyond any doubt that many faith-healers—Popoff among them—were obtaining information by subterfuge and then feeding it back as if it came from God.

The Electronic Evidence

During our investigations of Popoff, we recorded what were obviously unintentionally transmitted off-mike conversations from the trailer between Elizabeth Popoff and Pam Sherrill that demonstrated just how callous, arrogant, bigoted, and shallow were the "anointed." Elizabeth laughed and joked at the "boobs" and "big butts" of terminally ill women who were there giving their money and their confidence to the Popoffs. The two women made raunchy gags at the expense of many of their ailing victims. They discussed breast implants, recipes, and family scandals while Popoff pretended to heal the sick, snapping back into action only when the reverend went into a series of "amens" that signaled his need for a new data set.

On one occasion, Elizabeth Popoff left the transmitter switched on for 40 minutes following a performance, and the ensuing conversation with her husband and others of the inner sanctum was *most* revealing, as they discussed the results of the meeting and the individuals involved.

Our man was listening to all of this. While his tape machine and scanner hummed away, Alec Jason, our electronics whiz who detected the secret broadcasts, stood directly outside the TV trailer, staring at the sky as though he were a tourist and was undetected.

A Different Brand of People

Elizabeth Popoff is a Roman Catholic, with rosary and all, a fact not well advertised by husband Peter, and unknown to the Popoff following. (The Popoff family attends a Nazarene church in Upland.) Perhaps that is one reason she was able to operate the "Word of Knowledge" scam without too many serious qualms, because the victims were of the "wrong" denomination.

Following the "Tonight Show" exposure, though there were a number of personnel and public relations problems at the Popoff office, the money continued to arrive daily. Why did it take eight months for the Popoff organization to feel the effect of the devastating exposure? Had it involved any other sort of business, the result would have been catastrophic within 24 hours. But, as his former controller, Ira McCorriston, explained, Popoff had told his staff:

> Randi can hit me through the media, he can hit
> me through the news, TV, radio, but he can't
> hit me through the mailing list. That's the *only*
> way he could hurt me all the way.

He was wrong. But why eight months? The explanation for that delay lies in the lifestyle of the faithful. They rarely see any television other than Christian programming, certainly not a late-night show like Carson's that may allow naughty words occasionally. Even regular network newscasts are suspect to these people, because the personnel may not be Christians and could thus be tools of Satan. This isolation is encouraged by the leaders of many sects. A best-seller currently on the Christian merchandise list of the Dominion Network is a specially programmed and selective satellite dish receiver tuned *only* to 100 percent Christian channels. The rest of the world—the real world—can thus be effectively shut out. Ira McCorriston summed up the situation for me:

> You're not familiar with Christian people. They
> live in their own little world. A lot of them
> don't even read the paper. They're a whole
> different brand of people. If you want to
> understand them you have to think the way
> they think.

It seems that there isn't much thinking going on. In discussing
this closed world with Professor Joseph Barnhart of North Texas
State University, and others, I have learned that many fundamentalist, evangelical, and born-again Christian homes simply do not
watch television news or listen to radio news. Their preachers
have told them that the media are controlled by Satan, and they
fear invasion of their homes by doubt.

But through overheard conversation and gossip within church
circles, the shocking news eventually got around that Popoff might
not be quite what he represented himself to be, and the effect
was eventually felt in Upland. People began inquiring by mail
about the dreadful rumors they'd heard. McCorriston says that
Popoff decided simply to refuse to give any explanation, even to
those who telephoned or visited the headquarters with queries.

They'll Believe Anything

That "closed world" that refuses to know anything about the real
world can be sold any idea if it comes from an acceptable source.
Peter Popoff found that out even before he became a big media
personality. He sold booklets that confirmed the worst fears of
those who tremble at the words "demon" or "Satan." Some titles:
"Demons at Your Doorstep," "Calamities, Catastrophies [sic] and
Chaos," and "Six Things Satan Uses to Rob You of God's Abundant Blessings." From the first booklet, we learn the answer to
that age-old question, "What Is Collagen?":

> Doctors and clinics specializing in abortion have
> discovered a bonanza. In addition to the mil-
> lions rolling in as medical fees, there is another
> gold mine. I will begin explaining with this
> question: Have you ever wondered what happens
> to the aborted fetus? Perhaps it is flushed
> down a toilet or burned in a furnace? Oh no,
> they take that fetus . . . put it into a plastic
> bag and weigh it.

> Why weigh it? Because certain cosmetic companies pay around $5,500 per pound for that fetus! Why do they buy the fetus? For collagen. Collagen is the newest "miracle" ingredient in expensive skin creams that diminish wrinkles and purportedly maintain firmness. . . . What is collagen? Brace yourself. They take that tender, unborn baby—which often already had a heartbeat and had been breathing—they grind that tiny being in a processor and whip it into a cream. That's collagen. Yes, demons are at our doorsteps, even in our homes—their products even in our bodies!

As I relate such matters in these pages, it is difficult to realize that I'm not writing fantasy fiction. But it is clear that much of what I report, and what is believed by those who are duped by the charlatans, sounds like *National Lampoon* material. Popoff's insane story of the collagen conspiracy is a total invention.

The Popoff Camp Answers by Mail

On July 17, 1986, Popoff sent a letter to those who had written to inquire about accusations I'd made and the major news stories that developed about the Popoff radio device. It said, in part:

> The so-called Great [*sic*] Randi, a magician and avowed atheist, is trying to discredit anything and everything that is supernatural. He is attacking every charismatic ministry in this country. Most of his so-called charges are *out right* [*sic*] *lies*. . . . He says I carry fifty wheelchairs around the country and fake miracles. . . . I have *never* faked a miracle. I have never carried a wheelchair into my crusades. That is the absolute truth. . . . Randi has defamed my wife and prayer partner Elizabeth. . . . Yes, Elizabeth loves to greet you and shake hands with you at our crusades. But, I only pray for those whom the Holy Spirit prompts me to minister unto. . . . But the carnal mind cannot understand these things because they must be spiritually discerned.

That calls for a brief discussion. Popoff's statement puts all sorts of words in my mouth and intentions in my mind that never even occurred to me. The wheelchairs were 30 in number, not 50, and they were carried by W. V. Grant, not Popoff. His statement "I have never carried a wheelchair into my crusades" is clever. Note that he does not say that he never *rented* a wheelchair and sat someone in it. If I have defamed Elizabeth merely by describing her participation in the deception and quoting a small part of what she said in some four and a half hours of recordings we have of her transmissions, so be it. As for the statement quoted above, that he will "only pray for those whom the Holy Spirit prompts [him] to minister unto," it seems passing strange that, as mentioned previously, we found that the names of *all* those Peter was "prompted" to minister unto by the Holy Spirit were relayed to him by Elizabeth. Quite a coincidence. Finally, there must be a great number of dense, carnal minds out there in the real world who fail, along with me, to understand Popoff's explanation.

Backs to the Wall

Ira McCorriston told me that the Popoff camp was at last forced to face facts:

> We finally had a meeting, and sat down and said, "We gotta say something. We should have said something the first week. We've waited too long now." But Peter kept thinking it was all just gonna go away.

Mike Delaney, Popoff's former assistant, echoed this observation:

> [There was] no reaction at the office [though many phone calls were coming in] and the employees didn't think much about it. Most of them weren't very educated.

At this point, Popoff fired a number of people. He moved into a storefront location in an Upland shopping center, went off TV completely, and changed the name of his organization, dropping his name from it. The Peter Popoff Evangelical Association, as of January 6, 1987, vanished. The new operation which filled that void, People United for Christ, included, as directors, Peter Popoff; his father, George Popoff; and his sister, Ruth Ferguson.

Elizabeth Popoff, who had been a director of the PPEA, was not listed as a director of PUC.

Attendance at his crusades dropped precipitously, but those who know the religion business well feel that by radio campaigns alone, Popoff could still continue to bring in $100,000 to $200,000 a month as long as his face was not seen and recognized.

Some months later more personnel were fired, including one of the most important—controller Ira McCorriston. McCorriston was very close to the top. Before joining the Popoff entourage, he had been living in Tampa, Florida, working as a used-car salesman, and first came into contact with Popoff when his crusade came to that town. He told Popoff of his eight years of experience working for evangelist Leroy Jenkins, and as a result, in January 1986, he was engaged as the controller of the Popoff empire. He moved his family to Upland, where he bought a $500,000 house on the assumption that he would continue to receive a handsome $80,000 a year for his services, plus a percentage of the gross mail contributions. He is now back in Tampa, selling used cars once more. Ira had known Popoff's TV director, Rod Sherrill, for more than 20 years at the time he made the move, and he did it, he says, largely because Sherrill assured him of Popoff's integrity. Then Popoff fired Rod Sherrill. Both firings were enormous errors in judgment.

Before he was equipped with the electronic gimmick in September 1985, Popoff used a variety of means to obtain people's names. One trick was to examine the checks they handed in, which bore their names and addresses. This is a technique also used by W. V. Grant and others. But nothing any other faith-healer ever had beat the radio device for dramatic effect. Said Ira McCorriston:

> He didn't have much until he got the earpiece,
> and then that "made" him. When he lost that,
> well, he just didn't have anything.

Then, too, Peter Popoff still had four presses going in his private printing shop, churning out his carefully constructed begging letters to some 100,000 people, twice a month, by using the mailing list he still has. Even operating out of his garage, McCorriston says, Popoff could keep three or four employees busy and bring in $50,000 to $100,000 a month with his mailing list alone.

An Unhappy Toiler in the Vineyard

In July 1983, young Mike Delaney took a position as printer and general handyman with the Peter Popoff Evangelical Association in Upland. Soon, he was working in the radio production department, and in less than three years had risen to the position of manager of the tape-recording operation and general assistant to Popoff. He says that he felt from the first that the Popoff ministry was crooked, and many of his assignments convinced him of that suspicion. One of his functions was to dispose of the mountains of mail that came in every week. Unlike W. V. Grant, who simply threw out his letters in trash bags, Popoff had his professionally shredded, and Mike was in charge of that. Popoff was on guard against competing evangelists who would like nothing better than to go through his trash for additions to their mailing lists.

And Popoff made promises to his donors that Delaney says were not kept. Explained Delaney:

> He'd say [on TV], "Send your letter in and I'll pray over it." But he never prayed over them. They'd sit there in a big pile for a month, then they'd be shredded. I'd take them to the shredding company and they'd take care of it.

This was done, of course, after the money had been taken from the envelopes and the names, addresses, and other personal data had been entered into the IBM computer system to maintain Popoff's secret detailed file on each writer.

Popoff's security guards were in charge of checking the garbage for any unshredded documents. In the weeks before Delaney left Popoff's employ, a security man was told to follow him every time he drove the rented U-Haul truck into Los Angeles to have the material shredded. Once, just for a lark, Mike eluded his stalker simply by driving the truck into the U-Haul parking area and then joining other trucks as they drove off in various directions.

Delaney also witnessed examples of Popoff's callous attitude toward the people who supported him. When Popoff sent out a special-appeal mailing of 2,500 letters to donors who were known to be unusually generous, Delaney himself signed 1,500 of them because Popoff was tired. Often he watched as people showed up at the Peter Popoff Evangelical Association headquarters, down and out because they had given the preacher all the money they had. They even arrived in rented trucks with all their furniture stacked in them, desperate for help. When they asked to see Popoff, expecting a miracle, he was never in. They were always refused an audience.

As a result of my exposure of the Popoff organization on the Johnny Carson show, his failure to rise above the $8.50 an hour paid him by the ministry, and an involvement in one of Popoff's major scams, which will be discussed later, Mike Delaney left the Popoff organization. He gave two weeks' notice, but was dismissed the next day, July 12, 1986.

And Then There's the Other Sherrill Family

Reeford Sherrill, a very tall, well-groomed, white-haired Texan with a striking stage presence, went from being a small-time preacher to the position of right-hand "front man" for Peter Popoff. He says he and his wife, Pam, had to leave the Popoff operation when he discovered that it was, to quote him directly, a "crooked and foul'" system. Pam had first seen Popoff in operation when she was only 14 years old, and she was "thrilled" when first invited to have the opportunity of working with him.

Reeford was an old hand in the business. He'd had a church of his own in Mansfield, Texas, just south of Dallas. It failed, and his brother Rod, who at that time was running All-American Video for the W. V. Grant organization in Ohio, invited him to work there. Reeford accepted, and was put in charge of the camera department. He stayed with the company even after Dennis Jenkins, son of faith-healer Leroy Jenkins, left because of the trickery he saw being used to deceive the faithful. Young Jenkins had, and still has, considerable respect for the Sherrills. "I was real surprised to see Reeford stay on after that," he told me.

An Important Character

If there is a single Svengali behind the evangelist/healers we are discussing, Reeford's brother, Rod Sherrill, might be cast in that part. He worked in highly responsible and vital positions for Leroy Jenkins, W. V. Grant, and Peter Popoff. He grew up in the same neighborhood as Grant in Dallas. He was in the business well before he brought Reeford into it. He knew about chicanery that he must have felt Reeford and Pam would not have approved of, had they known about it, and he was in fact the originator of much of that flummery. To him, as with all of his efforts, it was "just doing my job."

Let us not forget though that it took Reeford and Pam some time to decide to back out of the Popoff operation after they learned about the secret transmitter Popoff was using. Other things, such as the pre-show interviews with the ailing in the audience and the high-powered money-making gimmicks, didn't seem to trouble them. Reeford even participated, regularly, in these interviews. Pam, for one, had been told by Elizabeth Popoff (during a crusade in Stockton, California) that there was $2 million in the family vault set aside for a rainy day, and she had seen the endless items of jewelry that had come into Mrs. Popoff's hands from admirers. But it was many months before she decided that she and her husband had had enough.

In all fairness, it was not easy for the Sherrills to quit their lucrative jobs with Popoff. Both Reeford and Rod had families with children to support.

One Broken Promise Too Many

One particular episode seems to have—understandably—angered Pam Sherrill more than most and might have been the final straw for her. It was not unusual, she says, during a service, for women admirers to reach out to place jewelry into Peter Popoff's hands or pockets as he passed them. During a crusade in Bakersfield, California, a smitten woman gave a diamond ring of several carats to Reeford Sherrill to give to Peter. Later, at the close of the service, Peter gallantly presented it to wife Elizabeth. Noticing Pam's expression, he promised her, "The next ring I get will be yours!" Not long after that event, an opportunity to fulfill that promise arrived during a Houston crusade, when Pam was approached by a distraught elderly gentleman who pressed a bulging manila envelope into her hands. It was held together with rubber bands and tape. He told her that his wife had Alzheimer's disease, and he wanted her jewelry to go to the Popoff ministry for God's work. She thanked him and hurried backstage to present the package to Popoff, fully expecting him to share the bonanza with her. He examined the shining treasure and waved her away, saying that they would discuss it later. He never mentioned it again.

Electronics to the Rescue

At first, when Peter Popoff began his TV ministry, says a cameraman who helped prepare the earlier shows, "there was nothing happening." Popoff was not very good at what he was doing. Former controller Ira McCorriston told me:

> [Popoff] can't preach a complete sermon. He'll start, then he'll begin rambling and telling you things that happened to him when he was 10 years old, and his father . . .

But Rod Sherrill was there to improve that performance electronically. A former photographer who learned video techniques from his foster father, evangelist Leroy Jenkins (he left that ministry just before Jenkins went to prison), Rod was well able to create appropriate TV images for his employers, and had no illusions about the strictly businesslike approach he was expected to take. Before the Popoff ministry collapsed, he told an independent filmmaker in San Francisco, "There are two kinds of people in the world." He said there were those who believed and those who didn't, and that he was dealing with the former. The latter were of no interest to him. Cameraman Gary Clarke echoed Rod's conviction, saying, "We have a certain kind of client . . . they just *want* to believe." It was also Rod's opinion that "a *real* Christian can't work in a Christian organization." But he did, and in case faith in his employer began to fade, Rod Sherrill was there to reinforce it by whatever means necessary.

The "Russian Bibles" Vandalism Scam

But Rod Sherrill did more than just enhance certain aspects of the Popoff performance. He was involved as well in at least one of Popoff's major deceptions. It was one that brought Popoff a huge financial return. A leading actor in this drama was Mike Delaney, the young handyman at the Peter Popoff Evangelical Association headquarters. Just before he left that organization, he had second thoughts about a scheme in which he had been intimately involved the year before while working for Popoff. To protect himself, he began asking questions and making notes. He felt that the whole organization would eventually unravel and that this plot would come to light. It did.

Delaney told us that he had known nothing of the electronic device with which Popoff accomplished his miraculous "Word of Knowledge" stunt. In fact, he said, no one then in the office but the Popoffs, Tisha Sousa, Volmer Thrane, and the Sherrills knew about it until my exposure of it on the "Tonight Show," though they were *all* aware of other fakery.

Through 1985, Popoff promoted a huge project. He begged his audience to send him money for the purchase of Russian-language Bibles that he promised to send behind the Iron Curtain by means of couriers who would smuggle them in their baggage to thousands of eager Soviet citizens starving for the Word. Several other totally hilarious, harebrained schemes were also suggested as alternatives to keep up the interest of potential donors. Up ahead, I will detail the "Great Balloon Caper" that he came up with to further flatten his fans' wallets.

The Plot Thickens

There was much more to the project than Popoff's patrons ever knew. My colleague David Alexander is the one who uncovered the entire plot, by interviewing many of the minor characters involved and gathering the physical evidence to establish the facts. What he discovered constitutes, in our opinion, a strong case.

Popoff needed two things: He wanted to bring in a great deal of money, and he had to explain the fact that his promise to deliver the Russian Bibles had not been fulfilled. Ideally, he could provide the explanation and at the same time attract the money. To accomplish this, he decided to fake a break-in at his head-quarters along with the destruction of the Bibles he had told his followers he had ready to ship. The results would be videotaped and shown to the nationwide television audience. He would earn sympathy and funds at the same time.

In May 1985, Delaney had entered the plan. He was approach-ed by Rod Sherrill, who offered him and a friend of his $25 each for an easy evening's extra work. Popoff and Sherrill set up a stack of "Russian Bibles" in the print shop and instructed the two to return later and wet them down with a hose and strew them around the shop.

The Vandals Strike

That night, at nine o'clock, Mike Delaney let himself and his friend into the print shop with a key that Rod Sherrill had given him for that purpose. They turned a hose on the "Bibles" and left. Early the next morning, just before the videotaping began, Mike returned to generally ransack the shop. The plan was to break a window as if that were the means of entry by unknown vandals, said Delaney. He left the printing equipment intact, but made enough of a mess for the resulting display on TV to be effective.

It is incredible how inept the operation actually was. Although Sherrill—with the full knowledge and enthusiastic approval of Popoff—had come up with this clever scam, he bungled the actual performance. For one thing, Sherrill told Delaney to put in an order for new glass for the front door of the office *three days before the glass was broken!* Delaney still has the original, dated receipt from the A-1 Glass Company in Upland.

When Volmer Thrane tried to break the window, he heaved a brick at it three times, but only cracked it. Rod Sherrill had to take over. When he successfully threw the brick through the window, he did so *from inside the office,* so that not only did all the shattered glass end up *outside,* but the flexible plastic laminate in the glass made the door bulge *from the inside out,* and this fact showed up clearly in the tape they prepared and eventually broadcast. The Three Stooges couldn't have improved on this performance.

To top it all off, Mike Delaney says he discovered that he had soaked only about 10,000 books, not the 100,000 claimed, and that they were not Russian Bibles at all, as Popoff represented them to his TV audience. They were simple 48-page religious tracts written in Russian!

When David Alexander and I interviewed Rod Sherrill in the company of his brother, Reeford, and his sister-in-law, Pam, Rod told us that he had not been aware of the Russian Bible vandalism scam until Volmer Thrane, a former Popoff employee, told him about it. Though it had been Peter Popoff's idea, Rod was in on the implementation of the scheme, and helped carry it out—badly.

The Appeal to Repair the Devil's Work

Having performed the fakery, Popoff now had to launch his money plea to the gullible. First, to establish among the staff that the break-in was real, he allowed them to come in later that morning and "discover" the damage. At that point, they were sent home, and the TV crew began taping a special segment for the next Sunday's broadcast.

Director Sherrill arranged a heart-rending shot of Peter, tears streaming down his face, standing before the smashed front door of his headquarters. Those tears were real, the result of Rod rubbing a cut onion over Popoff's cheeks. Choking—perhaps more with laughter than with histrionics—Popoff showed his viewers the broken glass and invited them inside to see what the "Satanists and secular humanists" had done to his office and printing plant. The wrongly broken glass door stood out for any mildly perceptive mind to wonder about, but Popoff didn't have to concern himself much with that possibility.

Inside, Popoff stood beside Liz, both of them sniffing back tears. A pallet was beside them, its contents spilled around and obviously wet. Peter launched into a disjointed account of how the vandals had tried to destroy these "Russian Bibles" that his viewers had been paying to send behind the Iron Curtain. He told them that he and Liz had decided to reach into their own pockets and use their credit card to help pay for the damage. He suggested that viewers should do the same.

The Smoking Videotape

We have in our possession the *original* videotape that was prepared for that broadcast, along with the out-takes (unused portions) made at the same time. And on that tape is damning evidence of the scheme that Popoff perpetrated on his viewers. There is information on the tape preceding and following the video image that none of the perpetrators could have known about.

First, color bars appear on that tape. This is standard procedure. Those bars and the accompanying "reference tone" on the sound track are necessary to establish the parameters of each recording, so that when the original master tape is sent out to be copied and distributed to the dozens of TV stations that will broadcast it, it will be of optimal quality. Next, the program material shows up, with Popoff leading his TV audience inside the office through the smashed window in the front door, to see the terrible damage wrought by the Devil. This is the text directly from program No. 134, broadcast on Sunday, May 12, 1985:

> Originally, I was going to do something else this week, but I want to show you what the Devil has done. Will you come with me?

Once inside amid the debris, he continued:

> Elizabeth, I'm in a complete state of shock. Friends, while you were at church, our headquarters were vandalized. Now, we've been experiencing Satanic opposition, but friends, I

never expected that the Devil would come right into our headquarters and smash our premises. And the thing that I don't believe was a co-incidence was—is that he came right for the Word of God. I want to *show* you what happened. I want to *show* you the Devil has attacked us and they *hosed down* the Bibles. Now these Bibles were on skids, ready to be airlifted to the Russian border, where we were going to bring them to the persecuted underground church in our annual gospel invasion. We were *excited* about this gospel invasion. But *now* it seems like the Devil's brought us almost to a complete standstill. Our van was vandalized. The *windows* were smashed. The *lights* were smashed. My *children* were *almost* in tears when they saw what was going on.

As the reader will know by now, this is a complete pack of lies. Amid phony tears, the Popoffs were outlining an entirely fictitious event. If the Devil brought this operation to a standstill, his initials were P.P. Next on the tape, they presented the appeal:

And right now, at this moment, as we are *both* in a state of shock, we can feel your needs, you see, because we suffer. We suffer with you. We hurt. I feel the hurt to the pit of my stomach. . . . Well, it really hurts to see Satan step in like this, and try to stop God's work in our tracks. But friends, I know that the Devil's not going to win. I know that we're going to break through. Yes, we *did* have some insurance, but it will never make up for what we've lost, at this moment. And friends, time is of the essence. Right now, these Bibles were to be airlifted, *now*, so that we could get them into the hands of our couriers, so they could *go*. I feel *hurt*, right now. I can feel *your* needs, because the *Devil* has attacked us, just like he attacks *you*. And I feel right now that God is going to let us see restoration, Elizabeth. And my wife and I had agreed—we felt this in our spirits—to *loan* $500 to Jesus, that we were

going to borrow on our Visa card. I didn't
know at that time what was going to happen,
but I felt led of the Lord to loan this to Jesus.
Well, now I know that we're going to loan this
$500 to Jesus on our Visa card, and Liz, we're
going to put it into the Word, and I know that
no man at any *time*, any*where*, has *ever* put
something into the Word, loaned something to
Jesus, whose life wasn't changed, who didn't
experience an overwhelming, abundant, press-
down,   shake-'em-together,   running-over
measure. And I believe that many of *you*,
friends, are going to stand with us. You're
going to loan to the Lord, loan to Jesus, and I
believe that God is going to make you a par-
taker of the blessings that we're going to see.

At the time Popoff spoke those words, assuring his viewers of
the hardship that $500 would mean to his family, he was pulling in
at least a million and a quarter dollars a month. And, incidentally,
it was Volmer Thrane who, according to Rod Sherrill, smashed up
the van so convincingly. I wonder if Popoff made an insurance
claim on that damage, and if so, whether the insurance company
cares that they paid off on planned destruction.

Selling the Snake Oil

Following this, Popoff offered an inducement to send in "a love
offering of $30 or more." Viewers could obtain a vial of very
special "anointing oil" which the Popoffs had obtained for them
"in the Holy Land, walking in the footsteps of Jesus," along with
"instructions on how to use it." I certainly hope that purchasers
didn't use it on salads. Unknown to all but a few of the Popoff
staff who prepared it, it was a mixture of olive oil and Old Spice
Shaving Lotion. That mixture, plus three of Popoff's cassettes,
would be accompanied by a special print of Jesus (drawn by Rod's
wife, Elsa) with His arms spread wide. The picture, viewers were
told, had been on the wall of Popoff's office when the terrible
vandals broke in, and the proof of its power was the fact that
those vandals had been "unable to pass this holy picture" to get
further into the premises. Mind you, they had been able to get to
the Russian Bibles and had wet them down, but this drawing had
stopped them. Said Popoff:

> In this day, when Satanic spirits are literally on the loose, isn't it good to know that Jesus with His outstretched arms covers you, your loved ones and your home?

But Popoff wasn't quite finished making a point. As we've seen, he was never satisfied with his flock merely sending in whatever loose cash they had available. He wanted every dollar that he could root out of them. An unemptied wallet was an abomination to him. On this tape, we hear:

> I believe that some of you have something in land, in cars, in houses, and your savings accounts, money that you were going to use for something else. You're going to loan it to Jesus now . . . and God's going to give it back to you many, many, many, many times over.

There we have evidence not only of insatiable greed and avarice, but there is a promise that the money sought is just a loan which will be repaid. It is also a promise of financial return made through the media, and in the opinion of several experts we have consulted, making such a promise may constitute a crime.

The Damning Evidence of Popoff's Personal Involvement

But between the segments of the May 12, 1985, tape is some very interesting incidental conversational material, following a microphone test of voice level. With no video on the screen, we hear:

Peter Popoff:	No, we can't tell you that right now. We need to let the kids come in and tape them, and then we want to get out by the van and do some taping out there.
Elizabeth Popoff:	What time is the window guy comin'?
Volmer Thrane:	At four.
Rod Sherrill:	Well, he'll be here a little earlier, but that'll be all right.
Peter Popoff:	Okay. That'll just take a minute. All we're going to do is just one shot. Volmer, which window's cracked?

Volmer Thrane:	We're not going to break it, 'cause I'm going to make a ventilation system out of it. [Giggling in the background] I'll just bust the one in the door.
Elizabeth Popoff:	(Giggles.)
Peter Popoff:	Okay.
Volmer Thrane:	Yeah, that'll be fine. That'll be such a mess to clean up. I'll have to pull everything out, and—
Peter Popoff:	Okay.
Volmer Thrane:	I think we'll get the point across with the door.
Peter Popoff:	Okay. I think so, too.
Rod Sherrill:	Are we ready?
Peter Popoff:	Volmer, are you going to help me bust this door? Or—
Volmer Thrane:	Yeah, I'll be back on it.
Peter Popoff:	Okay. Come back down in five, ten more minutes. We'll be done.

This conversation seems to indicate that the interior video shots were obtained *before* the window was broken by Volmer and Rod.

The Popoff Miracle Crusade program ended that day with one more appeal to shake loose any money that the faithful might still have been holding onto. Popoff reminded them once more of all the many sources of cash they might have that he might tap into:

> It may be part of your savings account, some antiques that you have, some real estate, a car that you're not using. Pray about loaning it to Jesus. Remember, God will do for you what you cannot do for yourself, if you will do for God what you can do.

The picture of a tear-streaked Peter Popoff standing with his faithful, distraught wife, Elizabeth, froze on the TV screen and slowly faded. Then, on the original tape, but unheard by the home viewers, Elizabeth is heard to give a great sigh of impatience: "Whew! I was already at the store!" The poor dear had apparently become restless with the taping and wanted to get away for some important shopping. Using her Visa card, no doubt.

The Mail Campaign

Prior to the filming of this effective video message, the Popoff office had already started work on the mail campaign. Dated May 16, 1985, a computerized letter went out along with a water-stained piece of Russian scripture. The Popoff mailing list was so extensive that they had run out of genuine "vandalized" text and had to have more material printed. The letter read, in part:

> Right now I am in a complete state of shock, I'm so mad at the devil! Never before has he brought this ministry so close to a complete standstill. Our warehouse and printing plant were vandalized. My heart sank as I walked in on Monday morning and saw all of the Bible portions that we were going to airlift to the Russian border scattered everywhere. Destruction was all around me. The vandals didn't destroy our equipment, all they did was try to destroy God's word. After scattering these Bible portions everywhere, they took a fire hose and soaked them with water. Our van was also smashed.

The letter went on to reveal a message from God, delivered to Peter Popoff from his father, George. Said Almighty God:

> My son, I am moving upon those that will in this urgent hour send an EMERGENCY RESTOR-ATION offering to stop Satan in his tracks. Some will give twenty, some will give fifty, some will prove me according to Malachi 3:10. Those that obey the leading of my spirit now shall see that I will literally open my good treasure unto them. For I shall bless all the work of their hands and pour out upon them an abundance that they will not even have room to contain. Satan will be completely defeated for God's word must go forth at this critical hour!

In this letter, the Popoffs told folks that they had borrowed only $100 on that Visa card to "loan" to Jesus, not the $500 they'd claimed on the TV show. Perhaps they had felt more ambitious while standing among the "Russian Bibles." I suspect that this letter was not written for Popoff by a professional, because God seems to speak of Himself in the third Person, and forgets to capitalize the pronominal adjectives and the personal pronouns. It is a sloppy job and most certainly did not originate with God. And it probably was not a Gene Ewing idea, either, because that source produced much slicker mailings—though just as corny.

This scheme by Peter Popoff, assisted as he was by several of his employees and his wife, was used to take money from TV viewers and those who received his mailing. It most certainly violates several laws and should put the perpetrators in serious danger of prosecution. But it doesn't, because of the inaction of law enforcement officials who refuse to bring the law to bear on these people.

What I find just as infuriating is the threatening phrasing of many of the Popoff appeals. An example:

> If you will prove God now to help us defeat satan, the Lord has a special golden prosperity blessing for you that you won't even have room to contain. This is your season of blessing. Liz and I are launching out in faith and proving God with $27 dollars [sic] each. This is a real sacrifice for us at this time, it may be for you too. But launch out in faith now and do your very best for our Lord. DON'T YOU DARE throw the GOLDEN PROSPERITY ENVELOPE away because many have thrown their miracles away. . . . DO IT NOW.

I wonder what Peter was promising God would send as a blessing that could be that large. An elephant? The Queen Mary?

No Refunds in the Religion Business

I have in evidence a complete file concerning a woman in Welland, Ontario, Canada. I will protect her by calling her "Mrs. A." (Unlike the evangelists who refuse to make the original material available, I *do* have the genuine original documents on file, and interested persons who are able to responsibly represent any source of assistance for this person will be allowed to see them.) Mrs. A literally begged, borrowed, and stole to satisfy Popoff's stated needs. She heard his insistent demands, and in 1980 she

Evangelist/healer Leroy Jenkins just after his release from prison in 1979.

Leroy Jenkins "heals" a woman by the "laying on of hands."

Pastor David Epley, before he took up his ministry in Fort Lauderdale. He had just been fined for soliciting funds illegally in Cincinnati.

UPI/Bettmann Newsphotos

The Reverend Roberts in 1987. He threatened that he would die unless his supporters could raise $8 million.

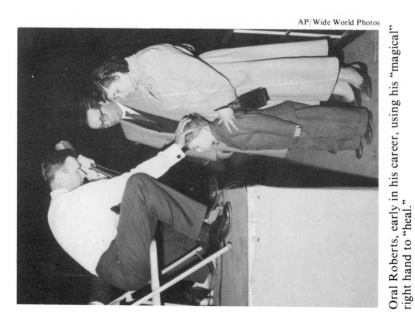

AP/Wide World Photos

Oral Roberts, early in his career, using his "magical" right hand to "heal."

AP/Wide World Photos

Father Ralph DiOrio, of Massachusetts, at one of his charismatic "healing" services.

Atlan/Sygma

The faith-healer who wants to be president of the United States, at a political rally.

The Reverend Ernest Angley, of Akron, Ohio, as he appears on television.

Ernest Angley laying hands on a subject in the healing line.

Don Henvick, as "Virgil Jorgensen," in a state of simulated ecstasy at a Peter Popoff meeting in Anaheim, California. On the left is Reeford Sherrill, Popoff's "front man." The bearded man with the glasses at the right applauding Don's performance is Shawn Carlson, my colleague.

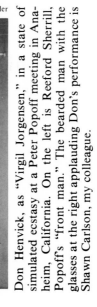

"Jorgensen" collapses at the touch of Popoff and is caught by an usher.

Elizabeth Popoff enters the TV trailer in Detroit to begin her clandestine radio transmission to husband Peter Popoff.

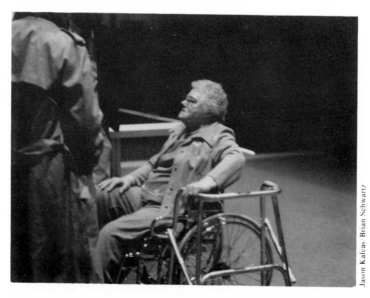

This Detroit lady denied she'd told anything to Mrs. Popoff, though we'd overheard their conversation. When her pastor discovered us talking to her, she told us that she had better not speak to us any longer.

Popoff crusade in Houston, Texas. The author (circled, bottom) is in the white wig. Mrs. Popoff questions "Travis Lamar," played by Steven Schafersman (circled, center). He was later "called out" to be healed by Peter Popoff, who was divinely inspired to give him exactly the same information Schafersman had given to Mrs. Popoff.

"Gae Devoe" (Dr. Gae Kovalick, another "mole" at the Houston meeting) is given the Popoff trickery.

Don Henvick in disguise as "Bernice Manicoff," preparing to enter the Popoff crusade meeting in Detroit.

MIRACLE OF THE MONTH!

Before

AFTER: This Milwaukee man was blind all of his life. After Rev. Grant prayed, he saw for the first time.

Dawn of a New Day

W. V. Grant claims a "miraculous healing." However, Mr. Kidd, the Milwaukee man, was *not* "blind all of his life."

W. V. Grant in Haiti, where he claims to feed thousands of orphans through his ministry.

THE BLIND
SEE
and the
CRIPPLED
WALK

This is the "How many fingers?" trick used by W. V. Grant on persons with impaired sight.

Dawn of a New Day

W. V. Grant seems to stretch this woman's left leg by prayer. In actuality, he has simply pulled her right shoe slightly off her foot, then pushed it back again to produce the illusion.

Dawn of a New Day

W. V. Grant as he appears on the cover of his publication *Dawn of a New Day*.

Letters of prayer partners salvaged from W. V. Grant's garbage following his Fort Lauderdale meeting.

Crutches at Santuaria.

Gary Morgan

The Gang of Four immediately after the Popoff exposure. Left to right: Don Henvick, Alec, Jason, James Randi, and Bob Steiner.

began sending him varying financial contributions. At first, she took money from a savings account established by her husband. When that was depleted, she borrowed money from her mother and from her son. Next, she took a loan at her bank to continue funding Popoff, who had instructed her that it was a sign of weakness to fail to do so. The Devil, he said, would try to stop her from supporting his ministry.

Mrs. A sent Peter Popoff well over $13,000 by these means, and when her family discovered what she'd done, she was forced to appeal to the Popoff office for a refund of at least part of that money. Letter after letter was ignored. She began sending registered letters, both to the post office box in Toronto, where the Canadian branch of the Popoff money machine was located, and to the headquarters in Upland. In one letter, she pleaded with Popoff to send her some of the money, and explained:

> I then started to receive letters from the ministry . . . so I started to send money from a small account I had. It so happened I had no money left and your letter said if I borrowed some to send it in God would bless us. So I started borrowing it from my son . . . about $3,000 in all. As I told you over the phone I read in the Bible about putting out a fleece. Because I would not know how much to send I would let the bible fall open to a page or scripture number and send that amount in. Then in Nov. 1980 I got desperate because I had no more funds and did not want to miss God. So I started to take out loans against a savings that my husband had placed into a Savings Certificate in my name. I also sold his centennial silver and gold coins . . . my husband was very hurt and angry that I did this to him. Despite all of that I still kept on writing to your ministry, afraid of losing contact, borrowing a few dollars from my mother or taking it out of my husband's pay. I am sorry to cause such a mess . . .

I have often been asked why I become so infuriated by the people I am investigating. I do not think that any reader can ask that after knowing the contents of this letter.

(The stunt of letting a book fall open for purposes of divination is well established in religion. The Greeks did it with Homer; the Moslems do it with the Koran. It is known as "stichomancy," and it is an established magic ritual.)

Finally, Popoff's Toronto representative answered her inquiries. Responding to a terse note that he had received from the California office saying merely, "We're sorry, payment can't happen," his letter doomed her appeal:

> We have checked, on our records, your record of giving to date. We do not have any donations on file.

And this answer was given after Mrs. A had forwarded photocopies of checks paid to the ministry amounting to over $6,000 as well as an official, signed Peter Popoff receipt for $893! As far as Popoff was concerned, the stone wall was up, and that was the last he wanted to hear of the matter.

A Plea from a Colleague

Mrs. A had her pastor in Toronto contact Popoff. In October 1983, he wrote Popoff that

> . . . the problem is that three years ago [Mrs. A] began to support your ministry with funds that she was siphoning off from a savings account that her husband had put in her name. That account was not her money, simply in her name and supposed to be accumulating towards the purchase of a vehicle. When she began to receive your very direct, compelling, "personal" letters, she took this money . . . and sent it to you. . . . It is unfortunate that your ministry did not demonstrate enough character or class to even as much as reply . . . especially from one of the "faithful" who had given so much. Your actions have called into question the *integrity* of your ministry, and the integrity of the gospel.

The pastor went on to say that, unless some reasonable answer was received, he would have to go to the Canadian solicitor general for satisfaction. Because this pastor and the church he represented are now out of business, we cannot know what, if anything, was the result of that threat. My guess is that Popoff didn't think twice about it.

Mrs. A then attended a Popoff crusade in Toronto, hoping to contact Popoff and make her plea in person. The Sherrills told us that at that crusade Reeford was under strict orders from Popoff not to allow this woman near him under any circumstances. In contrast, they expected another woman to be there who had donated handsomely to the ministry and was likely to continue doing so. Reeford was instructed to find this woman by any means possible and to conduct her backstage into Peter's presence immediately.

A Similar Case in Chicago

In November 1983, *Chicago Sun-Times* columnist Mike Royko wrote about an elderly woman there who had sent Popoff her life savings of $21,000. At that time, Popoff was pleading for money to enable him to send Russian Bibles into the Soviet Union by balloons, a scheme mentioned earlier. As with the woman in Canada, this victim needed some of that money returned, but Popoff refused to do so. Perhaps she had been persuaded to give the money by a *Chicago Tribune* article that had appeared a year previously. It was titled "Air Strike Hits Moscow With Barrage of Bibles." The piece by reporter Ronald Yates, quoted Popoff and his assistant Volmer Thrane as saying that they had launched 13,500 Russian Bibles from Finland aboard 700 9-foot balloons, which he claimed then floated over the border into Russia. Said Thrane:

> We used a formula to figure out just how far the balloons would carry. We didn't want them to go directly into the Kremlin, just to the outskirts.

That's quite a feat. Thrane was able to launch this armada at just the right moment so that the balloons would pop over the Moscow suburbs 550 miles away (Thrane said it was 700 miles) and deliver the cargo safely!

That same newspaper article was used by Popoff more than five years later, in a January 27, 1987, mailing. On a gold-sealed letter, he had printed:

> Partner, The things inside this letter cannot
> become public knowledge or they will jeopardize
> our outreach to the underground church behind
> the Iron Curtain. I send this letter to you as
> my very special inner circle friend in confi-
> dence. Partner, don't break the seal until you
> hold this letter in your hands and pray . . .
>   The things I am about to share with you I
> cannot share with just anyone. I cannot write
> everyone this, only a very FEW SPECIAL ONES
> LIKE YOU who the Lord has very specifically
> put on my heart. . . . Partner, you are on [sic]
> of my closest friends and therefore I want to
> share my vision with you. . . .
>   What I have written you in this letter
> cannot go public because any publicity will
> greatly hinder our effectiveness. That is why I
> am writing to you in the strictest confidence.

After putting in another overdone plea for money, Popoff insulted
his victims' intelligence with this ridiculous statement:

> I will go to my mail box daily TO LOOK FOR
> YOUR IMPORTANT LETTER. Your letter is
> MOST IMPORTANT TO ME AT THIS TIME
> because the Lord commanded me to write you.
> Don't put this letter down until you answer it.

That picture of Peter Popoff going to his "mail box" every day is
pretty funny when you realize that he was receiving his mail in
huge 100-pound sacks. The impression he created with those words
was of an impoverished preacher sorting through a handful of mail
looking for one specific letter containing a donation sufficient to
pay for the Russian Bible delivery. I also find it hard to accept
that God personally chose the recipient of that particular letter
for Popoff to write to. Especially because I was that recipient!
     Inside the gold-sealed envelope was the *Chicago Tribune*
article. Well, almost. The Reverend Popoff had carefully edited it,
omitting anything that would date it—along with his age—and
cutting it down to about a quarter of the original length, because
so much of the text betrayed its vintage. Notice that this information, *published in a major newspaper* five years earlier, was so
secret that Popoff could share it only with his 100,000-person

mailing list, all of whom were his "closest friends."

During the years that he developed the Russian Bible scheme, Popoff told his faithful that he was planning to charter a 747 jet loaded with the balloons which would waft the Bibles across Russia and drop them over Moscow, and also postulated a wild plan that would float styrofoam rafts across the Baltic Sea loaded with the Bibles. His third idea, to set hundreds of Bible-bearing balloons loose from Finland and drop them in a specific location—the *suburbs* of Moscow—by calculating altitude, direction, and velocity of prevailing winds, was the plan finally decided upon. No thought was given to the inescapable international fuss that would most certainly result, and the faithful accepted Popoff's Rube Goldberg plan as a big winner.

Expert Advice Is Sought—and Ignored

Obviously, the plan could not work. Even Popoff knew it was impossible. He had consulted Jamie Ali, a local expert on the subject of balloons, and was told that he was out of his mind even to dream of such a scheme. Regardless of the absurdity of the idea, Popoff purchased 300 ordinary party balloons and two small tanks of helium. All of those balloons together would barely have lifted *one* legitimate Bible.

High-Powered Mail

That woman in Chicago will never recover her money, nor will Mrs. A in Canada or the tens of thousands like her who gave all they had—and more. Perhaps they should be grateful that Popoff didn't ask for their lives, too. But they had been bombarded with ardent pleas for money, and we should examine that fact.

On the following pages you will find one of Popoff's begging letters addressed to one of my colleagues. The original was printed on what appeared to be pages torn out of a notebook. The same letter was addressed to all the people on the mailing list, but each person's first and last name was dropped in by computer. The top part of the first page was computer-typed, the only way this "drop-in" process can be done. You will see part of the first page of a second letter addressed to another of my colleagues, placed behind the first letter. As you may notice, the computer-generated names are different, in the salutation and in the fifth line. (With a female correspondent, the term "Sister" would be inserted by the computer at appropriate spots.) Popoff gave the impression that he was overcome with emotion and had to cease typing two lines into the second paragraph, changing over to handwriting. From that point on, both letters are identical, being offset-printed in blue ink to simulate handwriting. That portion of the letter could not have been personalized because it was not typed.

Read the letter through to know on what a low level the evangelists attack their subjects.

Dear Brother Morrow,

I am writing this letter, just the way God gave it to me. God awakened me last night and began to deal with me as he has dealt with me at only one other time in m----ntire life. Throughout the night until the first rays of dawn began to bre-------- floor, fell on my knees, then lay flat on my face, before the Alm -----ons and the earth. Joe, as God dealt with me tea -----bout your spiritual blessing and

I c

Dear Brother Lassner,

I am writing this letter, just the way God gave it to me. God awakened me last night and began to deal with me as he has dealt with me at only one other time in my entire life. Throughout the night until the first rays of dawn began to break I walked the floor, fell on my knees, then lay flat on my face, before the Almighty God, the Creator of the heavens and the earth. Michael, as God dealt with me tears streamed down my cheeks. He dealt with me about your spiritual blessing and also about your physical, spiritual, and financial well being.

As I write these words to you the Spirit is flooding through me constantly. I can't even type

Again last night God reminded me that He had raised me up and called and anointed me to bring HIS WORD into Russia and all of the 1/3 of the world that is behind the Iron Curtain. He called me to do it, He anointed me to do it because He wants it done, it has to be done, and it has to be done now!! This is God's time!

Timing is so important! This is often where we miss God, either we get ahead of God or we lag behind and then we miss God's blessing.

God showed me how to get into Russia with tons of literature for the underground Church. God spoke to me of the angels of God who are with me as they were with Paul in ACTS 27:23 where he said "The angel of the Lord stood by me." And with Peter in ACTS 5:19, when the angels opened the prision doors and let him out. And the angels with the prophet Elisha who was surrounded by the enemy and when his servants cried out for fear, he prayed to God to open the servants eyes and show him the angels, "that they who are with us are more than they who are with them." (2 KINGS 6: 15-17) And others who were especially anointed to heal and deliver had angels. I heard myself crying out to God I must have angels to help me break through this Iron CURTAIN. I must have angels as men of the Bible had. SUDDENLY I was aware that the angels of the LORD were encamped all around me! And the angels still are ALL AROUND ME as I write you these lines.

Since hearing from you last, God has kept you heavily upon my heart. I feel you have a great need. Has something happened since you last wrote?

I definitely feel led to tell you —

THAT A MIRACLE IS ABOUT TO COME TO YOU !! Will you refuse to open up and receive it or will you open the door of your heart and let God's miracle come in?

God knows just what your need is right now. He sees every ache, every pain, every problem. It makes no difference what kind of miracle you need. The way this miracle is going to come to you is by opening your spirit up to receive.

I know God showed me that you and I are to join hands "through the mail by the Spirit," and walk through the power of faith right into the miracle you need and I need right now.

TWO ARE STRONGER THAN ONE

WHERE THERE IS UNITY THERE IS STRENGTH

That is why Jesus sent out his ministers two by two. That's why God put YOU and ME together to do this great WORK for HIM!! When you get weak, I can lift you up in prayer.

I want to tell you that a miracle is about to happen. Now you can stop this miracle. Or you can open the door to the Spirit and let it happen to you. Let me explain exactly what I am talking about.

GOD TOLD ME TO GO to RUSSIA NOW WITH HIS WORD!!

The underground church is now bleeding for the cause of Christ and they don't have the WORD to fight the good fight of faith. I said, "Lord, I don't even have the money to ship the Bibles that we've printed at such great expense and SACRIFICE to our launch points. Many of our faithful couriers are stranded in remote areas because we have not been able to help them."

The Lord said, "someone who needs a MIRACLE BLESSING is going to be a part of this miracle of BREAKING THROUGH the Iron Curtain right now.

That's when I broke down and
FELL flat on my face BEFORE GOD ...

my soul was crying out to God.
I said, "God you told me to go, you
let me know that your angels would
make a way for me. This is a matter
of life and death to so many right now
who are suffering for Christ. I must
Go to them because God's power can
and will set them free. God told
me to DO IT and I MUST OBEY!

GOD LAID IT UPON MY HEART TO
WRITE YOU THIS LETTER AND, EVEN
THOUGH IT WILL BE A SACRIFICE,
ASK YOU TO STEP THROUGH THIS
GLORIOUS DOOR THAT GOD OPENED
AND GIVE A SPECIAL COVENANT
SEED GIFT (DO YOUR VERY BEST)
TOWARD THIS MIRACLE FOR GOD'S
GLORY!!

Now wait a minute!! Listen to God's
Spirit. Because He has a plan for you!
LISTEN with your spiritual ear. YES,
it's a sacrifice but remember JESUS
SACRIFICED HIS LIFE AT CALVARY.
Christians in Russia joyfully
their blood for Christ.

Now I have enclosed a special envelope along with some very special SEALS for Russian Christians. I _must_ hear from you one way or the other on this matter for GOD.

God is speaking to you right now Remember, anytime you feel an inclination to give, that FEELING COMES FROM GOD. BECAUSE THE DEVIL WILL NEVER INSPIRE YOU TO GIVE ANYTHING TO GOD'S WORK. You know you feel, right now, what you are to do. Obey His Voice.

Please answer my letter immediately. My hands are tied until I hear from you. So many are hurting right now. And so are you I have the answer. I MUST GO and tell the people behind the IRON CURTAIN that Jesus will set them FREE !

PS By FAITH alone I've told our couriers that I'd give them these 100,000 Russian Bibles. I know God will give you HIS HUNDRED FOLD return as you help me put HIS WORD into the hands of the underground church. Sign your first name only on these seals. I will put them inside a Russian Bible. Rush these seals BACK TO ME.

10
Oral Roberts and the City of Faith

Granville Oral Roberts is a 69-year-old evangelist/healer who never studied theology, though he attended a few college courses. He started with the Pentecostal Holiness church and is now affiliated with the Methodists, has been in the preacher business for more than 40 years, and is the guiding power behind the Oral Roberts Evangelistic Association, headquartered in Tulsa, Oklahoma. It is a $500-million conglomerate that has become a major part of that city's economy. It consists of Oral Roberts University, the City of Faith Hospital, and the City of Faith Medical and Research Center, a 60-story clinic, a 30-story hospital, and a 20-story research center at the corner of 81st Street and Lewis Avenue, augmented by several advertising, insurance, recording, and real-estate companies, a nursing home, a retirement center, a day-care center, some office condominiums, and considerable shares in several banks. The association employs more than 2,800 people.

Citizens of Tulsa are understandably quite happy about the city's biggest single tourist attraction, the City of Faith complex, with its collection of Disneyesque buildings. It has proved to be a powerful money magnet that attracts more than 200,000 visitors a year. They usually stay overnight and spend an average of $125 each for food, lodging, and entertainment before they depart. Few locals would want to see the Roberts operation fold, because many of their jobs depend upon its success.

The university was opened in 1965. An expensive experiment, the dental school, was forced to close in 1986; the law school, which also failed, was literally given to fellow evangelist/healer Pat Robertson. Oral's son, another evangelist healer named Richard Roberts, has repeatedly denied that financial problems had anything to do with the dental school's closing, the law school giveaway, or his father's constant begging for money. Insiders know otherwise. In fact, Oral himself has made that fact clear in his sermons. Richard should have paid better attention.

A Losing Proposition

As with most evangelical projects, the Roberts empire is in perpetual crisis in spite of the millions that are poured into it annually by the faithful. Half-way through, construction suddenly halted on Roberts's $14-million Healing Center. This part of Roberts's operation had been built over the objections of everyone except God. Tulsa was already oversupplied with hospital beds, and all those who foresaw disaster for this addition were ignored until it became obvious that economics was winning out over prayer. In an attempt to save the project, Roberts pleaded to viewers of a November 1985 Sunday morning TV show: "The City of Faith now is at the point it could be lost . . . I'm calling you to Tulsa." This was an attempt to fill the beds with paying customers, but it turned out that many of those who responded to the appeal were on health plans that did not encourage long, costly hospital stays at their expense. Also, about 60 percent of the flock from which Roberts draws both patients and donors is older than 65. As these "prayer partners" (contributors) undergo reductions in income or die off, they cease to support the Roberts machine, and Oral has not tried to, or has been unable to, attract a younger group of followers who would not be so likely to suffer these changes.

The hospital, which was originally designed for 777 beds (Oral has a fixation on magic numbers) and was finally licensed for only 294 when it opened in 1981, has since averaged just 125 patients. It cannot support itself, and Roberts has had to take a massive amount of money from other branches of his organization to put into the project to save it from going under. Much of this rescue money came from a university quasi-endowment fund accumulated in previous years when the ministry was raking in money at a much greater rate. In 1981, for example, more than $75 million came in for the university; that figure had dwindled to $20 million in 1982, and to $17 million in 1983.

Divine Financial Advice

Roberts has always claimed to obtain his instructions directly from God, and it began to appear, even to believers, that the evangelist needed a better financial adviser. But he chose to blame his problems on another entity. He declared: "The Devil is coming against me and this ministry in a way that is almost beyond belief." In other words, neither his own poor judgment nor God's had anything to do with it.

Financial experts advised Roberts that he could easily borrow on the land and capital improvements that he has in Tulsa to save the hospital. He declined to do so, saying that he would never borrow on those assets. But he failed to mention that the hospital was *already* in debt to the U.S. government for huge loans taken to get the operation under way. Who approved those loans—and why, in view of the infeasibility of the project—may never be known, along with so many other undiscoverable facts about Roberts.

The original God-given theory was that income from the hospital and clinic would support the university. Exactly the opposite took place. To quote former ORU official William Brunk, "Instead of becoming a blessing to the university, [the hospital] simply dissipated what was there." Roberts's financial adventure can only be described as disastrous.

Oral's powers of rationalization have seldom been equaled, in or out of the evangelical business. To excuse his dipping into the endowment fund, he observed that every university that has received and maintained big endowments has eventually departed from the faith. Thus, according to his reasoning, ORU was obviously better off without that fund.

In the mid-1980s, as Roberts's tearful pleadings for money were aired—and were largely unheeded by an audience weary of such constant begging—employees began leaving the organization, and others were simply pared from the payroll in order to try to save the entire operation from going under. According to a published statement from Roberts, those who were not interested in supporting him and ORU by either voluntarily resigning or contributing $1,000 apiece to help him out were "of the Devil." This reflects his callous behavior toward employees and those close to him. "You simply don't get in his way," say executives, who claim that he has often betrayed them and caused them to lose prestige among those with whom they do business, because of broken promises and misinformation that he has given them. Such auto-

cratic behavior is hardly surprising in a man who believes that
God guides his every move. In his mind, what Oral decides is what
God has decided.

Shortly before the exciting conclusion of what the press came
to refer to as the "Roberts deathwatch" early in 1987, Oral had
appeared at a Conference on World Evangelism to explain himself.
He had already tried to explain how he knows that God speaks
directly to him, a claim he often made to his followers. In the
April 1983 issue of his publication *Abundant Life*, he had said:

> It's something I'd stake my eternal soul
> upon—that I saw what I saw, that I have heard
> what I have heard, that I know that I know
> that I know.

So there! On March 2, 1987, Oral told possibly alarmed donors:

> As you know, the news media have questioned
> our motives and mocked and held us up to
> ridicule for weeks now. They've gone so far as
> to suggest our program be canceled on tele-
> vision. Also, certain religious leaders have
> mocked me for saying GOD STILL SPEAKS
> TODAY—and have jumped on me for saying God
> spoke to Oral Roberts.

For the folks at the conference, he was a little more specific
on that point. He set forth a scenario in which he explained that
everything Jesus ever said wasn't necessarily written down in the
Bible (one can imagine such omitted comments as "Isn't Jerusalem
dull on a weeknight?" and "If these crowds don't stop touching
my garment, I'll smite someone!"), and that therefore Roberts was
able to tune in to God and company and supply a lot of unwritten
holy words. Thus, what he reported God had told him would not
necessarily be found already written in the scriptures.

Get Thee Behind Me, Poverty

Then, because his high living has always caused some of the
attention focused on him, especially after his most recent threat
to die, he chose to outline to the conference delegates the logic
behind his luxurious habits. He really knows how to live in style,
and he's not shy about it.

A frequent honored guest of several presidents at the White House, Roberts enjoys an existence that amply reflects his view that poverty is one of mankind's greatest enemies, second only to Satan himself. I will quote this explanation here exactly as he himself gave it, with the strange syntax, incomplete thoughts, and grammatical chaos. After briefly mentioning the home, cars, clothes, and wealth about which the critics had tut-tutted, he said:

> What *is* our desire? [Saint] Paul says, "But I desire that fruit may abound in your account." Now, what *is* fruit? Something that grew from a seed. Fruit is called *what*? Produce! Is it not? When you went in to go to the market, you go to get *produce*! *Fresh* produce, if you can buy it! It came *from seed*! What do I desire? I desire that you might plant seed into *my* ministry, in *my* life to Christ, that *you* might get a harvest. *Produce*! Get it multiplied *back*, that you may have an account with God. When you write a check, and you don't have any account in a bank, the check will bounce. Right here is where there's big trouble! There's big trouble among God's people, sending up a demand of God and we've not planted seed! We've not given to his men and women who are taking the Gospel. When I give to my church. Alright? Let's just talk about that. Fine! Why don't you investigate what's happening to your money?

(Perhaps you can understand his logic. I cannot. Those at the conference went wild with enthusiasm over these words, so it appears they are better able than I to follow the thought that the Reverend Roberts presented to them.)

At that point in his "explanation," Roberts avoided discussion of what was happening to the money that was sent to *him* and spoke instead of another preacher who had joined the Roberts staff because he was not satisfied with the way his own funds were being handled. Then Roberts launched into a definition of why his ministry was a true representation of God's teachings and was worthy of donations. But he avoided the mystery of just what happened to all that money.

The Canvas Cathedral

Roberts claims that he entered the ministry and began speaking to God after he was divinely healed of tuberculosis at age 17, but the miracle dims somewhat when we discover that he has not produced any medical records except to establish that after his purported healing he had "clear lungs." Also, he was undergoing orthodox medical treatment at the time, and it took him months of such treatment before he was well enough to claim a cure.

At one time his tent show, which predated his TV show, accommodated 12,000 chairs, plus an additional 60 for the "anointed" and special visitors on stage. It boasted a 200,000-watt lighting and public-address system. According to his former managers, some 200 people would be taken by ambulance to each of these tent revivals. Former evangelist Marjoe Gortner said in his documentary, *Marjoe*, that Roberts at that stage was spending $300,000 a month on postage—an *enormous* sum in 1971.

Devotees can come up with the most incredibly naive reasoning to explain Roberts's successes and to ignore his failures. Two of his ardent fans, Tom and Beth Poole, quoted in the *Tulsa Tribune* in an extensive and excellent article on the ministry, gave their opinion that "Oral Roberts is a man of God. A country boy couldn't have done this if it hadn't been God's plan." The Pooles are apparently unaware that Harry Truman, Thomas Edison, and hundreds of other "country boys"—and girls—have been far more successful than Roberts, and without using contrived gimmicks to sell their abilities. They also lived up to their failures.

Economy-Size Miracles

Roberts is inventive, if nothing else. In October 1980, in response to a summons to the Tulsa command post, the eager media dutifully reported that Roberts had seen a 900-foot-tall figure of Jesus at exactly 7 p.m. on May 25 of that year near the City of Faith, in Tulsa. To quote Roberts:

> I felt an overwhelming holy presence all around
> me. When I opened my eyes, there He stood,
> some 900 feet tall, looking at me. His eyes . . .
> Oh! His eyes! He stood a full 300 feet taller
> than the 600-foot-tall City of Faith. There I
> was, face-to-face with Jesus Christ, the son of
> the living God. I've only seen Jesus once be-

fore, but here I was face-to-face with the King
of Kings. He stared at me without saying a
word. Oh! I will never forget those eyes! And
then He reached down, put his hand under the
City of Faith, lifted it, and said to me, "See
how easy it is for me to lift it."

Some were more than slightly skeptical about the claim. The
media failed to embrace this Roberts whopper, and he was the
butt of jokes for several weeks following the press release. Personally, I found it difficult to picture how Roberts could have
stood "face-to-face" with a figure that tall, and it seemed strange
that he had waited four months before telling the world of the
appearance of this holy colossus. Commented one observer, "It
takes a real man to keep a secret like that!"

In a six-page letter sent out to prayer partners that October,
Roberts appealed emotionally for money to keep the hospital
afloat, and he brought in the Super Jesus tale to press home the
need. Though it may appear incredible to non-evangelist-watchers,
it worked. Five million dollars poured in following his preposterous
ploy. Heartened by the result, he followed up with a tale of
another divine visit, this time by a somewhat smaller Jesus who
appeared at the foot of his bed and assured him that the City of
Faith would be a success. Said this Jesus in his familiar manner:

Oral, I'm going to put my blood back
into the City of Faith. And I'm going
to heal people like never before.

One wonders how and why His blood was ever withdrawn from the
hospital, and why He had been slacking in His healing efforts.

The Midas Touch

It seems that wonders just follow Reverend Roberts around, waiting to happen, and heavenly apparitions hover over him at all
times. Following this visit by the regulation-size Jesus, he reported that a large-size angel was left behind in his room. Not
one to lose the golden opportunity that suggested itself at this
time, Oral immediately commemorated the miracle by offering his
flock a 7-inch replica of that very angel and the simultaneous
chance to donate some money. Roberts seems to provide us with
the very definition of hucksterism.

Sometimes, offers like these that Roberts makes during his campaigns sound like supernatural mail-order catalog blurbs. Examples: For a donation of $20, you can get four "Expect a Miracle" coffee mugs. For a mere $120 (later slashed to $50), you will receive an Oral Roberts commentary Bible, with not only Roberts's name on the "genuine leather cover" in gold lettering, but your own as well. A jigsaw puzzle of Oral astride his favorite horse, Sonny, and an irresistible recording of Richard Roberts in full song can be yours for just $10 each. One mailing enclosed a tiny sack of cornmeal. The recipient was told to pray over it and return it with some cash, whereupon Oral would instruct his wife what to do with the cornmeal:

> I am going to have Evelyn mix the cornmeal
> and bake for me God's representative [sic] of
> the body of Christ.

Can anyone imagine Evelyn Roberts actually emptying out tens of thousands of itty-bitty bags of cornmeal into a huge bowl and baking up a Host from it? On the other hand, maybe that 900-foot-tall Jesus was coming to lunch.

A Few Paradoxes and Second Thoughts

In 1984, son Richard began his own daily TV program, and serious efforts got under way to groom him for taking over the ailing TV operation. He has been appointed president of the Oral Roberts Evangelistic Association, and his autobiography is available for purchase by the faithful. Another book, not as popular with Oral and Richard, is *Ashes to Gold*, written by Richard's first wife, Patti. In that book, she recounts that on their departure for their honeymoon, she and Richard were called into Oral's presence. Weeping, he warned them that, if either of them ever left the ministry, God would kill them in a plane crash. Ironically enough, when Patti left Richard and the ministry in 1977, Oral's oldest daughter was killed—in a plane crash.

Healer Roberts, in the days of his tent show, assured his success by calling only those holding certain selected prayer cards to come forward to be healed. Others, crippled or afflicted in such a way that they obviously could not even appear to be healed, were kept segregated from the main body of worshipers. As reported in a United Press International release about a Roberts crusade in Long Island in 1958:

> Ambulances pulled up to the doors to discharge
> children with grotesquely twisted arms and legs,
> hollow-eyed victims of palsy, of cancer, of
> rheumatic fever and polio. The saddest cases
> were brought into a ward-like special room safe
> from the eyes of others.

This procedure was reported many times by the media and was
witnessed by countless observers. But the truth is what Roberts
says it is. According to him:

> I never segregated my healing line. . . . You
> saw them healed or not healed. I took every-
> body. . . . [On the prayer line] all manner of
> diseases and all conditions were healed.

The truth is that only a small percentage of those who attend *any*
faith-healer's meeting will receive personal attention. Most are
only touched in passing, if at all.

Faced with the evident fact that *some* people will not be
affected by his magical and theatrical laying on of hands and
screeching for demons to let loose of a body, Roberts had to
change his official opinion, though that opinion had been given to
him by God. In 1957, he asked:

> Do you believe that everyone can be healed by
> faith in God? I'm going to get you out of your
> suspense. I'll give you my answer. Yes!

But just ten years later, the reverend had changed his mind:

> I used to think that everyone I prayed for
> would be healed. . . . What I was not reckoning
> with was the free moral agency of the person I
> was praying for. Nor was I reckoning with the
> sovereignty of God, nor the degrees of power
> that I might feel. There were a lot of things I
> was not reckoning with, because no one had
> ever told me and it wasn't in a book. You could
> only find it out by trial and error.

Roberts says he knows just where his magical power is centered, and in that we may find further evidence of the incredible

reasoning applied to examinations of these claims. Viewing the performance of Roberts, Episcopalian writer W. E. Mann was perceptive enough to know just where Roberts's magic originated. Mann said: "There is a power in his right hand." Oral verifies that and agrees that he has "God-anointed hands":

> When the Lord's presence came in my hand, I
> was really concerned about myself, whether I
> was just thinking I felt it. And I talked to
> brethren about it, and they warned me. But the
> fact was it was there. [My hands are] an exten-
> sion of the hands of Christ.

Amazingly enough, it seemed to make no difference whether anyone actually touched Oral's hand or not. He found he could place his magical appendage—via film—on the TV camera or—via recording—on the radio microphone and have it work just as well.

Oral Roberts has said to reporters: "Ask whatever you like. I'll do my best to answer." And consider his statement in a recent broadcast (this is an exact transcribing, again with Roberts's own confusing syntax):

> The Word has to be confirmed with signs and
> wonders. You got no right to give your money
> anywhere unless the Word is confirmed with
> signs and wonders. You got no legal right by
> *God*! . . . I'm up here talkin' the way I talk,
> and I started the Word must be confirmed with
> signs and wonders—the healing of the sick, the
> casting out of devils, the raising of the dead—
> that's what I said in '47, that's what I'm saying
> in '87!

In response to this suggestion, garbled as it was, on February 16, 1987, I sent a registered letter to Oral Roberts, marked "Personal and Confidential." Here is part of the text of that letter:

> I note that you have mentioned
>   (1) healing of the sick,
>   (2) casting out of devils, and
>   (3) raising of the dead.
> You have frequently, in the past, laid claim to
> the performance of at least some of these

"signs and wonders." May I hear from you
regarding your evidence for the performance of
these miracles as a result of your ministry? I
am aware that you believe God, not you personally, brings about these events. I am particularly interested in any claims of healing, which
would require medical evidence both before and
after the event. Thank you for your attention
to this request for information.

I received a reply a month later, consisting of three books
and a letter from the Reverend Roberts assuring me that the
answers I sought were there. They were not. All I found were the
usual scraps of anecdotal material, first names, initials, and foggy
designations. I was naive to have sent such a letter. Only later,
looking into previous attempts by others seeking to obtain such
evidence, and finding that they, too, had been rebuffed, I came
upon this statement from Roberts:

I don't try to prove [that] multiplied thousands
[are being healed]. I just say, "There's the
person. Let him tell you." [This is enough] to
me and the person. . . . I can't prove that any
person who ever came to me was healed, that is
I can't prove it to the satisfaction of everyone.

That's not what I have been looking for. A hungry man does not
demand a gourmet eight-course meal. A hamburger will do. I have
never required that Oral's healings—or *anyone's* healings—be proved
"to the satisfaction of everyone." Nor have I asked for evidence
that "multiplied thousands" have been healed. That would be
ridiculous. I have asked only that *one* case be proved for a small
group of expert, impartial witnesses. Obviously, Oral Roberts has
no intention of cooperating. His organization has abandoned any
effort to provide evidence of healing. The earlier efforts, in an
atmosphere which tolerated sloppy thinking, were disorganized and
produced only personal opinions of the believers who thought
they'd been healed of every conceivable variety of ailment—psychological, organic, and financial. As a result of such adamant refusal
to produce evidence, I can only believe that Roberts cannot produce it.

My challenge is only one of many made over the years to
Oral Roberts. In 1955, a Church of Christ repeatedly offered

Roberts the opportunity to collect $1,000 if a jury of competent physicians could find any evidence that miracles were occurring in his ministry. The Roberts organization did not respond to that offer, either, I think because he is aware that he has no need to respond and that he could not, in any case, succeed. A City of Faith spokesperson offered this clever explanation for Roberts's failure to respond:

> Suppose, for instance, Brother Roberts should take the time to answer those who offer $1,000 rewards for proof that one miracle has been performed in his meeting. The testimonies of the people who were healed would not be accepted by those making the challenge. The testimony of competent, believing physicians would not be accepted. Then where could an effort to satisfy the challengers end? Perhaps in a civil court to be dragged out with weeks of litigation that would do nobody any good. Meantime, the person who has been healed is still healed. He doesn't need proof.

Note that besides the implicit threat of a lawsuit against anyone who would dare to insist upon proof, this statement specifies the use of "believing physicians," once again implying that only believers can judge and evaluate these matters. In reality, of course, the attitude of the investigator in a properly controlled and designed test can have nothing to do with the result. But believers cannot master this kind of logic, because they think in a magical manner—when they think at all.

The official spokesperson, questioned by phone, would not even answer a simple query about whether or not the Roberts prayer plus medical-care combination was any better than simple medical attention. And he had no statistics to offer for examination.

The Ultimate Presumption

Finally, I abandoned my demand for proof of a healing brought about by Oral Roberts in June of 1987 when he startled most people (but not seasoned Oral-watchers) by declaring that he had frequently *resurrected the dead at his services*. He simultaneously announced that God had just informed him that if Oral died before the Second Coming, Oral would return with Jesus to sit with him and rule the Earth. Presumably the site of that split rule would be Tulsa, Oklahoma. Where else?

Son Richard, as usual, had to face the press and try to explain his father's atrocious claims. He said that there were "dozens and dozens and dozens" of documented cases of such resurrection, and I decided to switch the direction of my inquiries. Knowing full well that a mere healing is nothing compared to a resurrection, I sent this telegram to Oral Roberts on June 30, 1987:

> Please provide me with one identifiable case of a resurrection from the dead brought about by Oral Roberts, regardless of the source of the power used to accomplish this wonder. Since resurrections are not considered commonplace, I will accept documentation of such an event in place of any of the other evidences of healing by Reverend Roberts that I have been seeking.

Need I tell you that no response was ever received?

11
A Word of Knowledge
from Pat Robertson

Incredibly, it is possible that the next president of the United States of America might be a charismatic, Yale-educated TV evangelist faith-healer named Marion Gordon "Pat" Robertson. He has the money, the media exposure, and the following that could enable him to sweep into the 1988 race and take the top prize. He is seen daily by hundreds of thousands of people on the Christian Broadcasting Network's "700 Club," a religious "Tonight Show" imitation that he hosted until he decided to be merely a commentator. This show can be seen by 82 percent of the American TV public and is thus a powerful aid to his presidential ambitions.

It is interesting to note that Robertson, a law school graduate, has of late abandoned his Grant-style healing pretensions in favor of a tamer and less testable performance. He now says he considers himself as more a TV commentator than an evangelist, and compares himself to Walter Lippmann and William F. Buckley. From his television pulpit, he claims to dispense miracles of healing to the faithful across the country, and the fact that millions of Americans actually believe those claims may very well upset the predictions of political experts.

The Political Power of the Evangelists

Those White House aspirations may not be as fanciful as we could wish. Jerry Falwell, Jim Bakker, and Jimmy Swaggart are all fond of mentioning the contents of phone chats they've had with the president. Falwell, who began his ministry in 1956 with 35 members of his Thomas Road Baptist Church, is now a rich and powerful figure in religion and politics whose organization's gross income ($74 million in 1985) could easily support any political campaign he might choose to launch. He has declared that the idea of separation of church and state is an invention of Satan.

Bakker, a Bible-school dropout, created through his "PTL Club" a 2,000-acre religious Disneyland-style park called Heritage USA and has so far escaped attempts by the Federal Communications Commission to prosecute him. As a result of the recent scandal both Jim and Tammy Faye Bakker were swept out of the PTL pulpit and the organization was put in the hands of Jerry Falwell, though I doubt the world has seen the last of that pair.

Swaggart, named by the Bakkers as the head of a conspiracy to topple their clan, is certainly no stranger to accusations. He is still smarting from a move by the city of Baton Rouge, Louisiana, to extract enormous back taxes from him for sales of religious hardware. Swaggart ranks high among the top ten televangelists, with a total audience of 732,000 households weekly.

At a prayer breakfast during the 1984 Republican National Convention, Ronald Reagan declared that "religion and politics are necessarily related," thus giving the cue to Jerry Falwell. Taking advantage of this reassurance that they had access to the presidential ear, five TV evangelists promptly presented themselves before the convention's Platform Committee and claimed that they represented 30 million television viewers a week. This was a bold ploy to make themselves important to the media and thus available for "inside" clues to Reagan's intentions. But, again, reality tends to catch up with us all. The A. C. Nielsen rating service puts the viewer audience of all top *ten* TV ministries at 9.3 million, still a formidable figure but far less than what these five—who have serious theological differences with one another—have claimed for themselves. Facts and figures are invented and hyperbolized at the whim of these operators, with little fear that anyone will know the truth and care to correct them.

Because of his high profile and his presidential aspirations, Pat Robertson was my first choice for investigation when I began researching this book. But examination of his healing claims was far more difficult than I had anticipated. In his case, the task can be compared to trying to nail a handful of grape jelly to a wall. You simply cannot get hold of his claim because it is nonfalsifiable and well ventilated with loopholes provided by those who claim the marvels are genuine.

I concluded that Pat Robertson's current scaled-down perform-ance, which is similar to the "safe" act done by Richard Roberts, offered no opportunity for me to look into his preposterous claims. He is now immune to proper research. I had to turn to others in the field whose claims *could* be examined, and their claims are quickly shown to be spurious.

The new Robertson act is just plain tedious. He uses a simple "shotgun" technique. He and his sidekick, Ben Kinchlow, bow their heads and tune in to receive a "Word of Knowledge" from on high. In turn, they each describe what they ask us to believe they are being told directly by God. One announces that someone in the television audience has "a tightening in the chest" that is now being healed. The other says that a viewer somewhere "has a headache." Or:

> I have a Word of Knowledge that someone has trouble with a tracheotomy. God is miraculously healing it! . . . I see stomach pains at this moment. The Lord has healed you.

On another occasion, God zipped Pat around the map:

> There is a woman in Kansas City who has sinus. The Lord is drying that up right now. Thank you, Jesus. There is a man with a financial need—I think a hundred thousand dollars. That need is being met right now, and within three days, the money will be supplied through the miraculous power of the Holy Spirit. Thank you, Jesus! There is a woman in Cincinnati with cancer of the lymph nodes. I don't know whether it's been diagnosed yet, but you have-n't been feeling well, and the Lord is dissolving that cancer right *now*! There is a lady in Saskatchewan in a wheelchair—curvature of the spine. The Lord is straightening that out right now, and you can stand up and walk!

In 1986, soon after the full importance of the AIDS epidemic began to become evident, Robertson was attempting to cure it. Viewers of his program saw him pray over a man who had the dreaded disease. He invoked God's power:

> We rebuke this virus and we command your
> immune system to function in the name of
> Jesus.

Viewers were never told what the man's fate was. They were allowed to assume that he became the only person ever to be cured of that affliction.

It goes on and on, through a complete spectrum of illnesses. Pains, tumors, broken bones, scarred lungs, warts, headaches, and emotional problems, revealed to these holy men directly from God as they listen devoutly to His voice, are banished at a word from the two shamans. And it appears that the audience believes every bit of it. Why? Because it absolutely cannot be disproved, and Robertson makes no move to prove it.

Other Wonders, Too

Robertson handed the public a real whopper when he claimed on one TV broadcast that during a crusade in China he delivered his sermon in English, as usual, and was pleased to learn that his audience was miraculously able to understand every word because God had arranged for them to individually hear Robertson's words *in their own regional dialect of Chinese.* Another wonder occurs when people at home are healed by Pat by videotaped histrionics that were recorded weeks before. On one occasion, a woman's broken ankle was "healed" this way, and it was later discovered that *the video healing was performed before the woman broke her ankle.* Such discrepancies mean nothing to Pat Robertson—or to his followers, all of whom are apparently accustomed to this sort of logic.

A Sour Note from a Colleague

Gerry Straub, a former associate of Pat Robertson and his television producer, pointed out in his book *Salvation for Sale* the astonishing fact that God seemed able to time miracles to conform with standard television format. God would stop speaking to Pat and stop healing exactly in time with the theme music. He described his former employer's "Word of Knowledge" performance:

> There was nothing "mystical" to understand; it
> was simply "statistical." Robertson's little
> faith-healing procedure is a charade—he simply

"calls out" an illness and predicts its cure, and with millions of viewers the statistical probabilities are that *someone* will have the disease named and that they will naturally recover. People put their faith in the belief that God speaks to Pat.

Straub relates a nonmiracle he witnessed while still a believer in the ministry he worked for. He describes Robertson, at the close of a "700 Club" videotaping, shaking hands with members of the studio audience:

> He stopped when he reached a man sitting in a wheelchair. The elderly man looked as if he were moments away from death's door. Emaciated and jaundiced, his head and hands shook constantly. I felt sick just looking at him. Someone pushing his wheelchair whispered to Pat about the man's condition and that he wanted to see the show in person before he died. The man hadn't walked in months. . . . Pat . . . laid hands on him as everyone prayed for a healing. . . . At Pat's urging the man stood up. The people cheered as the man took a couple of very shaky, small steps. While everyone applauded God, I feared the man might fall. The next day we showed the nation the miracle [on the "700 Club" broadcast].

What has just been described by Straub is not untypical of many "cures" my colleagues and I have seen taking place with other faith-healers. What Straub describes next is also not unlike results we have experienced:

> I simply wanted to know if the old man in the wheelchair was permanently healed by God or if he temporarily thought that he was healed. A few weeks later I had an assistant track down the man's family in order to see if the cure had lasted. He had died 10 days after his visit to [the Christian Broadcasting Network]. We reported his "healing" but not his death.

That last sentence puts the finger on just where the deception takes place.

Straub sums up his experience with faith-healing in the Robertson ministry with these words:

> During my two and a half years at [Christian Broadcasting Network], I never saw one clearcut, "beyond a shadow of a doubt" type of healing; however, I did see a tremendous amount of faith in healing—cleverly created, I believe, by Pat Robertson. . . . The prophet-turned-healer could have been described as prophet-turned-fake for the sake of a profit.

Robertson has been criticized for his insistence that his followers can earn and control God's favor. In *Beyond Reason: How Miracles Can Change Your Life*, he implies that people can control miracles by using "faith strategies," and in the final chapter, "Master Keys to Miracles," he endorses what has become known as the "Pelagian heresy," which says that after one has followed the prescribed formulas, if a miracle is not granted, it is the fault of the supplicant. It says that those who demand favors from God have every right to do so, and God *must* grant this boon, according to contract. Faith-healer A. A. Allen may have originated the modern use of this idea, quoting as he did from Isaiah ("Command ye me") and from Job 22:28 ("decree a thing") to establish scriptural sources for the notion.

After seeing what he claims are "thousands" of miracles in his 25 years of preaching, it would seem that Pat Robertson would be willing to share at least one with me. On March 24, 1987, I sent him my final letter of three:

> Reverend Robertson:
>
> I am presently preparing the manuscript for a book to be titled *The Faith-Healers*. A certain portion of this book will deal with your ministry.
>
> You have frequently, in the past, laid claim to the performance of some of the "signs and wonders" referred to in Holy Scripture. May I hear from you regarding your evidence for the performance of these miracles as a

result of your ministry? I am particularly interested in your claims concerning healing of the sick, and I am aware that you believe that God, not you personally, brings about these events.

I require that any claims of healing should provide medical evidence both before and after the event. Thank you for your attention to this request for information.

I trust that *this* letter has come to your personal attention, since it is so marked, and that you will provide me with a response.

Though I wrote him over a period of several months, earnestly—and persistently—requesting such information, I was denied an answer. The only response I ever received was a note from administrative assistant Barbara Johnson, who wrote:

Your letter of March 24th to Pat Robertson has been received. He is away at this time, but I will share your letter with him upon his return, which will be next week.

That was five months ago.

A Redefinition

David West is Robertson's press coordinator, obviously a good man to have around when the questioning gets tough. When I made it plain that I was not satisfied with the wall Robertson had erected against my inquiries, West simply redefined the Robertson act:

What is happening is not faith-healing, and Pat Robertson does not fit my definition of a faith-healer. What happens in oversimplified terms is that prayer is offered for healing, healing occurs, and knowledge is given to the person who prayed. It isn't nearly as direct and specific as someone coming to town and holding a healing meeting.

West then said he believed that I did not "understand" and was not maintaining an open mind. He suggested that I contact "other churches" for the evidence I seek, or that I advertise for those who have been healed. Well, Mr. West, I have done both of those things, and none of my efforts has been successful. I know that does not concern you, because your concern must be the work and the reputation of the Reverend Pat Robertson. And Robertson has refused to produce *one case* of his that will stand examination. It does not take a genius to conclude that something is wrong here.

A friend of mine in the entertainment business who claims to have close ties to Robertson assured me that he would be able to produce evidence of genuine healing by the Robertson ministry, but after eight months of half-answers and no answers, he abandoned the attempt. Robertson simply would not respond, even to him.

But Pat Robertson is a man who, like Oral Roberts, *must* be right because he is convinced he is a spokesperson for Almighty God. He takes no criticism of any kind, for that would be criticism of God. He deals summarily with employees who displease him. An IBM-trained personnel manager who says he was hired by Robertson to evaluate the situation at the "700 Club" found a number of irregularities and submitted his report to Robertson. He was not only fired on the spot, but was physically ejected from the building. One thing he'd discovered was that Robertson was testing potential employees with a questionnaire that had been designed to test for criminal personality traits.

The TV Special to End Them All

In 1979, it appeared to Robertson's staff that their boss had been taking lessons from Oral Roberts. One plan CBN came up with sounded as if Roberts had thought it up and was acting as Robertson's publicity man. They proposed to film the Second Coming! Examining scripture, Robertson had decided that recent actions by Israel had indicated that this event was imminent, and his staff was so convinced of that idea that they decided to record it on videotape. It was decided to call this top-secret idea "God's Special Project" (GSP), and the staff began planning for the ultimate TV show. In *Salvation for Sale*, Gerry Straub admits that even he took the plan seriously for a while:

> The greatest show on earth was in our hands. I wondered where we would put the cameras. Jerusalem was the obvious place. We even

discussed how Jesus's radiance might be too bright for the cameras and how we would have to make adjustments for that problem. Can you imagine telling Jesus, "Hey, Lord, please tone down your luminosity; we're having a problem with the contrast. You're causing the picture to flare." . . . The concept of pulling together a project in which every person could witness the Second Coming of Jesus on his or her television—and in his or her own language—boggled my mind. . . . In the world outside the walls of CBN such delusional states are treated with hospitalization and therapy. Inside CBN, budget allocations are made for their development.

The project was not developed, but may still be under consideration in the mind of Pat Robertson.

Author Martin Gardner, writing on the Robertson ministry, found the GSP story easier to accept than one that Robertson himself told in his book *Beyond Reason*. He reported that a 12-year-old girl had been killed by a car as she ran out of the Mount Vernon, New York, church where he was assistant pastor early in his career. The following day, Robertson led the entire congregation in prayers before the open casket of the embalmed body, praying for her resurrection. I will let Gardner close the story:

Pause a moment to savor this scene. Here is a man who wants to be president. He actually believes that perhaps God, hearing his prayer, will revivify a corpse. Did not Jesus call Lazarus from the grave after his body (as Martha said) "stinketh"? Did he not turn water into wine? It would be no big deal—after all a miracle is a miracle—for Jesus to resurrect the poor girl and turn her embalming fluid into blood of the right blood type.

Robertson sees nothing unusual or funny about this incident. "She did not rise," he concluded solemnly, "and we buried her on Tuesday."

12
The Psychic Dentist and an Unamazing Grace

There comes a point where I must assure my reader that I have not invented any of the preposterous claims that I quote in this book. Indeed, I don't have the skill to think up the fantastic scenarios that I've come upon in the course of my investigations.

The field of faith-healing abounds with ridiculous claims, but none sillier than those we will now examine. The Reverend Willard Fuller, of Palatka, Florida, says he can insert dental fillings without drilling or even opening his client's mouth, turn ordinary silver fillings and crowns into gold, straighten crooked teeth, tighten dentures, cure periodontal disease, and grow new teeth in his clients—all just by calling upon Jesus to do it. He says:

> Sometimes you can watch a cavity fill up right in front of your eyes. You can actually see silver, gold or porcelain coming up until the whole cavity is full. It's amazing!

Skimpy Evidence

Fuller calls himself "The Psychic Dentist." Believers swear that all the above-listed miracles have taken place in their mouths at his command, though none of them has produced before-and-after X-rays to prove those claims. Much of Fuller's success depends upon the fact that most people do not know where fillings or other repairs are actually located in their own mouths. Also, the

faithful find wonders in every little twinge and tingle they experience while in the ecstasies of evangelical fervor. Add a little
carefully calculated and applied hoopla and tambourine-thumping,
and you have dental miracles.

The Fuller literature abounds with fantastic claims. It is easy
to simply spout accounts of miracles when no possibility exists of
their being checked out. In an October 1986 meeting in Rochester,
New York, Fuller claimed that, in Phoenix, an 11-year-old girl
with six cavities suddenly had no cavities and no fillings after he
cured her. A 66-year-old woman "in upstate New York," he said,
had *no teeth*. They had all been extracted. As a result of Fuller's
magic, he claimed, she "began cutting a set of baby teeth, and
eventually re-grew an entire new set of teeth."

At that same meeting, Fuller's wife, Amelia, declared: "We
welcome skeptics with an open mind [*sic*] who come to investigate."

Acting upon that invitation, Mark Plummer, executive director
of the Committee for the Scientific Investigation of Claims of the
Paranormal, who attended the meeting, tried to obtain the iden-
tities of the Phoenix girl and the woman with the set of new
teeth whom the Reverend Fuller had spoken of. The Fullers declined to supply that information.

Going to the Top

At the suggestion of Florida State Representative Art Simon, on
December 4, 1986, I wrote to the appropriate regulatory department of the Florida State government. Three weeks later I received a form which I returned with this letter:

> Department of Professional Regulation
> Dental & M.D.
> Capitol Building
> Tallahassee, FL 32301
>
> Dear Sirs:
>
> Enclosed is your form 0385, filled out and with
> accompanying documentation.
>   Briefly, the subject, Willard Fuller, is
> claiming that he brings about dental healing in
> the form of filled cavities, new gold caps,
> straightening teeth and changing silver fillings

to gold. His performance is dramatic and convincing to those who do not understand the psychological pressures brought to bear on them, and he takes money from these persons in every place he performs.

Fuller is literally claiming to perform medical services while he:

(1) is not in any way trained for such work,

(2) does not in actuality perform the services and

(3) collects money from his victims by fraud.

Furthermore, and this may be the greatest harm that Willard Fuller does, he passes through the audience carrying a glass of water along with a variety of dental tools, which he places into the mouths of his victims to examine their teeth and show bystanders where he claims the miracle healings have taken place! No sterilization of instruments is done. This can easily result in widespread infection of various sorts, passed from person to person on the instruments. The list of possible diseases that can be vectored by this means is very large.

Fuller's procedures are potentially very dangerous. I ask that the Department of Professional Regulation investigate his activities, and I wish to file a formal complaint at this time.

Sincerely,

James Randi

On March 17—three months later—I received a letter from Charlene G. Willoughby, senior complaint analyst for the Department of Professional Regulation. In it, I was told:

Your complaint has been reviewed by the Complaint Analyst Section of this department. An analysis of your complaint has resulted in

referral to the Bureau of Investigative Services
of this department. A status report will be sent
to you in sixty days, or sooner if possible.

It was 96 days later that I received a form letter addressed to
"Randy, James" about "Subject: Filler, Willard." The letter
assured me that reports were being reviewed and that a decision
would be made as to whether there was "probable cause" to bring
charges against Fuller. It also notified me that "this process
normally takes several weeks."

In the eight months since I first notified that Florida state
authority, Fuller has met and possibly infected hundreds of people.
As this book goes to press, I am still waiting for a response from
the state.

Trouble Down Under

It would seem that checking out Fuller's claims is a simple matter,
when and if he will allow it, which he won't, and when and if the
appropriate authorities will try to do so, which they won't. But
there has been at least one exception to this last general rule.
When the 72-year-old Reverend Fuller and his wife visited Australia early in 1986, the Dental Board of New South Wales took
him to court and charged him with breaching the Dental Act by
falsely advertising himself to be a dentist capable of filling cavities and straightening teeth. The offense was found to be proved,
and he was ordered to pay court costs of $435; but, says Fuller,
because of his saintly nature and his religious orientation, the
conviction was "not recorded." This is a nice way of saying that
they decided to go easy on him. The Fullers left Australia immediately.

Improving the Account

Fuller immediately began rewriting history. In the July 1, 1986,
edition of his newsletter, the *Lively Stones Fellowship*, he exulted
that "we issued the order for prayer power and 150 angels to
march into the courtroom with us." He went on to say that he
had been "invited to court by the Dental Board," that "the case
was dropped," and that "the judge read a two page statement as
to how 'the character of the Fullers and their ministry is beyond
reproach.' "

These quotes are simply not accurate. Fuller was not "invited" to court; he was, in the words of the summons issued to him and served on him by a court official, "commanded to appear under penalty of law." He had no choice in the matter. The case was not "dropped." It was heard in court in all its detail, from beginning to end. The case against Fuller was proved. And the judge never declared on the character of Fuller; the words Fuller quotes never appeared anywhere except in his newsletter, and he himself invented them. The fact that Fuller claimed, in court and under oath, that he was "living on Social Security" in the United States might have colored the opinion of the magistrate, had the truth been known. As for the crowd of angels in the courtroom, they were not noticed by anyone, nor were they reported in the press.

Dentistry by Alchemy

How can Fuller's victims possibly believe that God puts crowns made of gold or porcelain, or fillings made of silver, into their mouths? Why doesn't He restore the original tooth? After all, He made the original, didn't He? Fuller is credited with a "miracle" when people see in their mouths silver fillings that have turned to gold. First, gold fillings simply are not used in real dentistry. Second, Fuller uses a small, penlike flashlight to look into the victim's mouth. Its feeble glow is rather yellowish, and could make silver fillings appear golden. In fact, many recipients of this Midas touch complain that the next day the miracle is found to have reversed itself, the gold having degenerated back to silver.

How does Fuller claim to perform his magic? His explanation is typically crackpot-style, incorporating basic, accepted facts followed by sheer nonsense. He says:

> Everything in the universe, including our bodies, is made up of atoms. The atoms can be manipulated, and when you get into the right relationship with God, you have a great source of power at your disposal.

A Serious, Direct Health Hazard

The dangers of Fuller's operation are many. As I informed the Florida Department of Professional Regulation, Fuller wanders about his audience, poking a dental mirror into mouth after mouth, swishing it in a glass of something or other between pokings. Such a procedure is certainly not sufficient to sterilize the instrument, and he has the potential of spreading deadly diseases from one infected person to all those he touches. Especially when we are so concerned with the transmission of the AIDS virus, Fuller's practices appear to be exceedingly dangerous.

Perhaps one reason that people like Fuller are so popular has to do with an observation by the director of communications for the Dental Society of the State of New York, Chris Florentz. He believes that the Fullers may hold some attraction for dental phobics, of which there are upwards of 30 million in the United States, by the society's estimate. Says Florentz:

> Dental phobics are people who will avoid receiving dental care under almost any circumstances. I can see this sort of thing appealing to that sort of person.

But Florentz was not optimistic about the possibility of prosecuting the Fullers. "There is a further consideration involving the First Amendment and freedom of religion that adds to the complexity of the issue," he said.

Yes, and only after some serious illnesses have occurred as a result of infections brought about by the Reverend Fuller will anyone trouble to begin defending us from this perversion of the First Amendment.

I have one simple question regarding Willard Fuller: How is it that he not only wears thick glasses to correct his eyesight, but also has six missing teeth himself, while the rest are badly stained and contain quite ordinary silver fillings? Physician, heal thyself.

The Shirley Temple of Faith-Healing

"Amazing Grace" is the show business name of Grace DiBiccari, a former beautician and singer turned circuit healer. A minor actor in the faith-healing business, she dresses like an aging teen going to a '60s senior prom. After watching the woman on a major TV program, a Toronto-based newspaper reporter wrote that

> Amazing Grace, unfortunately, gives the impression of someone for whom the word "bimbo" was coined, and her contribution is mostly restricted to generating mayhem and an endless string of non sequiturs.

Grace offered me, as proof of her powers, a claim that she had cured a liver condition suffered by a Connecticut woman. That lady (the subject, not the healer) showed up in person at the TV broadcast referred to above to confront me with this evidence, and though that TV audience will never be presented with what I discovered, I will share it with you here.

It had been agreed during the television presentation that I would follow up on the case Grace had produced for examination, but when I attempted to intercept that woman as she left the studio, I was blocked by Grace and a man who accompanied her. I fought my way past the pair and reached the woman as she exited the building. I asked for her address and telephone number, and she informed me that she never gave anyone that information. After a few minutes of haggling with her, I managed to extract the post office box address of "a friend" through which I could reach her, and she hurried away.

Upon my return home, I wrote the woman at that address. My letter came back marked "Addressee unknown." However, shortly afterwards I received a phone call from a man who said he knew the woman in question, and he gave me a telephone number which proved to be correct. I finally reached Grace's prize example—much to her surprise—and found that she was apparently willing to cooperate.

She gave me the name of her current doctor, whom I contacted. He assured me that the original diagnosis had been made by a reputable physician. The subject was believed to have a hepatoma (primary liver cancer), which does not usually respond well to chemotherapy, but the subject was given such treatment for six months. About one person in five reacts favorably to this treatment, and this subject possibly did, since she was apparently free of symptoms of the hepatoma for four years after the first diagnosis. According to her doctor, the fact that she reacted this way was "fairly amazing."

But this woman is far from cured. Even before she was diagnosed as having the hepatoma, she had sarcoidosis, a "not generally malignant" liver condition but one that can be fatal. It is a chronic disease, and this woman is still being treated for it. When I asked her physician whether there was anything miraculous about her apparently improved condition, he told me: "I don't think faith-healing has got anything to do with how she's doing right now."

When she was asked by Dr. Gary Posner, a physician who has traced many of these cases for me, to supply him with her medi-

cal records, which she said were at her home, she balked at sending them. She said she *might* send that material after she had an
examination by her doctor the next month. When it did not arrive,
Posner called to ask about the status of her case. She said that
her appointment with her doctor had been postponed, and she
questioned Posner about why he wanted her records, though the
reason was quite evident and had been made known to her. She
also, strangely enough, did not want her association with DiBiccari
to be mentioned in this book. She said she did not credit Di-
Biccari with having cured her, but believes that her own prayers
did the job. From someone who was willing to stand before a TV
audience of hundreds of thousands of people with Grace at her
side and declare her miracle, this attitude needed explaining.

Questioned by me about how the miracle claimed by DiBiccari
was supposed to have taken place, this woman admitted that she
hadn't even spoken to the healer at the service she attended.
Amazing Grace walked past her as she sat. Grace never even made
an *attempt* to heal this woman, yet raved about her success.

As we go to press, months after having asked for the medical
records to establish the case, we still have not received them,
though the woman continues to say that she "might" send them.

Six More Failed Examples

Reporter Doug Margeson, of the *Bellevue* (Washington) *Journal-
American*, had no better luck finding anyone healed by DiBiccari.
He attended a huge meeting in the Seattle Center Arena, where
this colorful performer failed dramatically in every case he was
able to record. He made a list of those she treated.

(1) Kendal Walker, from Tacoma, Washington, was paralyzed
from the waist down as the result of a 1978 accident. Grace said
he was cured. He is the same now as he was then.

(2) Carolyn Rogala, of Seattle, had her ankle crushed in 1980
and still suffers severe pain. After Grace ministered to her, there
was no change.

(3) Gladys Chase suffers from osteoporosis and arthritis, was
touched by Grace, "felt better," but left wondering if the feeling
would last.

(4) Gloria French, a tiny woman from Tacoma, had pain in her
knees. Grace made no change in her condition. In fact, Grace
declared that Mrs. French had been in a wheelchair for ten years,
which Mrs. French later denied. "I tried to explain that to
Grace," she said, "but she kept insisting."

(5) Jamie Kitts, 7, of Lynnwood, wanted to be cured of certain birth defects and asthma. Her parents had to take her home early. The next day the little girl was taken to the Children's Orthopedic Hospital, very sick as a result of attending the meeting. Her mother, Sharon, said:

> I noticed that Grace didn't approach anyone who was incurable like Jamie. We talked about it on the way home. We all decided we don't buy it.

(6) Finally, reporter Margeson submitted to Grace's divine touch. He suffered from back problems, but went away no better off than before.

An Amazing Lack of Evidence and Loss of Memory

Grace DiBiccari's biographer, Elizabeth Fuller, makes some startling statements about her, particularly about her early life. As usual, this subject of an official biography has come up with fascinating anecdotes to glamorize her history. On one occasion, says Fuller, who has taken her subject's word as gospel without troubling to check the facts, young Grace refused to go on a car ride with some friends because she had "an overpowering feeling something bad would happen." Moments later, Fuller reports, the friends were all dead in a car wreck. Asked about the names of her friends and the date of the wreck, Grace could not remember any of them. Nor could she recall the name of a man in Danbury, Connecticut, who, she told Fuller, was instantly able to walk out of a wheelchair when she "called him out." She also had a memory lapse about what happened to him following the healing.

"We have nothing to hide," she told Margeson. She claimed that "healed" people were followed up by her staff to see if the healing had worked. All the evidence that Margeson—and I—have gathered shows that they would have little to report back after an investigation.

In response to criticism of her claims, despite her repeated offers to prove her claims and her failure to provide that evidence to the media, DiBiccari surprises no one by declaring in the same breath that she has no need to document any of her healings: "As long as the results are there, I don't care if the skeptics laugh."

Well, we're *not* laughing, Grace. We weep for the tens of thousands that you and other "healers" have talked out of their money, their reason, and their lives. The "results" you claim to obtain just aren't there.

The Gift of Knowledge Backfires

Robert Steiner, a Californian who has pursued Amazing Grace for some time now, made it quite plain that her Gift of Knowledge is the result of clever guesswork and "cold reading" techniques whereby she appears to be telling the afflicted things that have been divinely revealed to her. A man she had just called out of the audience and "healed" in front of Steiner on a San Francisco TV show asked her how she knew about his ailments. She explained it all for him:

> How did I know? Well, see, it's called the Word of Knowledge. It's a small inner voice of the Lord, for anyone else that would like to know. . . . It's called the Holy Spirit. . . . He speaks to me in a small inner voice . . . and He'll even show me who that person is.

Really? Well, Steiner at that point asked Grace if God—or the Holy Spirit—ever makes mistakes. Answered Amazing: "Never!" That was proof enough that God had had no communication with DiBiccari. Steiner then revealed that the man she had just called out of the audience was none other than the ubiquitous Don Henvick, chosen once more by another faith-healer and "healed" of yet another nonexistent disease. Despite the floundering post-mortem that Grace then launched into to explain away this faux pas, it was obvious that she had been trapped in her own game. To avoid the discussion, she merely turned away from Steiner and Henvick and declared, "Listen, I don't want to get on this anymore!"

Just say goodnight, Gracie.

13
Father DiOrio:
Vatican-Approved Wizard

Until recently, the Catholic church had kept claims about the healing sanctuary of Lourdes separate from claims made by the faith-healers. Specifically mentioning healer Oral Roberts, the National Catholic Welfare Conference declared that though

> medical evidence from doctors is frequently included in the testimony of the cured, [in Roberts's reports, there was] no effort on the part of the Roberts staff to gather extensive medical and psychiatric evidence.

The conference pointed out that the church had been very careful to establish "rigid tests of acceptance as miracles" for the cases reported from Lourdes. I found that at least one modern Catholic healer also makes such a claim, and I made every attempt to examine it.

There are a number of Roman Catholic healers who operate within the church and with cautious Vatican approval. This group includes Fathers Ralph DiOrio, Dennis Kelleher, and Edward Mc-Donough, along with Francis MacNutt (a former priest from Florida), and Barbara Shlemon.

Father McDonough divides healings into three categories. They are physical, emotional, and spiritual, with the last being "the greatest." He says:

> The greatest healing is a happy death. Then we
> are completely restored. Every other healing is
> temporary. What we try to teach people about
> miracles is that they are signs of God's love,
> goodness, and mercy. . . . Many times, people
> intellectualize healing. They try to make it too
> complicated.

Feeling that I might complicate Father McDonough's life too much
by asking simple questions about healing, and seeing from his
published comments that this faith-healer would not be likely to
enlighten me further, I decided to examine only the superstar of
all the Catholic healers.

Charismatic Catholic Father Ralph DiOrio, of Worcester,
Massachusetts, is by far the best-known of them all, largely
because of an article in the *National Enquirer* in 1977 and subsequent coverage on NBC-TV news. At age 14, he says, he was
dedicated to the priesthood. He joined a Chicago seminary through
the Missionary Fathers of St. Bartholomew's Church in Fitchburg,
Massachusetts, and was ordained in 1957. Healing abilities apparently came early to him. He says:

> . . . At the beginning of my priesthood, every-
> one I anointed with holy oil, every lay person
> was healed. . . . God has been preparing me all
> my life for this work.

DiOrio made his commitment to the healing movement on the
very day that healer Kathryn Kuhlman died, and he made his first
attempt to heal on the anniversary of her birth, apparently believing that he had inherited her position. He certainly had studied
her techniques and even today uses her "shotgun" method of
healing. An example:

> There is a healing taking place now in some-
> one's leg. I'm not sure if it is arthritis. If
> someone feels a healing taking place in their
> leg, if they feel less pain, tell us.

Consider the possibilities in these three sentences. Among 1,000 or
so devotees, *any* leg problem will qualify. If it is arthritis, so
much better the "hit." If not, DiOrio has already declared that he
is "not sure" about that angle, so he's covered. Notice he says

that "if" anyone feels they are being healed they should respond. "If" anyone feels "less pain," he wants to know about it. Should there be no response, he can just go on to something else that will elicit an answer. Nothing is lost. Also note that he is first fishing for a "healing," then drops the caliber of the miracle to just feeling "less pain" or a diminution of symptoms. This is classic "shotgun" technique, as is the "14 people have just been healed of scoliosis" ploy.

Father DiOrio also does the leg-stretching stunt. As W. V. Grant does, DiOrio sits his subject in a chair, prays over the "short" leg, and it appears to grow longer. It's the same routine, but he wears a cassock.

DiOrio also features "slaying in the spirit," a part of his (and Kuhlman's) ritual in which the afflicted person falls over suddenly when the healer gestures. This is an expected reaction, learned and accepted by regular customers.

Father DiOrio claims he has healed every conceivable kind of emotional, physical, and spiritual defect in his time. However, consider the testimony of one healed devotee of Father Ralph, "healed" during his Detroit appearance at the Joe Louis Arena. This was published in 1986 in the pages of *Fate* magazine, not a periodical apt to doubt many miracles:

> I suffered a neck injury . . . a long time ago
> . . . and I have had breathing problems and
> pain. . . . I attended Father DiOrio's charis-
> matic service. . . . I was sitting high in the
> third balcony. . . . I heard [him] call my name,
> saying, "There's a Helen here with a cervical
> problem, a neck problem—I feel it happening—a
> healing is taking place." Out of all those
> thousands of people, I was not certain he meant
> me, because nowhere was my name or ailment
> given. But he *did* mean me. . . . [Now] I do not
> have pain.

True, this woman's name is Helen. But how difficult was it for Father DiOrio to hit on a Helen with a neck pain in the Joe Louis Arena, jammed with thousands of believers? It is probable we could find such a combination. And if not, are all the non-Helens ever going to know it? Of course not. This woman never indicated at the meeting that she was the one healed, and had there been no one there to match that description, the result would have been the same. A faith-healer can never be wrong with such a maneuver. And was there perhaps another, very different problem that someone, anyone, might also answer to, given that description? "Cervical" can refer to problems of the uterus, too, and the alternative problem would have applied to Helen, had she been so afflicted. This fitted-evidence tendency is typical of many reports of miraculous healings, as we shall see in the in-depth study of the evidence in Chapter 16.

Down Syndrome "Cured"

Father DiOrio's claims cover a wide spectrum. He says, for example, that during one of many hundreds of miraculous performances, he instantly changed the facial features of Sarah DeMoon, a Down syndrome child, by the touch of his hand. The child's father had brought her 1,200 miles from Addison, Illinois, to be healed by DiOrio. Following the charismatic service, the girl's father, Carl DeMoon, was ecstatic:

> I not only think Sarah is cured, I think she's a
> genius. She's alert, attentive, doing everything
> that's expected of a normal 1-year-old child.
> Science and medicine don't have all the an-
> swers. God still has the last word.

Naturally, I was *very* interested in looking into this claim, because Down syndrome is a basic birth defect, and *there has never been a recorded reversal of this condition in medical history. Never.* So I wrote to all concerned, asking for some evidence.

At first, Carl DeMoon agreed to be interviewed about the healing, but now will not discuss the matter with anyone. Several letters I have sent to DiOrio's organization (the Apostolate of Prayer for Healing Evangelism, in Leicester, Massachusetts) asking for information on this specific case have been unanswered. In fact, similar inquiries simply asking for information on a medical validation team that DiOrio claims to have in operation have all been ignored. If the validation group cannot be identified, of what use can it possibly be? Or does it actually exist?

So that the reader will understand that my inquiries have been simple, direct requests for information, I will present here in its entirety one of the letters sent to this healer. The letter is typical of others I have sent to other faith-healers:

Fr. Ralph DiOrio
Apostolate of Prayer for Healing Evangelism
761 Main Street
Leicester, Mass. 01524

December 14, 1986

Dear Rev. DiOrio:

I have before me an article from the *Albu-querque Journal* of November 22nd, 1986. In that article, you are quoted as saying that the APHE "has a medical team that documents . . . healings [brought about by your services]." I should like to know how I might obtain the evidence that this team has gathered which establishes these healings.

The article also quotes you as saying that some healings are "inexplicable by medical standards." May I know what cases these are?

Is it true that your services have brought about healings of deafness to the point where people no longer need their hearing aids, as claimed in this article? Has your medical team evidence to support this fact, if you accept that claim?

I am preparing material for a book on faith-healing, and I would much appreciate the answers to these questions. Thank you for your attention to this request.

Please note that I was referring to claims made in the press and wanted to know if there was any truth to them. DiOrio did not respond to my requests for information. I believe he has good reason for not doing so. Surely, with almost 200 volunteers helping him at his headquarters, he has time to answer a simple request for information.

A Superior's Opinion

Father DiOrio's failure to respond is supported by the Reverend George Lange, the bishop's representative to the charismatic movement in Worcester, Massachusetts. Commenting on the matter of faith-healing to a newspaper reporter, he said:

> Everyone wants to know whether [Father Di-
> Orio's] cures are real or not. I say that they
> are. Sure, some are psychosomatic, and some
> hysterical, and some can be explained through
> natural reason. I don't have any problem with
> that, because they're still real. There's no great
> reason to prove them because when a doctor
> provides the means of healing, you feel God is
> working through him. God is working through-
> out a person's life. It's not that important to
> prove that it's extraordinary or divine inter-
> vention.

I can understand the Reverend Lange's insistence that it is
"not important" to examine DiOrio's claims of being able to heal.
If it were allowed to become important, *all* of the church's many
supernatural claims might become subject to close examination, and
the very survival of the church depends upon a continuing, persistent faith that allows no skepticism at all. Blind belief is an
absolutely necessary foundation for magical thinking.

More Incredible Claims, But No Evidence

DiOrio of course admits that some of the seeming cures that pour
from his fingertips can be of a psychosomatic nature. But, he
says, he believes that in such cases the "spirit" needs to be cured
before such a cure becomes permanent. He adds:

> But when we have a case of one leg shorter
> than another or curvature of the spine, or
> deafness, and that is healed, that is a real
> miracle.

That is exactly what this book has been trying to establish.
And Father Ralph DiOrio has been of no help in the investigation.
Cases for which we have been able to examine the evidence with-
out DiOrio's help do not support his claims. For example, Cecile
Boscardin of Fitchburg, Massachusetts, a victim of cancer, visited
DiOrio in 1976 and was thoroughly convinced that she had been
cured. Her doctor had told her that hers was a terminal case, and
she testified that she had been healed by Father DiOrio during a

"slaying in the spirit" experience. Less than a year later, Cecile was dead of cancer. Questioned by the press, DiOrio replied:

> Why are some healed when some others, even
> with the same affliction, are not? I don't know
> the answer; only God knows.

Perhaps the answer is—as it appears to be—that *no one is cured.*

The Catholic church has no problem with the claims of such Catholic healers as DiOrio. Its foggy reasoning on the subject, was expressed in the April 1985 issue of *U.S. Catholic* magazine:

> God's healing power is not a matter of faith; it
> is a matter of mystery, as inexplicable as the
> omnipotent force to which it is credited. And it
> will remain so. It operates beyond the will of
> those who purport to be its vehicles, the clergy
> and laypeople who say they have shrunken
> tumors, relieved arthritis, or restored hearing.

With the attitude so far shown by the Catholic church with regard to providing any evidence of actual healings brought about through its "vehicles," this power is certain to remain forever "a matter of mystery."

Sidestepping the Question

In its statement, the Catholic church avoids any logical discussion of the claimed healing phenomenon by simply declaring it to be a permanent mystery that cannot be examined and therefore need not be explained. This escape is not tolerable to rational people, though most if not all of the people involved in the cultural phenomena we are examining make no pretense of belonging to the rational mainstream. In fact, they proudly proclaim their refusal to tolerate any discussion, doubt, or examination of the notions they regard as absolute truths.

Social psychologist Dr. Carlo Lastrucci, in his book *The Scientific Approach*, discusses what science is, and makes this observation:

> A discussion of the legitimate object of scien-
> tific study (i.e., the observed object or event)
> often raises the question of assumedly spiritual

(i.e., extra-natural) or supernatural phenomena. Put another way, it is often asserted that science cannot study—and therefore cannot legitimately answer such questions about—supernatural events. The scientific answer to such an assertion is quite simple. Philosophically, science is neither theistic (i.e., a belief in god or gods) nor atheistic; but it is objective insofar as it studies phenomena having behavioral attributes or consequences. If something exists or occurs having such attributes that it can be objectively ascertained and confirmed, then it can be studied scientifically. Whether it has been "caused" by a "natural" or a "supernatural" force or agent is a separate and wholly different kind of question.

Of course the question we must answer before any other is whether or not there are any phenomena here to explain, and several years of investigation have produced no convincing evidence that this emperor has any clothes. This question of evidence for faith-healing will be discussed later.

The Heavy Burden of Guilt

Both his church and DiOrio disagree with the other TV faith-healers who insist on putting a guilt burden upon those who fail to summon enough faith to "keep the healing" they have been given, or to achieve it in the first place. In stating his position on this Father DiOrio says:

> Our prayers do not change the mind of God. Our prayers keep us in tune with the Lord's will. As I continually stress, healing from God does not depend upon our quantitative faith or upon our good works. God's gift of healing flows completely from the mercy and love of His bountiful goodness.

I have seldom encountered a more nonsensical, paradoxical statement from a supposedly educated person. DiOrio is saying, in effect, that the afflicted must ask God for His gift of healing. Because God has *already* made up His divine mind about the matter, all the afflicted can hope for is understanding of that decision. But even though that decision is unchangeable, the afflicted person is told to beg for an unobtainable divine "gift." Why? Does God so much need and require continual abject groveling and vain pleading? From what Father DiOrio says, it appears that He does. At least the other faith-healers preach that you can *ask*—if not demand—favors from heaven. The paradoxes that present themselves are obvious.

Finally, the Roman Catholic church, through the Jesuit magazine *America*, ran a damning critique of the Oral Roberts ministry and the healing claims made on his show. Titled "Faith-Healing Over T.V.," it said in part:

> There is certainly a reasonable doubt that these programs are in the public interest. Of their very nature, they play upon the hopes and fears of the credulous and ignorant. There is no positive proof that some of the "cures" are not rigged. At any rate, standard medical treatment seems to be flouted. We can wonder how many, viewing such programs in their homes, are impelled to neglect ordinary medical treatment.

Does the fact that Father DiOrio wears a woolen cassock, rather than a tasteless polyester suit, make him *more* believable, more genuine, or less dangerous than Oral Roberts? If Father DiOrio *and* Reverend Roberts would favor me with a simple response to my inquiries, I might be able to tell if there is any qualitative feature by which to differentiate the two.

Plus exemplo quam peccato nocent.

14
The Lesser Lights

There are a multitude of minor figures who belong in this discussion, but will be lumped together in this chapter because their histories do not add anything substantially new to the faith-healing picture. However, there are certain flavors and novelties to be found here that color in the picture somewhat. I can safely predict that faith-healers who fail to find themselves listed here or in the main body of this book will crow to their audiences that they escaped mention because they are genuine. That is a false assumption.

Danny Davis

Willard Fuller is not the only divine dentist. In Bakersfield, California, the Reverend Danny Davis conjures amalgam every Sunday. One amusing aspect of his miraculous tooth-filling is that recipients often notice that the "new" fillings are "cross-shaped," and Davis declares that shape to be "God's seal of approval." What he fails to mention is that ordinary dental fillings more often than not are cross-shaped to provide physical strength to the structure. But, it might be argued, God of course knows that, and uses the best configuration in His work, too.

Once, when Davis took his act to the state of Virginia, investigator John Whipple from the State Department of Health was sent to check out his claims. He concluded:

> I heard about Davis and decided to see if he
> was practicing dentistry without a license. I
> expected to find a mobile dental clinic, but I
> didn't. In fact, there was no physical dentistry
> going on—nothing that would involve my depart-
> ment—unless you think we should license God.

And that was the limit of this man's investigation. He had no
interest whatsoever in whether people who attended the Davis
show were there to receive actual dental attention, as promised in
the advertisements. He was concerned only with whether there
were tools of the trade in use, and whether Davis had a license to
use them. There was no further investigation of Danny Davis, and
he was free to continue his flummery unchecked in the state of
Virginia.

Kathryn ("The Great") Kuhlman

Kathryn Kuhlman was a colorful Pentecostal Baptist faith-healer
who dressed in flowing, filmy garments very much in the image of
a wrinkled, red-haired angel. In 1967, she was presented with the
key to the city of Philadelphia, which gives one a good idea of
how secure that city is. Dr. Robert Nolen, in his book *Healing*, did
long-term follow-ups on 23 of Kuhlman's claimed healings. There
were no cures among those cases. One woman who was said to
have been cured of spinal cancer threw away her brace and ran
across the stage at Kuhlman's command; her spine collapsed the
next day, according to Nolen, and she died four months later.

Kuhlman depended upon a limited number of stunts to accomplish her performance. As mentioned previously, she is credited
with developing the sit-'em-in-a-wheelchair gimmick. She was also
adept at the "shotgun" technique whereby she announced (as do
W. V. Grant, Father Ralph DiOrio, and Pat Robertson) that a
certain number of people in the audience were being healed of a
certain disease, without specifying who they were.

(Alan Spraggett, a would-be parapsychologist who investigated
Kathryn Kuhlman, was ecstatic to discover in her claims similari-
ties to those made by psychics. He quickly accepted Kuhlman as a
genuine operator because she matched the "paradigm" he expected.)

Kathryn Kuhlman, who at one time appeared on more than 50 TV stations every week, died in 1976 of pulmonary hypertension following open heart surgery, in Tulsa, Oklahoma.

Daniel Atwood

Daniel Atwood is a healer originally from Lake City, Florida. At one time, he employed David Jones—son of Thea Jones, a well-known faith-healer who owns the Metropolitan Theater in Philadelphia—as his "front man." They constituted one of the more entertaining pairs in the business. In 1974, they were in the small town of Waycross, Georgia, for a week of healing shows. It turned out to be a mostly black crowd that attended, and because the two operators were white, they asked their black organist, Bill Williamson, to mix with the crowd and casually obtain pertinent information—such as names and ailments—from individuals who were there to be healed. Bill refused, wanting no part of such a scheme.

He watched from the sidelines as the pair talked one woman out of $500 and made arrangements to meet her after the service on the last evening of the show to get more. But the mayor, the police chief, and a local judge were there when the pair showed up, and they arrested them both. The judge said that he had been at the service every night that week and that he had observed how Atwood and Jones had "manipulated people." He said they had been "taking all our niggers' money," and that he—the judge—would find those swindled people up before him in court soon for not being able to pay their utility and tax bills.

The chief of police, Williamson said, told them that he'd be happy to see them "make a move" so he could take a shot at them. The message was very plain indeed, and the latest victim's money was quickly refunded on the spot as the officials watched with satisfaction.

But the pair of rogues didn't want any of their other visible assets seized to repay other complainants, so they told Williamson to sneak out the back and drive their customized Eldorado to the next town, where they'd meet him. He did, and they were never seen in Waycross again.

Jones, a notorious drug abuser, died a few years ago. Atwood is making a comeback as an associate of the unsinkable Reverend Leroy Jenkins, who hauled him aboard the ever-leaky but still floating Jenkins ferryboat.

David Epley

Based in Fort Lauderdale, Florida, out of the Church of the Good Shepherd, Pastor David Epley got started in St. Louis, where I am told he still has a substantial church. The act he offers is very much like that of W. V. Grant, though his mailing pieces are rather juvenile compared with others of similar status. The wording appears to be almost identical to that of begging letters sent out by New York's Reverend Ike, from whom Epley might be borrowing ideas. He appears to pop on and off television, perhaps having difficulty paying for the air time.

In 1986, Epley voiced his bewilderment during one of his television shows that "Randi the magician" had not come to witness his wonders. Accordingly, I sent him this letter by certified mail on August 19, 1986:

> I have taken some time to get around to examining your claims, since those I have already investigated were "passing through" and were therefore handled sooner. However, since you publicly mentioned me in your last broadcast, I can consider that a "throwing down of the gauntlet" which officially opens the investigation and signifies your acceptance of my challenge.
>
> Accordingly, I will offer you the same challenge offered to Peter Popoff. I told him that I would accept evidence from an independent, medically qualified panel that would examine any *five* of his cases and declare that they received healing as a result of his ministrations. I told Popoff further: "You have now announced that you will soon present personal testimonials from selected individuals. If you should choose to present on your television program, as further evidence, video interviews with persons who have received healing through your ministry, any proper evaluation of that evidence would require that you supply us with the names and addresses of each person so interviewed. It would also be proper that we receive *all* names and addresses of those with whom you conduct those interviews, whether

they are selected to appear on the program, or not."

I will await your response to this challenge. Should you be able to meet the simple conditions of this test, I will present you with my check for $10,000. I will also declare in writing and in person that I believe you have the direct anointing from God to be able to bring divine healing to people.

A further point: Since we are bound to be very careful and specific about details of all statements pertaining to this matter, I must point out to you the error in your statement during the recent broadcast. You have brought up the old chestnut about "there can be no counterfeit if there is no genuine item." That is not true. Anyone can print a counterfeit American three-dollar bill. It will be obviously counterfeit, but that does not mean that there ever was in actuality a genuine three-dollar bill.

Pastor Epley, to prove that you are not a three-dollar bill, I suggest that you provide proof of your ability to bring divine healing to those in your ministry. And, as I also informed Peter Popoff, "I can assure you that I am a tenacious and determined investigator. I will not abandon my inquiries until this matter is settled satisfactorily." Since you have accepted my challenge to witness your claims, please take this challenge seriously.

This letter was sent, frankly, because a Florida newspaper had heard Epley refer to me and asked me why I did not take him up on his challenge. After I sent this letter, none of the newspapers followed up on the matter, for reasons only they can know. I suspect that they were cowed by Epley's religious stance.

Epley is a very small fish in this very large pond. But you should know this: In 1986, the Reverend Epley underwent surgery for a brain tumor. He visited a regular hospital, had regular anesthesia, and recovered in the normal way. It was a process he would not have recommended for his congregation.

Brother (Reverend) Al (Warick)

Brother Al, a flamboyant character who operates out of Fresno, California, owns racehorses at Monterey and a private jet. He got his start working as a "front man" for evangelist/healer David Epley—whom we have just discussed. One night about 15 years ago, according to a former colleague, Brother Al walked away with the entire offering at an Epley service and went into business for himself, working on radio alone to start. He has been very successful.

Reverend Al's *Enquirer* ad.

Most of Al's current income appears to be derived from advertisements dropped into supermarket tabloids (an expensive form of advertising) asking that a selection be made from a list of eight needs. For a mere $1.25, a "scriptural bracelet" will be sent you. At first glance, this seems not to be a worthwhile investment for Al to make. Mailing of even the cheapest trinket costs, in labor, packaging, and postage, more than $1.25. But the profit here is in the name and address, which not only can be used by Reverend Al, but can be sold to other evangelists. Anyone who answers such an ad will be predisposed to believe all sorts of things and can be counted upon to contribute to unlikely causes.

Al seems proud that he writes his own begging letters. In a 1985 mailing, he told me:

> I hope you also look close at my letters and replies to your needs and realize "*I do not hire*" (like other ministers) writers to do my work.

Maybe he should.

David Paul

The Reverend David Paul, son of an evangelist, hails from Chesterfield, Missouri, and now operates out of St. Louis. He got his start working for another healer, Don Walker, Sr., in the late 1970s. Paul had a home in a small town in Illinois, sold it, and made a $40,000 profit which he invested in radio time across the United States. In four months—the usual time it takes for turnaround of such an investment—he was in business and making money. Then the opportunity of using TV came along, and he dropped radio in favor of the more powerful medium.

He uses Don Walker, Jr., who lives in Stockton, California, as his "front man." Being of the old school, Paul took a long time to avail himself of modern methods for the purpose of recalling his boldly gathered, pre-digested information to offer his congregation. In the "Word of Knowledge" stunt, he used a quite simple method which was already well known to the last generation of evangelists. He was for a long time content to store his information on small slips of paper inserted in his Bible, apparently put there to mark passages to which he would refer from time to time. Those who formerly worked with him describe how Paul would burn those slips in a wastebasket following every show.

Getting all the necessary data onto a small slip is rather easy. All that is needed is a name, a disease, and perhaps an address number and street. Suppose you have on the slip, "William Parsons," "Dr. Brown," and "heart attack." Those six words can be expanded into a minor melodrama. To wit:

> I have an impression of you clutching at your chest. The pain is more than you can bear. It's enough to make you cry out in agony. You fall to your knees. "Dear God!" you are saying, "Take this burden from me! Let this travail pass!" The doctors are working over you, doing what they can for you. But they can't do anything except get you to bed, and Dr. Brown is saying, "Take it easy, Bill. You're a sick man." But doctors are only human. Only *Dr. Jesus* can do what you need, Bill. I want you to go home—because I see an angel of the Lord standing at your front gate right now, Bill—and tell all the folks there that Dr. Jesus has put a whole new heart into your body! It's done! Hallelujah!

(This is taken from an actual recording of David Paul in action.)

Paul's performance in Stockton, California, where I first saw his live show, was a startling event. The preaching part of the performance was drama at its best. Like a medieval rabble-rouser, he conjured up in the minds of his audience imaginary entities that I am sure some of them actually saw before them. He sprinted about, pointing out the Devil to his enthusiastic audience, and stomping on him with cries of "Take *that*, Devil!"

I attended in the good company of several colleagues and Joan Smith, a reporter from the *San Francisco Examiner*. Smith later described his act:

> [Paul] sings and cavorts like Mick Jagger without the pelvic thrusts. For nearly two hours he preaches the gospel, working the microphone like a musical instrument, his voice a bellow and a growl, a staccato blast and a rich glissando. . . . He selects people from the crowd, emphasizing that he's never seen them before

and that he hasn't read the cards they filled out at the door. The crowd gasps as he addresses apparent strangers by name and refers to personal problems God has told him will be healed.

This is Paul's use of the "Word of Knowledge" gimmick. He is not at all shy about telling his followers that he speaks directly with God as he stands before them in person. He distinctly addresses God and stands there listening as the Divinity speaks to him, apparently informing this Anointed Person of the name and ailment of the afflicted. At one point in the Stockton meeting, it appeared that God told him about a bearded man sitting on the aisle, and Paul called him to the front, by name. He assured the audience that he had never spoken to this man before, and proceeded to describe the man's problems and declared those problems solved. The unfortunate chap thereupon fell to the floor and appeared to be in the throes of either ecstasy or death.

Reporter Smith and I watched with more than average interest as David Paul "called out" this victim. I had asked the reporter to note how the preacher had repeatedly told his audience that he obtained his information by divine communication. During that service, among other similar statements, he had clearly said to his audience:

(1) I'll be ministering to those that God sends me to.
(2) Only way I can know about you is if God speaks to me.
(3) God spoke to me. By the Holy Spirit, "R" stands for "Roger"?

He'd also specifically asked those he approached whether they had been questioned earlier:

(1) Anyone ask you anything about yourself?
(2) Anyone come up to you and ask you anything?
(3) Nobody came up and asked you anything?
(4) Some say to me: "Call me out. Tell me where I live, what my illness is." I can't do that. Only if God sends me to that person.

As we watched, the Reverend Paul spoke to the bearded man: "Tom or Thomas—isn't that your name?" The man agreed. Paul then groped about in the air and divined that Tom had serious marital and drinking problems, and again obtained agreement from him. Then the preacher put his hand on Tom's head while inserting his foot in his open mouth when he reached just a tad too far, and gave Smith the evidence she needed:

> Some people have condemned you because— because of your financial status. . . . The only way that I can know about you is if God speaks to me. . . . God says he will heal you.

Perhaps Reverend Paul—or God—is confused. It *had to be* Paul's wife who gave him that information, because, as Joan Smith knew, the man Paul "called out" was a bachelor, doesn't drink, has a secure federal job and is not named Tom. *But when Mrs. Paul had approached him earlier in the evening to strike up a conversation, he'd given her that false information.*

("Tom's" real name is Don Henvick. We first met him back in Chapter 8 and then again in Chapter 9, as he pursued Popoff. He is a member of the Society of American Magicians and of the Bay Area Skeptics, the latter a group that was instrumental in catching the faith-healers in the act of cheating. He's the same man, referred to earlier, whom Reverend Popoff "cured" of uterine cancer in Detroit when Don attended a service dressed in drag as a decoy. The Stockton meeting with Paul was the first of many times Don would be "cured" of non-existent ailments.)

David Paul isn't much of a prophet, either. In his booklet *Seven Prophetic Events that Will Change Your Life in 1986*, he told his followers that "the Spirit of God has revealed" to him that in that year:

(1)   The Soviets will try to negotiate a withdrawal from Afghanistan.
(2)   The Ayahtollah Khomeni will be put out of power or will be killed.
(3)   Continued unrest and trouble in the Middle East. [How did he know?]
(4)   There will be a surge in the U.S. economy starting in April.
(5)   Economic collapse in South Africa.

(6) "The Lord showed me that two of America's leading ministers will fall from their religious pedestals . . . [There was a substantial rumor in evangelist circles at that time of the coming PTL scandal with Jim and Tammy Faye Bakker, but it waited until 1987 to materialize. Tough luck!]

(7) Many more people will "come to God."

These are the sensational revelations David Paul said "God has given me." And, said Paul, without any reservations whatsoever: "THIS WILL HAPPEN IN 1986!" If that's the best he can do at prophecy, he should get out of the prophet business.

Ernest Angley

Akron, Ohio, is the home of Grace Cathedral and a squeaky-voiced faith-healer named Ernest Angley. In 1986, I attended a service at the cathedral accompanied by Buffalo philosophy professor Paul Kurtz. It was quite startling in many ways.

The church is a meticulously kept, very attractive house of worship. The choir is excellent, and the musicians are top-quality performers. But the worship service can only be described as a pathological experience. By the time Kurtz and I had gone through four and a half hours of Angley's squealing and bellowing, we were ready for a rapid retreat. Such an encounter is an exercise in endurance.

Stuffed into a silk suit and a Rolex watch, Reverend Angley covers his pate with what appears to be a cast aluminum hairpiece. His heavy Southern accent gives him the flavor of a comic performing an impersonation of a preacher. He is often parodied by well-known comedians. In fact, he is the faith-healer most easily recognized because of his bizarre habits and appearance.

His sermon was simply a mind-numbing, disconnected, rambling series of mild admonitions and folksy anecdotes. Two hours of that, and then the "healing" session began, with no surprises whatsoever. At one point, he got into trouble. A 10-year-old boy, in the company of his mother, stood in the healing line. Angley spoke softly with her. Suddenly beaming, he decided to let her tell her story.

She enthusiastically recounted how her son had been suffering from a tumor on his head "big as a baseball," and that she had brought him to Angley to be prayed for. The preacher put words in her mouth: "And today this little boy is *healed* of that cancer! Is that right?" he asked. "Yes," said the mother, "and praise Jesus, he has no cancer or pain now after coming here to Grace Cathedral to be healed!" Then Angley put both his Florsheims into his open mouth. "So he was healed right *here* by prayer?" Said the mother, "Yes! You see, after the doctors cut off that tumor, he was feeling poorly, and you prayed for him to get better fast after the operation, and he did!" Angley quickly snatched the microphone away from the woman and went into a series of screechy hallelujahs, looking around for something to take the footprints off his tongue.

Angley also uses the "shotgun" technique of pointing into the audience in a vague fashion and yelling to diabetics, high blood pressure victims, and migraine sufferers: "Receive the miracle!"

He also does the "slaying in the spirit" demonstration, to which I subjected myself at his meeting. I stood before him and two huge "catchers" stood at my sides. He placed one hand at the small of my back, pressed the other to my forehead, and easily pushed me over. Kurtz was not such a "pushover." He decided to resist, and though Angley pushed him hard three times, Kurtz remained firmly standing. Disgusted, Angley muttered to him, "Well, then, take the healing for your friend!" and went on to more pliant victims.

The ritual that followed the healing portion of the service was really frightening. Kurtz and I saw how otherwise intelligent, quiet people could be manipulated into a frenzy by a sort of hypnotic, paralyzing repetition of a short phrase ("God is good!") endlessly chanted, while Angley "conducted" the chant with a bemused smile. It went on for 26 minutes, as evidenced by my tape recorder.

We regarded the Angley performance as more of a circus than a service. He is, to me, a ludicrous figure; to his parishioners, he is a God-inspired preacher. One thing surprised me greatly: We found that most of those in attendance at the church were accustomed to being there *every Friday night*. It was their "night out" in very much the way other folks go to the drive-in movie or the bowling alley once a week. Angley provides them with entertainment, essentially, and it is one of the community activities to be there when he is on stage.

Two professors of philosophy from the University of Akron were with Kurtz and me, and they later commented in *Free Inquiry* magazine:

> If Angley were only in the entertainment business, the matter could be left there. But the remaining possibility is of a more serious nature—that he is taking money under false pretenses by claiming to do something that he doesn't do and cannot do—heal the sick.

Ernest Angley appears to be a relatively harmless, probably sincere preacher. There has never been any complaint about his handling of money, and there is little in the way of serious objection from the community around him. Akron seems to like him and to tolerate any silliness that may rub off by association. Unless some major scandal descends on him, Angley will probably have little trouble holding onto his ministry.

Two deaths are known to have occurred during Angley's services. One was in Charlotte, North Carolina, and another in Zurich, Switzerland. For practicing medicine without a license in Munich, Germany, in July 1984, Angley spent a short time in jail. But no other accusation of any consequence has been leveled upon him—other than his bad wig—and he appears to be a relatively benign character in this otherwise rather seedy assemblage.

Though he claims to have virtually a 100 percent rate of successful healing, that is obviously only wishful thinking. As other healers, he deceives himself and doesn't know when to stop. We saw people at the Akron meeting who told us they were healed every week, and they saw nothing incongruous in that statement. I think the difference between us was in our definitions, nothing more.

Angley is fond of invoking God's wrath upon those who offend him. He gleefully tells his supporters that the city of Munich suffered a major hailstorm shortly after he was jailed there, and as punishment for the investigation that Kurtz and I did of his operation, he declared: "God's likely to strike them dead. It's just a mercy of God that He didn't." I rather think that God's vengeance would be worse if I had had to sit through another hour of Ernest Angley. *That* would be worse than divine lightning, I assure you.

The Happy Hunters

Frances and Charles Hunter are referred to as the "Ozzie and Harriet of Faith-Healing." They are billed as "The Happy Hunters," and they present a cheerful, effervescent attitude to their work that makes many other faith-healers look like grumps. Upbeat gospel music, seeming almost sinful in its rousing tempo, fills their services. But then they refer to their meetings as "Healing Explosions."

As investigator David Alexander discovered, there is much more to the Happy Hunters' activities than just attempting to heal the faithful; they specialize in conducting *lessons* in how to heal. They say that they do not charge for these services. However, participants are required to read a book published and sold by the Hunters ($5), watch 12 hours of videotapes conveniently sold by the Hunters ($175), and listen to 12 audiotapes also available for sale by the Hunters ($36).

Frances is a living testimonial to Charles's abilities. She says that he rebuilt her heart, liver, and pancreas. The fact that he left these retooled organs in a 71-year-old body makes one wonder. Perhaps when Frances dies, the mortician will have to beat her liver into submission with a stick.

Not ordained into any recognized church, the Hunters happily announce that they have been ordained "by God." This, apparently, is enough to satisfy the IRS, because the Hunters pay no taxes on money raised at their "explosions." They teach and encourage "speaking in tongues" and perform the Grant leg-stretching trick. I cannot imagine that any person who regularly performs this trick as a demonstration can possibly fail to know that it is a deception.

Alexander attended a Happy Hunters meeting in Anaheim, California, in 1987. He was appalled by what he saw and what he learned by following up on some cases. He reported his findings in *Free Inquiry* magazine. He said that one man, urged to accept a healing that failed to relieve his pain, was taken aside by Frances and scolded for still feeling the pain. He was accused of denying what God wanted for him. Another man, who said he had three herniated discs, was now supposed to be healed. Says Alexander, this man who had been put through the process, and who had then "demonstrated his healing by bending over and touching his toes was [now] leaning against some chairs and looking as if he had been hit by a truck; his face registered great pain."

More seriously, Alexander reported: "A man who had brought his wife for healing was contacted by this writer one week after the service. I was told that the woman had cancer, had slipped into a coma, and was not expected to live much longer."

Alexander also followed up on one Beverley Thacker, of Fresno, California, who had been incorrectly reported in a newspaper account of the event as having suffered a paralyzing stroke six months before. The crowd had cheered as she left the meeting (excuse me, "explosion") pushing her husband in her own wheelchair. Alexander wrote:

> Mr. Thacker informed me that his wife had suffered from a brain tumor, not a stroke. She had been operated on in March of 1986, and though she could walk without assistance and a cane, had not completely regained her sense of balance.

In other words, what Mrs. Thacker did was something she could do when she walked into the Happy Hunter Healing Explosion.

The Hunters at least have one positive, blatant miracle that one might think offers itself for examination. I will let Charles Hunter, a former certified public accountant, outline this wonder:

> A boy about fourteen years old came to the altar. The glory of God was shining all over him and he was crying with joy he couldn't contain.
>
> We asked, "What would you like for Jesus to do for you?"
>
> He stuck out his left hand and said, "Grow me a new thumb."
>
> His thumb had been cut off when he was four years old. It was a peculiar-looking amputation, because it looked like the skin had been pulled together and tied, rather than left smooth.
>
> Glory to God! This was our first opportunity to see a cut-off limb grow back!
>
> We said, "Stick out your hands!" He did. We commanded it to grow and nothing happened. Frances said, "Put out both arms and put them together."
>
> He stretched forth both arms, side by side, so we could watch both arms and thumbs at the same time.

Again we commanded, "Grow, thumb, grow, in Jesus's name!"

In fact, we yelled at the thumb. Our faith was high, because we had just read in the Bible that this had happened with the disciples of the early church.

Suddenly, with the whole audience standing, watching to see what the power of God would do, the thumb stub began to grow. Slowly, slowly it moved forward!

It grew right out to full size, just like the other thumb!

. . . We will see cut-off arms and legs grow just that way in this generation!

Hold on a moment, folks. Let's go back to that regenerated thumb before we start staring at arms and legs. Surely the Hunters recorded the name of this lucky lad. I'm sure they followed up this major miracle, so much above and beyond the ordinary biblical miracles, which do not encompass such organic restorations.

Well, maybe and maybe not. Charles Hunter, in his enthusiasm, had quoted a scriptural reference to such wonders. He said that he took his reference from the Living Bible, while I've taken mine from the New English Bible. Let us compare the two. Hunter's version of Matthew 15:30-31:

[They] laid [the sick] before Jesus, and he healed them all. What a spectacle it was! Those who hadn't been able to say a word before were talking excitedly, and those with missing arms and legs had new ones; the crippled were walking and jumping around, and those who had been blind were gazing about them! The crowds just marveled, and praised the God of Israel.

Compare that with what I find in my Bible:

. . . they threw [the sick] down at his feet, and he healed them. Great was the amazement of the people when they saw the dumb speaking, the crippled strong, the lame walking, and sight restored to the blind; and they gave praise to the God of Israel.

In the latter version, there is no mention of restored limbs. But regardless of a perhaps too enthusiastic and inventive interpretation of the scriptures, the grown-again-thumb story fascinated me. Learning of this miracle that supposedly had taken place not far from where I live, I fired off this telegram to the Hunters:

> Please provide me with the name and address of the church in West Palm Beach, Florida, where a new thumb grew back on the left hand of the young boy. Please also provide the name of the young man, so that I may include this wonder in my new book on faith-healing. You may call me, collect, at the number below if you wish. Thank you for your attention to this request.

On July 13, 1987, I received a reply. The Hunters informed me that they did not remember where that major miracle took place, except that it was "at a Methodist church in West Palm Beach, Florida." And they "did not get the name of the boy."

Attempting to discover at which church the wonder might have occurred, I telephoned every Methodist church listed in West Palm Beach. Two were disconnected. Three told me a distinct "No." Three never responded, though I left messages. Two were "not sure" whether the Hunters were ever there. I'm sure that signifies that they were not there, because such a marvel would certainly have been remembered. Again, no evidence was available for a major miracle claimed in print by a faith-healer.

The Hunters may be Happy, but I believe they are Unhappy about answering such queries.

15
Practical Limitations of Medical Science

He was standing one day at his door on Ludgate Hill, when a real doctor of Physic passed, who had learning and abilities, but whose modesty was the true cause of his poverty.

"How comes it," says he to the Quack, "that you without education, without skill, without the least knowledge of science, are enabled to live in the style you do? You keep your town house, your carriage and your country house: whilst I, allowed to possess some knowledge, have neither, and can hardly pick up a subsistence?"

"Why, look ye," said Rock, smiling, "how many people do you think have passed since you asked me the question?"

"Why," answered the Doctor, "perhaps a hundred."

"And how many out of these hundred, think you possess common sense?"

"Possibly one," answered the Doctor.

"Then," said Rock, "that one comes to you: and I take the other ninety nine."

(From "The Northern Impostor," the life of a celebrated quack, 1786, reprinted in *The Natural History of Quackery* by Eric Jameson, 1961.)

Why do so many people turn to faith-healers for help when their performances, even to the casual investigator, are so obviously high-powered quackery? For one thing, there are cultural biases that predispose some people to believe in the possibility of faith-healing. For example, Taiwanese and Mexican patients—among others—recognize in their own cultures two general healing modalities. They can be labeled "temple" (magical) and "biomedical." Traditional temple methods, they accept, result in much slower recovery than newer Western (biomedical) processes. But the temple methods are easier for them to understand and to relate to and do not involve frightening technologies. Besides, practitioners of magical methods promise much more than doctors do, and they have many rationalizations available to explain away failures.

What Does Medical Science Offer?

Important clues are found by examining the largely erroneous view that is generally held of legitimate medicine and its practitioners. Belief in this view is greatly encouraged by the healers, who assure their victims, as one California-based operator does regularly in his preaching, that physicians "want to cut on your body and put chemicals in your stomach. Dr. Jesus doesn't use chemicals, and he doesn't want to cut you with anything but the Sword of the Spirit!"

As I discovered when I began researching this subject, anyone who assumes he has a basic understanding of physicians and their work may be poorly informed. The correct answers to two questions—"What do doctors actually do?" and "What do they actually offer their patients?"—are both probably unexpected.

As a layman, I was surprised to learn that, except for certain types of surgical procedures (kidney stone removal, appendectomies, etc.) and some biochemical procedures and substances (such as dialysis and antibiotics), much of modern medical practice is devoted to diagnosis and evaluations that have nothing to do with relief of symptoms. One medical authority, examining this situation, stated:

> Roughly three-quarters of non-surgical physician's care today (both general and specialist) is not curative but supportive.

"Supportive" means treatment designed to prolong the life of the patient *before he eventually succumbs to the ailment.* Of course, this does not imply that the "supportive" treatment is without positive value. Nor does it mean that such treatment does not require a high order of skill and the use of extensive technology. Treatment of diabetes is an excellent example. This disease results from failure of the pancreas to produce insulin, a substance needed to control the sugar content of the blood. Now that diabetes can be treated by injection of insulin or oral administration of other medications, the disease can be controlled quite effectively. But the patient is under dietary constraints, and after many years of surviving quite well with medication and discipline, he may begin to show long-term effects of the ailment. Many diabetics live out their lives quite "normally." Some others have 20 to 30 years added to their lives by the prescribed treatment. However, diabetes is not cured. It is *treated* effectively, and well within the limits we should expect of medical science.

Even such seemingly miraculous substances as antibiotics only slow down the reproduction of invading bacteria so that the host body's natural immune system can obtain an advantage in the battle. Dr. Albert Schweitzer, commenting on the supposed secret magic techniques used by African native healers he had observed, wrote:

> The witch doctor succeeds for the same reason all the rest of us [doctors] succeed. Each patient carries his own doctor inside him. We [doctors] are at our best when we give the doctor within each patient a chance to go to work.

Schweitzer's statement does not imply a supernatural source for healing. It simply points out the wonderful defense and repair mechanisms of the organism.

But not all ailments respond to the immune system. The fact is that medical science does not have good validating evidence for the efficacy of measures currently employed to treat ailments like cancer, heart disease, rheumatoid arthritis, and AIDS. The first three problems, incidentally, are the ones for which people most commonly visit faith-healers. Naturally, some faith-healers are taking advantage of AIDS victims, knowing—as with all terminal cases—that their audiences never will see the eventual sad finale, only the momentary exultation of the victim reacting to the healer's suggestions and to his own enthusiasm.

The Attitude of Orthodox Physicians

As part of the propaganda to sell their case, most, if not all, of the "alternative healing" disciples and promoters have nasty things to say about orthodox medicine. Those criticisms, whether well founded or not, are often heard by receptive ears. Many of us have, at one time or another, felt that a physician was not being quite frank with us, or was perhaps less authoritative than we would have liked. That, as they say, goes with the territory. Faith-healers play on those uncertainties and encourage them to their own advantage. Then, too, most doctors understandably tend not to extend much sympathy or attention to patients who have trivial ailments that the sufferers believe deserve more of their professional time.

Physicians make an excellent living from their trade. I, for one, will never argue against their right to do so; they are highly trained and dedicated to an important and vital profession. But those who use the money argument to discredit the medical profession in favor of alternative forms of treatment, such as faith-healing, have failed to consider that those practitioners, too, make handsome sums from their labors. Self-appointed expert Hans Holzer, writing about acupuncture, mentions that the medical profession has viewed this ancient Chinese notion less than enthusiastically. Discussing the strenuous objections of orthodox medicine to this quackery, he says:

> Possibly, the complainants against the thriving
> acupuncture clinics were losing business in their
> regular hospitals or private practices.

He wrote that comment before those clinics began shutting their doors all over the United States, and before the British medical journal *Lancet* published in May 1984 the definitive article on the subject, which removed any enthusiasm that formerly supportive, responsible academics might have had for the practice.

The Experts Speak Up

Dr. David Tyrrell, a British physician and chairman of the British Medical Research Council, has expressed the opinion of that group in regard to faith-healing. Angered by claims of Tom Johanson of the Spiritualist Association of Great Britain, who insisted that AIDS patients treated by its healers "improve and do remarkably well," Dr. Tyrrell condemned such procedures as "misleading magic":

> Prayers are tried as a sort of magic which will suddenly make things melt away. They can give comfort, but to consider prayers as a genuinely successful treatment is totally misleading. Laying on of hands is for desperate people clutching at any hope. AIDS sufferers, unfortunately, will grasp at straws.

Another U.K. claimant to AIDS healing is Ray Branch, who runs a healing sanctuary in Surrey. He says about AIDS patients:

> We can give them hope and doctors can't. There's no known illness that hasn't responded to our kind of healing.

As for offering proof of that statement, we hear no more from Branch. However, the Royal College of General Practitioners began in January 1986 to allow faith-healers from the Confederation of Healing Organizations to work alongside its members at Leeds General Infirmary, adding the ceremony of "laying on of hands" as the doctors tended to 60 victims of rheumatoid arthritis. Other planned projects involved terminal cancer patients, cataract cases, and those suffering chronic pain. The project, budgeted at £500,000, involved physicians from London, Ipswich, and Liverpool, and was backed by Prince Charles, a devout believer in homeopathic medicine as well. I have been unable to discover what the results of those tests showed, or if the tests were ever completed. It should be added that in Britain and Ireland, faith-healers—as well as practitioners of many other "alternative" medical methods—may practice freely so long as they do not claim to be "registered." The subtleties of difference between "registered" and "nonregistered" are not known to me.

"Spiritual healing" can be purchased for up to £18.50 ($30) an hour by AIDS patients at two London-area hospitals: St. Stephen's in Fulham and St. Mary's in Paddington. The service can be paid for through the National Health Service. Consultant psychiatrist Dr. Farrukh Hashmi gave a negative opinion of this practice:

> No healer has a cure for AIDS and anyone who claims to is bogus. I am concerned that spiritual

healers who build up false hopes are doing serious damage.

The UK health minister, Tony Newton, promised in April 1987 that the government would look into the exploitation of AIDS victims.

The French Attitude

Faith-healers in France are known as "guérisseurs" (which translates as "healers" without any reference to the element of faith), and in 1965 stiff laws were passed to impose penalties on such practitioners. They were almost impossible to enforce, because many physicians felt—along with many laymen—that the healers performed a useful function. Perhaps one Paris doctor put it best when he told the press:

> [The guérisseurs] keep a lot of hypochondriacs
> and hysterical cases out of my surgical practice
> and then let me get on with my proper work,
> dealing with people who are really sick.

France has long been known for the profusion of quack medicines and procedures it has produced, and acceptance of faith-healers does not seem out of character in that country. Germany and Switzerland are not far behind France in their naiveté.

An Interested Anthropologist Looks at Faith-Healing

Anthropologist Dr. Philip Singer, who looked into W. V. Grant's healing claims in detail, found *not one case* that provided evidence that Grant was healing anyone. I have used some of Singer's findings in preparing the material on Grant for this book. Says he:

> As a concerned American citizen and as a medi-
> cal anthropologist, I view what is going on at
> the faith-healing rallies as examples of
> traditional superstitious healing. I would like, as
> an anthropologist, to see the "natives" move
> toward a more rational health-seeking behavior.
> However, given the strength of religious beliefs
> in our culture this is not a likely prospect . . .
> The paradox that emerges in the popularity of

faith-healing today is that never before in America has there been greater demystification and deprofessionalization of medical knowledge and medical personnel and never before has there been greater popular access to all kinds of medical knowledge; yet, at the same time, because of the chronic, degenerative, terminal nature of some diseases today, there is a greater reliance on, and acceptance of, all forms of quackery and conjuring. The healer's self-proclaimed "gift of grace" is thought by believers to be the most esoteric, mystical "knowledge," and apparently no amount of rationalism can counter it.

Singer also quotes colleague Alfred Louis Kroeber:

To the degree that a culture disengages itself from reliance on magic and superstition, it has advanced. To the degree that it admits magic in its operations, it is primitive.

Evangelists as Friends

An emphasis on a proffered friendship is typical of all the media preachers. It is their equivalent of the physician's "bedside manner," and they flourish or fail according to the quality of their smiles and kind words. The modern electronic church has succeeded largely because there are millions of lonely people "out there" who are seeking a friend. They are told by the preachers that they will be prayed for and accepted as friends and confidants. Computerized letters are sent to these people that are personalized and appear to be written and directed solely to them. Of course—they are told—all of this takes money, and in order to keep their new-found friends and to assure that those welcome letters will continue to arrive, they must contribute money to pay those costs. Their newly purchased friends also quickly achieve the status of soap-opera actors and are sought out in the same way that groupies pursue rock stars. To approach, witness, perhaps even touch these people seems to be part of their admirers' goals in life.

Perhaps the devotees are not totally swindled when they give their money to the stars of the electronic church. The $5 or $10 they periodically surrender might be buying them just what they want and think they need: contact with a glamorous entity who has supernatural connections and the confidence that comes with that contact. It is very likely that the televangelist is aware of that need and carefully sets out to meet it.

The Aim of Medical Science

A large percentage of those who turn to faith-healers rather than depending on medical science have the erroneous expectation that competent doctors should be able to diagnose and cure, in a straightforward and speedy manner, whatever disease is presented to them. This is simply not true. Medical doctors do their best to make life longer, more comfortable, and more productive for their patients. They strive to cancel out and repair the effects of injuries and infections. Relief is their goal, and they seldom have the satisfaction of returning total recovery to their customers. Their promises are few, and with good reason.

There is a point beyond which medical science—at least at present—cannot go. The normal attrition of later years, disease, and death are all part of the life process. We can combat the causes and the symptoms of some diseases. Specific medications and techniques attack bacteria and viruses and either remove the invading elements or arrest their attacks upon the orderly progress of life. But death—premature or not—often results simply and naturally from a series of failures of various smaller systems that are links in the life process and part of the support of our existence rather than from any catastrophic event.

With the passing of years we break down, with, it is hoped, a certain amount of grace and with the support of friends and a social system that respects and accepts our increasing failures to perform as previously. Reaction time becomes greater, perceptions are less sensitive, and memory serves us less efficiently. Perhaps the accompanying lessened awareness is an unplanned but welcome mercy of nature that eases passage; certainly it seems to be an advantage, given the inevitability of death.

I find no injustice in death, probably because I recognize the advantage to my species of a limited lifespan and the need for a great number of generations to improve the stock through selection. That process has enabled some of us to visit the moon and one of us to compose the "Moonlight Sonata."

To those who cannot summon up such a philosophy, death is an enemy. Disease and geriatric failures are his allies, seen as precursors to the end of life. It all seems so unfair, and faced with evidence of these failings, unable or unwilling to accept the medical facts, many people harken to joyful promises of cures for a multitude of ailments—biological changes that are actually inevitable and quite natural. They seek magic, and the promise of a miracle is held out to them—on a barbed hook.

16
Where Is the Evidence?

> Most of us discover soon enough that the world is
> full of misinformation. Some of it is the result of
> ignorance or its sibling, carelessness. Some, unfor-
> tunately, is spawned by self-serving interest or
> malice. And much misinformation is either the result
> of wishful thinking—we want it to be true, and so it
> must be—or represents a kind of symbolic truth: it
> ain't necessarily so, but it really ought to be.
>
> (From *Time-Honored Lies*, by Tom Burnam.)

In researching this book, I began to relate every experience and
fact I came upon to the faith-healing phenomena. News broadcasts,
magazine articles, conversations, and correspondence all went into
the hopper, and I tried to extract from them significant relation-
ships in order to make sense of the bizarre data I had collected.
Then I received a call from the manager of Alice Cooper, a rock
star for whom the word "bizarre" might have been invented.
Cooper's real name is Vincent Furnier. Much like the Frankenstein
monster/Boris Karloff relationship, Alice Cooper/Vince Furnier is
aware of who's who. Furnier can switch out of the Cooper character, pick up his golf clubs, and play nine holes without so much
as two notes escaping his lips. He "disconnects" very smoothly.
    I traveled with Cooper's remarkable show a few years ago,

working special effects. His manager was calling to ask if I'd like
to attend an upcoming concert near my home in Florida. I readily
accepted, needing a break from investigating the faith-healing
business and feeling that a different form of make-believe might
be a welcome change. Now, as I saw the latest version of the
show, with the stage lighting, the roaring loudspeakers, the
screaming star, it suddenly struck me that what I was watching
was not too different from the meetings of Peter Popoff, W. V.
Grant, and David Paul. The litany and the dress were different,
but the crowd was reacting in much the same fashion. They were
there to see a star they recognized. He had a message, albeit
incredible and wild, that they wanted to hear and accept. He was
loud. He was colorful. He loved them, and made that plain. But no
one questioned whether his real persona matched what they saw
on stage.

Another notion occurred to me. I thought of professional
wrestling, with its blatant fakery, overacted dramas, ersatz blood,
and phony injuries. The long hours of dedicated practice, the
careful placing of each blow, the choreography—that, too, fit into
this strange picture of human beings abandoning reason and entering a drama as actors, willy-nilly. The fans, in accordance with
some unwritten but understood rule, will not allow themselves to
wonder whether the blood, the moves, and the results are real;
they are content to pretend.

I see a strong parallel between the rock concert, the pro-
wrestling scene, and faith-healing. The one obvious common thread
is this: No one ever stops to ask the most important question: Is
it for real? It is an uncomfortable, obscene, blasphemous, and
impolite query that is just not tolerated.

Ancient Precursors

Writing in 1665, author Seigneur de Saint-Evremond (Charles de
Saint-Denis) wondered why people continued to believe they had
been healed in the face of quite contrary evidence. He made
surprisingly modern and astute observations on the psychology of
the victims of a faith-healer of that day, Valentine Greatraks:

> An idea of health made the sick forget for a
> while their maladies; and imagination, which was
> not less active in those merely drawn by curi-
> osity than in the sick, gave a false view to the
> one class, from the desire of seeing, as it

> operated a false cure on the other from the
> strong desire of being healed. Such was the
> power of [Greatraks] over the mind, and such
> was the influence of the mind upon the body.

He went on to explain why those who knew the truth failed to
speak out:

> Nothing was spoken of in London but [Great-
> raks's] prodigies; and these prodigies were
> supported by such great authorities, that the
> bewildered multitude believed them almost
> without examination, while more enlightened
> people did not dare to reject them from their
> own knowledge. The public opinion, timid and
> enslaved, respected this imperious and, appar-
> ently, well-authenticated error. Those who saw
> through the delusion kept their opinion to
> themselves, knowing how useless it was to
> declare their disbelief to a people filled with
> prejudice and admiration.

Saint-Evremond's observations are as applicable today as they were
more than three centuries ago. The costumes, the calendars, and
the names change. But a certain percentage of the population
continues to fall for the Popoffs as they did for the Cagliostros.

What You See Is Not What You Get

It is evident that in religion, there is, unfortunately, no "truth in
advertising" rule. Outrageous claims can be made without fear of
censure.

The greatest dread for the faith-healers is straightforward,
rational, scientific evaluation of their claims. The Christian
Science church is the prime example of a head-on attempt to
reconcile religion with science. The church's claims have been
looked into extensively, and the conclusion has not been favorable.
Other religions have attempted, ineffectually (except to the faithful), to meld scientific thought and dogma, utilizing fuzzy anal-
ogies and leaky logic that does not survive close examination.

Many people are unable to evaluate such reasoning properly
because they are unaware of what science does and does not
claim. Science appears to be a remote, ivory-tower idea that

cannot be dealt with by the average person. Writing in his book *The Scientific Approach*, Carlo Lastrucci puts forth the basic principles of the scientific reasoning process, one of which is that

> . . . all events have a natural cause. . . . This postulate epitomizes the great historical break of modern science away from fundamentalist religion, on the one hand, and from spiritualism and magic on the other. It implies, in effect, that explanations shall be sought in natural causes or antecedents . . . It eschews supernatural definitions of phenomena, and rejects the notion that forces, agents or agencies other than those found in nature operate to influence the cosmos, the earth and its flora and fauna. When a supposedly supernatural or extranatural explanation is offered for a perplexing phenomenon, the scientist assumes that the answer will be found in natural forces or events. And until such time that he can explain the event in natural terms, he rejects the belief that some other order of explanation is necessary. If the history of science proves anything, it proves that the scientist has not yet had his confidence in this belief shaken to date.

Obviously, when the claimed phenomena have not yet even been established, it is doubly illogical to offer "supernatural or extranatural" explanations for them. Until we taste the cake, we cannot discuss the flavor. But the faithful do not require that the cake be produced. As Lastrucci said to me, they have loose criteria for accepting a simple physical sensation or an inspiration as a miracle, and will gladly approximate Descartes by declaring, "I felt it, therefore it is."

An M.D. Refuses to Answer

The September 1986 issue of *Charisma* magazine contained a lengthy article written by James Hayes, M.D., of St. Augustine, Florida. The doctor described a remarkable recovery he'd made which he said had puzzled other physicians and for which X-rays were available. He ascribed the healing to his Christian faith, and not to medical treatment. Learning of this evidence, I thought that I might at last have someone who would be willing to provide the needed data. He is himself a physician and could easily supply the information without having to go through the process of obtaining permission from others. I wrote to him on December 24, 1986:

> I just read your remarkable article in *Charisma* magazine (September 1986) and I've a number of questions that I'd like to ask you concerning that article. I should like to know if you would answer a few questions on the matter of your divine healing(s).
> Please let me know by using the stamped, self-addressed envelope I have provided.
> Thank you for your attention to this request!
>
> Sincerely,
>
> James Randi

Having received no reply by January 3, 1987, I telephoned Dr. Hayes. During our conversation he told me details of an 85-year-old man's "terminal cancer" that was "completely cured," but he refused to give me the names of the doctors involved. He said they were not believers and might not provide truthful accounts of the case. However, he said that he would provide me with that information after he had spoken to them. That was more than eight months ago. I never received any further information about this healing, only one of "hundreds of documented miracles" Dr. Hayes told me he was aware of.

He seemed amused at my interest in his claims, and most of our telephone conversation concerned his questions about my "attitude," my "motives," and my personal beliefs. I pointed out that those factors could have nothing to do with the validity of his claims, and that for starters I only wished to know, as my letter had stated, if he would answer some questions. He told me that he wasn't sure whether he was willing to do so, and asked me whether I was "willing to be born again." I told him that I could not enter into such matters and that I would send him the questions by mail.

I reproduce here the form I sent him, again with a stamped, self-addressed envelope:

In response to the inquiry from James Randi:
(Answers, yes or no, may be simply circled.)

Re #1: Do you have radiographic information
showing that:
(a) your pelvis was "twisted,"
(b) your one leg was thus shortened,
(c) your pelvis is now no longer twisted?

a: Yes No   b: Yes No   c: Yes No

Re #2: May I have:
(a) the name of the osteopath mentioned,
(b) your permission to know of your medical
record from this person in this regard?

a: Yes No   b: Yes No

Re #3: Is the statement attributed to you, that
the osteopath "couldn't explain [your] 'remarkable improvement,' " a correct quotation? (Because the article was actually written by Angela
Kiesling, I must allow for the possibility that
the quotation was incorrect.)

Yes No

Re #4: You told me today that the form of
infertility that was involved consisted of a low
sperm count. I would like to know if:
(a) a medical opinion about this is on record,
(b) whether, in your own or another's professional opinion, a pregnancy might still have
resulted with this condition existing?

a: Yes No   b: Yes No

Re #5: You mentioned in our telephone conversation that you had X-ray evidence of a "fusion
of the lower spine" in your case. Is that fusion
still evident in radiographic scans?

Yes No

I waited for months, and no answer came. Finally, in July 1987, seven months after I made the first inquiry, I sent a final letter to Hayes. I repeated everything I'd said previously and sent him copies of all my previous letters. The last paragraph of this letter said:

> I do not wish to report to my readers that an M.D. has refused to answer simple inquiries concerning quite straightforward claims made in a widely circulated magazine. Such a refusal would, fairly or not, imply that these claims cannot stand examination. I am sure that, if your claims as stated in *Charisma* are true, neither of us would want that implication to be made by my readers.

No response of any sort was ever received.

A Nineteenth-Century Case and Its Conclusion

In an early nineteenth-century book titled *The Great Physician*, by W. E. Boardman, M.D., a startling case of instantaneous healing of a bone fracture was reported. Several believers in faith-healing have quoted and requoted it, at times enhancing the story somewhat. It is said to have originated with "Dr. Reed, a physician of Philadelphia," the father of the boy in question. The account goes like this:

> The children were jumping off from a bench, and my little son fell and broke *both bones of his arm below the elbow*. My brother, who is a professor of surgery in the college at Chicago, was here on a visit. I asked him to set and dress the arm. He did so; put it in splints, bandages, and in a sling. The dear child was very patient, and went about without a murmur all that day.
>
> The next morning he came to me and said: "Dear papa, please take off these things."
>
> "Oh no, my son, you will have to wear these five or six weeks before it will be well."
>
> "Why, papa, it is well."

"Oh no, my dear child, that is impossible!"

"Why, papa, you believe in prayer, don't you?"

"You know I do, my son."

"Well, last night when I went to bed, it hurt me very bad, and I asked Jesus to make it well."

I did not like to say a word to chill his faith. A happy thought came. I said, "My dear child, your uncle put the things on, and if they are taken off he must do it."

Away he went to his uncle, who told him he would have to go as he was six or seven weeks, and must be very patient; and when the little fellow told him that Jesus had made him well, he said, "Pooh! pooh! nonsense!" and sent him away.

The next morning the poor boy came to me and pleaded with so much sincerity and confidence, that I more than half believed, and went to my brother and said: "Had you not better undo his arm and let him see for himself?" . . .

My brother yielded, took off the bandages and the splints, and exclaimed, "It is well, absolutely well!" and hastened to the door to keep from fainting.

That seems like a very convincing story. (I will ignore the unlikelihood of such a silly, story-book conversation taking place between the father and the child, and the very expected reaction of the terrible, skeptical doctor as he tried to cover his embarrassment at witnessing a genuine miracle that he was convinced could not have taken place.) In spite of the well-known fact that children's bones mend quickly, we cannot accept such a rationalization in this case. We may ask: Did such a doctor exist in Philadelphia and did his son have such an accident? The answers are yes and yes. But when J. H. Lloyd, M.D., of the University of Pennsylvania, looked into this very famous and much-touted claim in 1886, he published in the *Medical Record* journal the following, which he received in response to an inquiry:

Dear Sir: The case you cite, when robbed of all its sensational surroundings, is as follows: The child was a spoiled youngster who would have his own way; and when he had a *green stick* fracture of the forearm, and, after having had it bandaged for several days, concluded he would much prefer to go without a splint, to please the spoiled child the splint was removed, and the arm carefully adjusted in a sling. As a matter of course, the bone soon united, as is customary in children, and being only partially broken, of course all the sooner. This is the miracle. Some nurse or crank or religious enthusiast, ignorant of matters physiological and histological, evidently started the story, and unfortunately my name—for I am the party—is being circulated in circles of faith-curites, and is given the sort of notoriety I do not crave.

Very respectfully yours,

Carl H. Reed

So a letter from the grown-up child, now a physician himself, puts the matter in a different light altogether. It is seldom that we have the advantage of such serendipitous evidence, available to us only because someone cared enough to investigate the matter and report the results.

Willful Blindness

In specific cases that have been presented to me by colleagues, interested correspondents, and various preachers with whom I have been in correspondence, I have met with repeated disappointments. I will share with readers a few of these inquiries.

In September 1986, I was sent a newspaper article from the *Ka Leo O Hawaii* newspaper in which a correspondent, Antonio Rosa, took on skeptics who doubted faith-healing. He cited

an example of an authentic psychic healing of a cancer patient: Religion Professor [at the University of Hawaii] Mitsuo Aoki's wife was healed by psychic healer Greta Woodrew.

I immediately sent a registered letter to Professor Aoki, asking for medical evidence of Greta Woodrew's ability to heal. I felt that Aoki, as an academic, would feel obliged to offer some support for the claim. Alas, the gentleman apparently did not feel any need to be of assistance, for I never heard from him, even after sending a second registered letter.

The reason became apparent when Rosa wrote to me. In part of a three-page letter explaining why no such response could be given, he said: "I do not have any evidence . . . of the healing I referred to in my article . . . I *believe* in the account given me." Rosa went on to tell me that I had "evil purposes" and that I was taking "an evil position."

Not quite so, Mr. Rosa. My investigation has led me right up to a stone wall of ignorance, superstition, denial of truth, and desperation. It is a structure to which you have added a few pieces.

One person consulted on the matter was quite willing to offer an opinion. Dr. Stanley Krippner, a prominent parapsychologist, director of the Saybrook Institute in San Francisco and former president of the Parapsychological Association, gave his opinion to the University of Hawaii concerning the "healer" in question, Greta Woodrew:

> In my opinion, James Randi has more of a standing among serious parapsychologists than does Ms. Woodrew (who has no standing whatsoever). I would suggest that your campus initiate a debate or discussion between people with opposing points of view on this issue. If the parties are somewhat informed, and not just giving polemical speeches, this joining of the issue would be beneficial to students.

This, from a respected academic authority on such matters, reflects the attitude of *thinking* people in regard to the matter of truth. Truth is not arrived at by sticking one's head in the sand; clear vision and determination are the minimal requirements.

The Case of Rose Osha

When I let it be known that I was actively seeking examples of genuine faith-healing for this book, I received a large number of references to miraculous healing claims. Most could not be checked out. But from several people I received copies of a booklet written by Rose Osha, of Washington, Indiana. There I found a claim of major healing through prayer. Having carefully read the information it contained, I wrote to her at once:

> I have been sent a copy of your booklet *Rise and Be Healed*, in which you report that you have been healed of cancer after 16 years. The account certainly is remarkable, and I intend to report it in my book. In order to substantiate the facts you relate, I would request that you answer the following questions for me:
>
> (1) What are the names and addresses of the two doctors mentioned in your account, referred to as "Dr. Jim" and "Dr. Joe"?
>
> (2) What is the name of the hospital where you were treated during the time that the major miracles took place?
>
> (3) Do you have evidence (X-rays, etc.) that will substantiate the details of the regeneration of the two toes, as referred to in your account? If you do not have this evidence, is it available either through the two doctors or through the hospital? (There are several references in your account to X-rays that were taken to establish your healing, and these films must still exist, either in the records of the physicians or in the hospital files.)
>
> (4) Will you please send me a photocopy of the remark by the "Surgeon General of the U.S. . . . written across [your] medical records in bold red letters saying, 'Healed by the Power of God Only' "?
>
> In attempting to obtain similar information from others claiming miraculous healings, I have been refused. Because your account is quite remarkable and you have stated at the close of the *Rise and Be Healed* booklet, "I would like to have you see what a great and wonderful thing my Lord has done," I trust that you will furnish me with the requested information so that I may publish it in my book, which will have major distribution worldwide.

I have enclosed a stamped, self-addressed envelope along with the above questions printed out along with space for the requested inform- ation, for your convenience. You need merely write in the names of the doctors, the hospital involved, and a short response to question No. 3, and obtain a plain photocopy of the state- ment written by the Surgeon General of the U.S. So that you will incur no expense in making the photocopy, I have included $1 as well. Thank you for your attention to this request.

I prompted Ms. Osha—after a few weeks—with a second copy of the letter above, and finally I heard from her. She wrote:

In regards to your letter I received yesterday about receiving no reply from me about your manuscript you were writing. I would like to say this: I get several letters on this same thing and we figured if we give it to one then we would feel we would have to give it to all who write, so that is why there is no reply. Enclosed, find the $1.00 refund you had sent. It is not that I am unwilling but feel it best this way.

I telephoned Rose Osha on July 4, 1987. She acknowledged that she had received my letters, and said that she was quite willing to talk with me about the matter. Encouraged, I asked her these simple questions:

(1)   Do you actually have the names of "Dr. Jim" and "Dr. Joe"?
(2)   And do you have the name of the hospital where you were treated, and do they have the X-rays to substantiate the details?
(3)   And did the surgeon general of the US write across the document, "Healed by the power of God only"?
(4)   And do you know who the surgeon general of the US was at that time?

To the first three of these queries, Osha replied in the affirmative. She said she was not sure of the fourth. Then I asked:

> (5) And you can't even give me the name of
>   the hospital?

I was told, firmly, no. I replied: "It seems to me relatively simple just to tell me the name of the hospital, which would not mean that you'd have to give it to anyone else."

Osha was adamant. None of the requested information would be given out. Yet she had stated that she wanted so badly to let everyone know about her miracles that she had published, at her own expense, a 14-page booklet testifying to those events. There she had told how "Dr. Joe" had seen a mass of "739 clamps and tubes dissolve." In fact, she said:

> One hour after they had taken that first X-ray
> . . . another one was required. In front of eight
> people the Lord had dissolved all of the re-
> maining clamps and tubes in my body. I was
> completely free from any plastic tubes and
> stainless steel metal clamps . . .

But Rose Osha will not name *any* of those eight people who witnessed this wonder. Nor will we ever know whether or not two of her toes—she says "they had completely rotted off"—were actually restored miraculously "sometime during the night."

She told me that she could provide me with "photostatic copies of letter after letter" of testimony supporting her claims, but *none of the information I had requested.* She repeatedly said that she would not do so because she would "have to do it for everyone." Another stone wall had gone up.

There are two dozen or more other cases that were submitted to me for examination by well-meaning people who believed that they might be true. Most of them could not be examined at all because of the lack of traceable data. Others presented the same kind of problems that have been described above.

So What Harm Is Done, Anyway?

Let me answer two questions frequently asked of me following my lectures. The first one is:

> Even though they don't heal, don't the healers
> at least bring hope to their subjects and, if so,
> what harm do they really do?

By teaching people dependence on magical practices, faith-healers take them back to the Dark Ages, convincing them that they are only pawns in some great game they cannot comprehend, the rules of which are concealed in sacred writings. The victims are told that these writings need careful interpretation and that can be provided by the healers along with the transfer of healing powers from a divine source. Faith-healers take from their subjects any hope of managing on their own. And they may very well take them away from legitimate treatments that could really help them.

A second question I often hear is:

> As long as healing takes place, why question
> how the healers do it?

My opinion is that miracles are *not* being done, by healers or by anyone else. And, of course, the question that supersedes *all* the others in this discussion is: Do any evangelist/healers actually do any healing? My answer is no. But that answer requires much explanation, which I will preface with the admission that I am not a medical expert, I do not have scientific training, and I am writing on this subject from the point of view of a reasonably observant layman with normal abilities to consult appropriate sources of information. This book is an account of my earnest efforts to discover *one* example of faith-healing that can stand examination. I have found none.

The Nature of the Ailments

Two classes of ailments are brought to faith-healers and legitimate physicians: imaginary and real. Some are obviously psychosomatic in nature. Such ailments, by their very nature, are going to be susceptible to faith-healers' ministrations. It is a recognized fact that suggestible individuals, immersed in an emotional, theatrical atmosphere and surrounded by thousands of others who *expect* a miracle, will be swept up by it all. Their symptoms may well vanish, either temporarily or permanently. But that result can also be achieved by a sufficiently good bedside manner or by any one of a hundred placebo treatments—in which category the healing ministries belong, when and if there is any observable result from their incantations and ritual.

Organic diseases constitute another matter altogether. No healer will accept someone who needs a new finger or a nose to be grown back. The healers typically choose for their audience demonstrations people who have such problems as arthritis, diabetes, and heart trouble. "Healings" of such ailments cannot be proved one way or the other at the scene of the performance, but only upon subsequent examinations. Information gained from any such examinations will never be communicated to those witnessing the show.

The Elusive Proof

Author Eve Simson, in a lengthy study of the subject, *The Faithhealer: Deliverance Evangelism in America*, says:

> Over the years . . . I met individuals who testified that they had received a miraculous cure, and I witnessed many claims to instantaneous cures at the revival meetings. But I was not able to obtain enough proof for any of them to convince me that they were true miracles of healing. At no time did I encounter anyone who testified to something like the regrowth of the severed arm or leg. Nor am I, according to some of the devotees of faithhealing, likely ever to witness it, because, they claim, to see a severed limb instantaneously restored would destroy faith by pushing it into the realm of certainty.

That last comment is most interesting to me. In at least two other instances, I have seen that "out" used by claimants who fell back on it in desperation. One case involved the Maharishi Mahesh Yogi and his Transcendental Meditation claim that his adepts can levitate their bodies through mind power. When we ask to witness this wonder, we are shown only a hilarious demonstration of TM-ers hopping about on mats while in the "lotus" position. This is highly entertaining but nothing more than acrobatics of dubious value. The TM-ers insist that their people can actually levitate into the air and *stay* suspended there as well as zoom about like

Peter Pan, but they refuse us that remarkable sight because, they say, if we were to *know* that levitation is a fact, we would not need to summon up the faith to blindly *believe* it, and faith is needed to perform levitation.

Similarly, a now-unfrocked "psychic" named Uri Geller was pressed at one time by serious parapsychologists to submit to test conditions while he did such parlor tricks as bending spoons and deflecting compasses. He declined to do so, saying that if he were to pass their simple tests, his psychic powers would be definitely established and he would no longer be a controversial figure. As it turned out, he is no longer a controversial figure *because* he refused to be tested, and no responsible people in science now believe that he has any powers that a 12-year-old amateur conjuror does not have.

George Bernard Shaw had a penetrating observation on almost every facet of human behavior. He, too, was bothered by the fact that no organic healing seemed to be taking place in the faith-healing business. His comment on the shrine of Lourdes was:

> All those canes, braces, and crutches and not a
> single glass eye, wooden leg, or toupée.

The Mystery of the Discarded Crutches

Various shrines around the world exult in displaying walls covered with crutches, braces, and other orthopedic devices that have been discarded by people healed by the water, vibrations, earth, atmosphere, or prayers there, and joyously left behind as material evidence of their cures. Is this not positive proof that the cures have taken place? If it is not, what happens to those people? The answer is that they simply fall down.

I cannot say that this is the case for *all* shrines, but I can relate my personal experiences with two. I was recently lecturing at the Los Alamos National Laboratory, in New Mexico. Taken on a sightseeing trip by my hosts, I visited the Santuario de Chimayo, a shrine about 20 miles east of Los Alamos. There I found supportive devices hung about the walls, and in the souvenir shop I was able to buy various photos of these adornments. But no two photos were the same. That is, the display of crutches and braces changed from time to time. The reason for this was well known to an orthopedic surgeon there. He knows the Santuario because he visits there about every six months. Why? To reclaim the orthopedic devices left there by his own patients, often poor people who cannot afford to replace the expensive mechanisms that they discarded. The priest at the Santuario knows this physician and permits him to remove what he recognizes as the property of his patients. By this time, however, they may have already been photographed.

A Personal Experience in Canada

In Montreal, Canada, St. Joseph's Oratory occupies a prominent position in the city's skyline and mythology. A gardener there, named simply Brother André, became famous as a result of healing miracles claimed by hundreds who visited the church both before and after his death in 1937. Those who said they were cured were mostly those who believed themselves affected by Brother André's relics. This diminutive, humble worker is commemorated at the oratory by the preservation of his personal belongings and the "cell" where he lived out his last years. He died at the amazing age of 92, whereupon his heart was removed from his body and can be seen today, preserved in formaldehyde, suspended in an illuminated container at the oratory. Veneration of this man is so great that he is at the stage of being termed "blessed" and on the way to official sainthood.

When I lived in that city, I would frequently visit my maternal grandparents, who lived near the oratory, then go over to the shrine and watch the long lines of faithful supplicants painfully "walking" up the long flight of stone steps on their knees to earn their confidently expected rewards. Inside the shrine, rows upon rows of crutches, canes, braces, and orthopedic devices covered the walls. Testimonials to the miracles wrought in the name of Brother André were posted everywhere, and the air was saturated with the sweet odor of burning candles.

Off to one side was the inevitable souvenir shop, where one event took place that convinced me, at age 12, of the fakery practiced there. I was squatting at a sales counter reading one of the comic books that told the story of Brother André's life. I was out of sight of the young man who approached—on the other side of the counter—and began refilling the many bins of medals, crucifixes, beads, rings, and buttons that were for sale to the faithful. There were two adjacent bins of crucifixes, one labeled "Blessed at the Oratory," and the other "Blessed at Rome." The hand of the clerk appeared above me and poured half a paper bag of crucifixes into the first, then emptied the rest of them into the second. Seeing he had gone to the far side of the counter, I stood up and looked at those bins. I discovered that though the holy items were not differentiated as represented—coming as they did from the same bag—they were at least both the same price. It started me thinking.

But it was my father who gave me the biggest jolt concerning the oratory's souvenir business. At that same counter, I'd seen a row of two-inch squares of cloth stapled to gold-colored cards. These were being sold as pieces cut from the very cassock worn by Brother André on his deathbed. My dad told me that he'd been employed by the tailor shop of Morgan's Department Store in downtown Montreal when I was a boy, and that on one occasion his manager had sent him and his close friend James Hamilton, who was my godfather, to St. Joseph's Oratory to deliver a bolt of heavy wool cloth.

His boss had instructed them to stay there after delivering the goods and do some "cutting" for the priests. They were given two large pairs of pinking shears to take along with them. To my father's amazement, the two found themselves assigned to marking the wool fabric into two-inch squares with tailor's chalk and then cutting it up for sale in the souvenir shop!

(James Hamilton became a Christian Scientist. He and my dad later traveled as advertising salesmen for Bell Telephone Company in Canada. Hamilton died of a heart attack in his hotel room right in front of my father, refusing to call a doctor and asking my father to pray for him instead. The doctor, summoned by my father in spite of Hamilton's pleas, arrived too late.)

The Anthropologist's View

Philip Singer, a medical anthropologist at Oakland University, in Rochester, Michigan, long interested in alternative healing possibilities, looked carefully at eight cases of claimed miracles by faith-healer W. V. Grant. Seven took place during a revival meeting in July 1982 at Cobo Hall, Detroit, and one was featured on a Grant TV broadcast in Detroit at that same time. Singer was assisted in the investigation by his students.

One case consisted of Grant's declaring that there were 49 diabetics in the crowd who had just received healing, but Grant made no attempt to identify a single one of these people. Singer decided that

in [these cases] it would seem clear that what is involved is fraud on Grant's part. . . .

"Healing" the 49 people of sugar diabetes would certainly seem to qualify as a "fraudulent practice" intended to get money from those "healed."

In the remaining seven cases, Dr. Singer found that the subjects either:

(a) had already been healed by orthodox medical methods by the time they visited Grant, but refused to believe it,
(b) still had the disease, with no abatement or cure,
(c) had only imagined non-existent diseases,
(d) accepted Grant's word that they had been healed and had no intention of checking it out with a physician.

Another patient he heard of had been to see Grant and was told that her diabetes and high blood pressure had been cured. She believed it. She stopped her medication and suffered a diabetic crisis followed by cardiac arrest.

Singer also independently discovered that Grant had been using quite transparent means of learning the names and other details about his subjects to perform his "calling out" procedure. His big favorite, the sit-'em-in-a-wheelchair stunt, turned up in Singer's investigation, too.

Singer concluded that Reverend W. V. Grant not only performed no cures for those he ministered to, but also used conjuring techniques to convince them that he spoke with God and that he had the power to heal.

Many Similar Conclusions

The Bay Area Skeptics, the Houston skeptics group, and the Southern California Skeptics, three groups that work in cooperation with the Committee for the Scientific Investigation of Claims of the Paranormal, appointed teams to trace examples of several popular healers' results. In carefully neutral, fully reported case histories, they found *not one* example of an organic disease healed. Other researchers over the years have looked into healing claims by the hundreds. Believers and non-believers were involved in these investigations, and they have had the same results, though many ardently believed in at least the possibility that such healings could be brought about.

In more than 40 cases that we were able to follow up, the victims were willing to tell us that they were not healed at all and that they were angry and frustrated. Frequently, we were asked what they could do to get their money back and whether there was any hope that something could be done about the deception that they had fallen for. We could offer them no satisfaction.

A Proudly Quoted Miracle

Popular accounts of seemingly amazing healings achieved by psychic means or by faith are plentiful. One writer, Jess Stearn, is dedicated to promoting such stories, and in one book, *The Miracle Workers*, he has a chapter titled "Miracles Without Medicine." I will quote from this chapter to show how a clever author can present convincing data to sell a case, including the damning facts, and end up with a story that still seems plausible to the unwary.

Stearn writes of a woman who testified thus:

> I had lost my sight, and the doctors could offer no hope of my ever seeing again. Something had gone wrong with a blood vessel feeding the optic nerve. . . . Originally, I lost the sight of my right eye, but soon the other eye went, too. The doctor said my sight might return within a few years or never.

Note that she has been told her loss of sight is not necessarily permanent. But she is "blind." She has "lost [her] sight." Or has she? In any case, she decided to visit a psychic healer, and on the next page author Stearn tells us:

> She began to notice improvement after her second visit. The shadows were getting clearer, and she saw blurs where she had seen nothing before.

Here we learn that she was seeing "shadows" before, which indicates that she had *some* sight. But was she receiving any medical treatment? In the text, we find that "in the meantime, she was receiving spinal adjustments from an osteopath. . . ."

Now, I am not much inclined to believe that chiropractors or osteopaths can adjust the spine to clear up eye problems. There are no connections whatsoever in the spine that can affect eyesight. However, the woman had sought other help, and as we shall see, some of it was legitimate, orthodox treatment. Says Stearn:

> Her sight did not come back at once, but improved gradually, until she regained her normal vision—in her case, 20/25.

Sight in *both* eyes? If in only one eye, which eye? Well after she had been to the healer, her doctor gave her a written summary of her case, which stated:

> As you recall, I first saw you in my office [nine months ago], at which time you had a visual defect of the right eye . . . I felt that the diagnosis was a blockage of [an artery] and we treated you with cortico-steroids. . . . I remember that you did have some similar complaints in the left eye, but, according to my records, there was never any defect of the visual fields. . . . The condition improved and the last time I saw you [the right eye] looked very good with the blocked vessel appearing to be open. . . .

So regular medication *was* administered in this case, the left eye was *not* visually impaired, and the woman's description of having "lost [her] sight" is now revealed as rather premature and hyperbolic. The woman's doctor's report went on to give his medical opinion about her recovery:

> I don't see anything particularly unusual about your spontaneous recovery, either. I would feel, though, that the medicine we did give you helped to a certain extent.

That last statement was enough to enrage author Stearn. Said he:

> [The doctor's] reaction to a claim of psychic healing reminded me of another physician's

> dismissal of a psychic cure as a spontaneous
> remission. The healer . . . asked, "Why is it
> *they* don't have these spontaneous remissions?"

First, the doctor did not state, nor did he imply, that the recovery was a "spontaneous *remission*." That would have to be a complete reversal—by definition—*"without external cause"*; and there were causes brought to bear on the condition, which *improved*, but did not constitute a remission. The ailment was not untreated, and the result was not a great surprise to the physician. But his refusal to accept a supernatural explanation is regarded by the believers simply as stubborn insistence on ignoring miracles. In response to the other healer's question, the answer is simple: Doctors *do* see spontaneous remissions occur, quite often, and they are thoroughly documented. In most cases doctors simply don't know why they occur. But at least they are trying to find out, rather than stepping into Wonderland for an explanation.

I must share with you a final observation on this particular healer Jess Stearn discusses. Asked to explain the case of another woman he had treated for eye problems and who simply went blind while he was treating her, the healer said simply, "She didn't *want* to get well." So, again, if the patient recovers, it's because of the magic; if the patient does not recover, the patient is to blame. It's never the healer.

A Physician Answers My Request

On April 5, 1986, Peter Popoff brought onto his TV program a physician named William Standish Reed. This man did not offer Popoff any direct support of that particular ministry, but he chortled at the things that had been said against Popoff by me and by others. He openly pitied those who could not accept miracles and related in detail a wonder that he had seen happen in his organization, the Christian Medical Foundation International of Tampa, Florida. I wrote to Reed, asking four simple questions and guaranteeing that his answers, if any, would be published in full in this book. I will not bore you with his responses here, but because they are excellent examples of this sort of shilly-shallying, a copy of his letter may be found in Appendix II. However, I will mention one of Reed's comments:

> With reference to the "lady patient" who
> suffered from ovarian cancer, this patient

> appeared on the Christian Broadcasting Network
> 700 Club on April 2, 1986 so her personal
> testimony has been on national television and
> therefore does not need my statements to
> further verify her cure.

Does Dr. William Standish Reed, M.D., M.S., really believe that "personal testimony" from a patient is sufficient evidence to *prove* a miracle? If so, how did he arrive at those standards of proof? And *he* was the woman's doctor? When asked for information by another physician, he even refused to give *this responsible colleague* the name of the patient involved, citing "the doctrine of privilege"! We do not even know if that woman is still *alive,* let alone if she is cured.

The Newspapers Have a Go at It

On the rare occasions when the media have seriously attempted to investigate faith-healing, they have had no better success at finding genuine healings than scientific investigators have had. Back in April 1956, the *Fresno* (California) *Bee* surveyed those who had been treated by faith-healer A. A. Allen in a three-week revival meeting there. They covered some 400 miles, interviewing everyone they could find who had experienced Allen's efforts. They found that some of the claimed illnesses were entirely imaginary in the first place and had been self-diagnosed. Though a few people still claimed they had been healed, not one case could be confirmed by any medical authority. Of those who had permitted Allen to quote their cases as examples of his powers, some confessed that their illnesses either had never really been cured or had returned. One Colorado victim had traveled 1,000 miles to get treatment from the evangelist, had been declared cured of liver cancer, and had returned home, only to die of the disease two weeks later.

Perhaps media in other countries have a more skeptical point of view than those in America. In early October of 1986, ten million West German viewers sat entranced before their television sets as ZDF—one of the country's two largest networks—offered them a program titled "Healing Currents That Flow Through the Entire Cosmos." The periodical *Der Spiegel* called it "a new low point in television and at the same time a high point in healing promises, con artistry, and quackery." The program featured a couple from Switzerland, the Wallimans, who held forth in a

Hannover TV studio jammed with 2,000 paying guests, including many who were blind, asthmatic, and rheumatic, and a large number of cancer victims. Unknown to the TV audience, some 50 wheelchair patients were kept out of sight of the cameras.

Bild, the West German equivalent of the *National Enquirer*, had run ads claiming that the audience would be seeing "today's greatest faith-healers, live on television." A prominent medical society, generally said to be right-wing, described the event as "deceptive medieval superstition"; Cologne's archbishop, Joseph Höffner, was content to comment that the program made him "very uncomfortable." Protestant pastor Wilhelm Haack declared that the show was "occultism" and "religious trickery, information from the far side of the moon, a massive advertising event for the Walliman family."

German newspapers were not deceived. The *Hamburger Abendblatt* thundered that the producers of the program had brought forth the "bluff of the year." The *Munich Abendzeitung* reported:

> The mass healing was nothing but a flop. Truly, it is seldom that the fears and hopes of millions of sick people have been exploited in such a foolhardy manner. It is blasphemy for some, obscenity for others. . . . It is nothing more than an attempt at mass suggestion, a spiritualist séance presented under apologetic terms like "healing meditation" and "autogenic training." . . . No one kicked away a wheelchair, and no one regained mental capacity.

Professor Hoimar von Ditfurth, a science writer and physician with whom I have appeared on West German television, has long been a foe of these irrationalities. He said of the program: "[It is] a scandal that ZDF, under the temptations of high viewing ratings, threw their responsibilities overboard." Even the presiding judge of the Circuit Court of the City of Mannheim was moved to comment to *Der Spiegel*: "The Federal Republic of Germany has become a training ground and a playground for magical healers."

Why Do They Continue to Believe?

Astronomer Carl Sagan, in "The Fine Art of Baloney Detection," which appeared in the February 1, 1987, *Parade*, wrote:

> Finding the occasional straw of truth awash in
> a great ocean of confusion and bamboozle
> requires intelligence, vigilance, dedication and
> courage. But if we don't practice these tough
> habits of thought, we cannot hope to solve the
> truly serious problems that face us—and we risk
> becoming a nation of suckers, up for grabs by
> the next charlatan who comes along.

A much earlier scientist/philosopher offered a more specific comment to his readers. Ben Franklin was aware of that strange quirk of human nature that elects the victim as chief supporter of the trickster. He said: "There are no greater liars in the world than quacks—except for their patients."

A Poor Body of Proof

For something so popular, faith-healing has a remarkably undocumented success rate. But this is flimflam of a somewhat different style from real-estate schemes, vitamin frauds, and get-rich-quick hoaxes. It bears religious, semi-scientific, and emotional labels that lend it a considerable—though quite false—pedigree.

Evidence to prove faith-healing must be of good quality. No number of purely anecdotal accounts can suffice. Before-and-after medical evidence is absolutely essential, along with careful consideration of the possibility that any remission may be within the probable incidence of such occurrences and not at all remarkable in itself, though we still do not understand the causes behind, for example, cancer remissions. In 1956, a British medical board of inquiry organized by the archbishop of Canterbury concluded that

> we can find no evidence that there is any type
> of illness cured by spiritual healing alone which
> could not have been cured by medical treat-
> ment.

This is a limited censure of faith-healing; my quest has been much more pointed.

The Devil Known as Science

Pat Robertson, among others, is quick to identify science—and thus all scientific procedures and standards—as tools of Satan. Thus, it is hoped, skeptics will not insist upon rigorous proof of unlikely claims. Amateurs like "parapsychologist" Hans Holzer, who writes endless accounts of miracles without any demand for good evidence, even accepts the infamous "Delawarr black box" as a working tool of the healer. This "diagnostic" device—an absurd, crackpot, electronic horror named after the quack who first introduced it—has become a popular item with collectors of such bizarre items. It was long ago shown to be prime hoax material, but Holzer hasn't heard about that, or chooses to ignore it. His criterion for whether or not a healer is the real thing reflects his rather loose standards: "If you have been helped, the healer was genuine." Holzer is not *entirely* without common sense, however. When speaking of "alternative medicine," he says he admits that "eye of newt or the head of a toad" treatment is "nothing but fantasy." Overlooking his mutilation of Shakespeare, I agree.

The Refusal to Know

It is a common aspect of all religious groups that they simply do not wish to know the truth, but they are fond of saying that they seek the truth; in some cases, they do seek truth, but on their terms and with their definitions. I will spend some time here giving examples of this kind of thinking.

The Christmas season of 1986 brought a media blitz of articles and interviews about yet another miracle of the bleeding statue/weeping icon variety, this one of a Virgin Mary painting in Chicago that was said by church authorities to exude "a very thin, oily sweet substance very similar to the [liquid] we use to baptize children or [sic] unction for the sick." These authorities firmly declined to have the "tears" examined by chemists, saying that

> to further analyze [this phenomenon] would be almost blasphemy. The Archdiocese thinks [investigators] should not subject [the substance] to a scientific analysis, which is not a very religious procedure.

Little wonder that there was such reluctance to look into the matter. The previous year, a similarly attractive myth had collapsed when another religious figure, in Montreal, Canada—this time a combination weeping/bleeding statue—turned out to have been smeared with a quite mundane mixture of the owner's own blood and K Mart shaving lotion. The resulting fuss was no surprise to experienced observers of these matters. Media exposure of the hoax brought a barrage of hate mail to the local bishop. The letter writers felt that in spite of the evidence—a direct confession from the hoaxer—the bishop still should have declared the event a genuine miracle.

A Religious Parallel

The Mormon Church offers us another example of this refusal to know. Faced with exceedingly uncomfortable facts that cannot be reconciled with their dogma, the Mormon elders have stonewalled investigations and research into their claims concerning the authenticity of the Book of Mormon, the text upon which most of the philosophy of that church is founded. Skeptics believe that the book simply was invented by Mormon founder Joseph Smith, who certainly had the wit to do so. But modern historians have questioned how, for example, the Book of Mormon can mention the Book of Revelation, when the latter was not supposed to have been written until more than 700 years later. Steel, not in existence at the time the book is claimed to have been written, is spoken of in its pages, and it has Jesus Christ being born in Jerusalem, not Bethlehem.

Back in 1911, Brigham Roberts, a prominent Mormon historian, loudly challenged skeptics to thoroughly examine the Book of Mormon. They did, and to Roberts's dismay, they found it contradictory and loaded with errors. The Mormon elders are putting an end to such inquiries, telling young Mormon historians to ignore scholarly standards and to defer to church dogma rather than scientific methods when doing research. Ernest Taves, in *Trouble Enough*, a book on the Mormon Church, denounces this stance:

> What [Mormon elders] want, then, is Accommodation History, a primitive kind of spoon-feeding of goodies . . . that will not bring doubt to those of insecure or uncertain faith; history, that is, by platitude, half-truth, omission, and denial.

The Mormons need not concern themselves with such problems. In the words of the Mormon Church dogmatists, "When the leaders speak, the thinking has been done."

The Art of Rationalization

The glaring and uncomfortable fact is that the vast majority of those who go to be healed by faith-healers are *not* healed except for, at best, temporary symptomatic relief. Certainly there is no proof that *any* of those suffering from actual organic problems are healed, and it seems obvious that those who believe that they have been healed are simply wrong in that delusion. The April 1986 issue of the magazine *U.S. Catholic* offered a startling rationalization of this obvious fact while maintaining the unproved claim that "some are healed." It offered that

> redemptiveness is a way of explaining why some are healed and others not. It injects purpose into the equation. Once, a blind friend and fellow priest asked [two Catholic healers] if they thought his sight could be restored. Will being able to see make you able to love more? they asked him. No, he replied. Then the healing was unnecessary and counterproductive, they concluded.

It appears that a quick shuffle is possible even in a cassock.

The Overlap of Magic and Science

There is an interesting similarity between religious faith-healing and modern psychoanalysis. Writing on the concepts and mechanics of perception in his book *The Body Human*, Jonathan Miller says:

> Psychoanalysis has had an influence which is quite out of proportion to its scientific credibility . . . In Freud's case the discrepancy between social influence and scientific reality has led some psychologists to despair at the gullibility of the general public, and there are many more who resent the money that can be made out of something which they regard as a seductive fraudulence. It's difficult, however, to believe that the success of psychoanalysis can be explained in terms of public credulity and the extent to which Freudian ideas have penetrated and replaced some of the more tra-

> ditional views of human nature implies that
> they have a recognizable truthfulness which
> cannot, and perhaps ought not to, be weighed
> by the standards which are applied to labora-
> tory science. . . . Some of the more uncharit-
> able skeptics . . . conclude that the Freudian
> enterprise should be classified as a religious
> dogma and not as a scientific theory.

Miller's observations on psychotherapy apply equally well to
faith-healing, and I can share the resentment that so much money
is made by those who promote highly questionable or obviously
fraudulent theories and claims. But, much more, I resent that
those fortunes are earned from innocent victims who often surrender their health, their emotional stability, and even their lives
along with their money. While I can easily believe that psychotherapists believe in their professional efforts, I cannot think the
same of faith-healers.

In common with many philosophers of science, Miller seems to
find it difficult to believe that nonsense can become accepted by
the public—and by a significant percentage of scientists—simply
because it is attractive, satisfying, and exciting, and because it
offers a great amount of evidence, though admittedly of poor
quality. As a non-scientist, I have no difficulty accepting this. The
additional fact that it is often endorsed by people recognized as
authority figures—whether or not their expertise derives from an
actual study of the phenomena in question—seems to fix it in
history as proved, established knowledge, when it never deserved
recognition as anything more than mythology, a joke, or a novel
notion.

The Placebo Effect

Professional evaluations of the efficacy of psychotherapy vary; few
of the in-depth studies have pleased the psychotherapists. One
major 1971 study concluded that "while some therapies produce
positive client change, the majority either effect no change or
lead to client deterioration."

Some recent studies indicate that in cases of neuroses and de-
pression, almost any type of psychotherapy is better than none at
all. This could well be due to the well-known "placebo effect."
The word is Latin, and means "I shall please." It is defined as "a
process or substance, of little or no known worth in itself, which

is applied to a problem in order to produce an encouraging or 'pleasing' result."

A placebo effect takes place when a patient is exposed to a satisfactory "bedside manner" and/or when medication, manipulation, or other means (any or all of which may be entirely ineffectual in themselves, but are seen by the recipient as unique, special, or advanced) are applied to the problem. Such effects may also take place when the patient feels in control of his situation, or when he has surrendered that control to another in whom he has confidence. This is a simple case of what is known as "transference." Encouragement leads to hope, and hope to better self-care and self-interest. Many types of chronic pain, because of the emotional condition of the sufferer, are associated with chronic anxiety. An efficient and caring physician, knowledgeable about the placebo effect, can largely alleviate that anxiety and thus improve at least the symptoms of certain ailments.

The Endorphin Effect

Without question, a positive attitude provides a somewhat better environment for healing, if for no other reason than that the patient nourishes himself better and is more willing to follow prescribed procedures. But it may go much further than that.

Reflecting what is now a very questionable idea about the relationship of attitude and susceptibility to cancer, evangelist Oral Roberts declared in 1949 that the "greatest protection from cancer . . . is to live a life free of tensions, fears, frustrations." It appears that the Reverend Roberts does not follow his own sensible advice. No one, in recent years, has publicly exhibited more fear, frustration, and worry than this man. To hear him tell it, he is assailed by Satan, threatened by God, reviled in the press, and living under threat of bankruptcy. And he is constantly before us on television wringing his hands in despair over his unhappy circumstances.

Leo Abood, a neurochemist at the University of Rochester, New York, Medical School, says he believes that it may be possible for external as well as internal factors to bring about the production of endorphins—organic chemicals that produce effects on the brain similar to opiates—in the body. If this is true, some of the faith-healers' results could be due to certain neurological and/or biochemical effects of endorphin release, which, regardless of whether Abood's conjectures are correct, is known to take place under stress or in highly emotional environments. Abood quotes research that showed almost one-third of more than 1,000 cases of simple illnesses (colds, angina, headaches, seasickness, anxiety, and post-operative pain) responded well to placebos. How long these effects will last, and whether such symptomatic relief is an unmixed blessing to the afflicted, however, are other questions that must be answered.

Even Oliver Wendell Holmes had an opinion on this matter:

> Healing is a living process, greatly under the influence of mental conditions. It has often been found that the same wound found received in battle will do well in the soldiers that have beaten, that would prove fatal in those that have just been defeated.

I would hope Holmes considered the possibility that a defeated army might have less effective medical treatment available than that afforded the winning side.

Psychotherapy vs. Faith-Healing

The practice of psychotherapy, as we have seen, is seriously questioned by many scientists in the medical field. Interestingly enough, investigators have noted that the *major* result of psychotherapists' efforts is diagnostic, and that *their predictions are based upon observations of the patient's characteristics.* This appears to be the skill upon which faith-healers like Leroy Jenkins largely depend, if other more certain methods of obtaining medical information are not available or are not preferred by the operator.

It has also been shown that, in psychotherapy, actual methods of treatment and the involvement of the therapist seemed to add little to the outcome. Attempts to parallel these studies by comparison with the faith-healers' impact upon their clients have led to roughly similar conclusions.

Keeping the Victims Dependent

There are cases in which psychotherapy and faith-healing might be expected to have essentially the same end results, because in some ways the processes are similar. But the basic *purposes* are quite different. The former will say that problems are generated by unresolved conflicts, and the latter will declare that the problems are due to attacks by demons and devils, allowed to control the patient because of a lack of faith, piety, or sacrifice.

It is said that the basic aim of psychotherapy is to create in the patient the feeling that he is autonomous, is in control of his own destiny, and is assuming that control. A "cure" is said to have occurred when the patient has in fact become self-sufficient and is able to function in society. The faith-healer, however, promotes in his victims a feeling of total dependence on the operator, based upon a mythology which the operator himself has created by specialized interpretation of various writings and authorities. Coupled with this is the strong message that the world outside is infested with evil elements (demons, science, pollution) which are not "of God" and thus are to be despised.

Faith-healers are in no way concerned with allowing their victims to gain insight into the reasons for their own behavior and failings. They perpetuate in the client a belief that the only source of relief and continued security lies with the faith-healer and the divine intervention that he or she can deliver. They denounce any inclination of the client toward behavioral independence and summon their strongest curses for the dreaded secular humanists, who, they say, have the presumption to declare that man is able to function without divine assistance, this being a sin of unparalleled arrogance.

Standards of Evidence

A friend of mine is closely connected with the evangelical movement and earnestly believes in faith-healing. He tried for a long time to come up with an example of genuine healing for me to include in this book. He chose his own criterion for a genuine healing: He would require it to be instantaneous. Until I consulted him, I had not included that in my list of standards, but when this man pointed out to me that healing as related in the Christian Bible was *always* instantaneous in nature, and because he speaks for several charismatic Christian organizations, I have adopted his requirement. However, Dr. Morton Smith, professor of ancient history at Columbia University, has observed that nowhere in the Bible is Christ said to have replaced any body part, and no modern-day evangelist is going to call on any person who needs a new ear or a finger to be grown back. It now begins to appear that Christ may have been simply one more of the many performers of that period who "cured" hysterical conditions like paralysis, loss of speech, deafness, and blindness—all of which are known to be brought on sometimes by entirely emotional causes. Indeed,

Christ's modern faith-healing imitators are rather close in their performances to what we are told about the original.

Canadian writer Arthur C. Hill, M.D., a devout believer, fortifies this strict view of judging genuine healings by faith, observing that the miracles attributed to Jesus Christ in the Bible have these characteristics:

(1) Wherever the name of the problem was mentioned in scripture, it was incurable then and remains so today: blindness, deafness, dumbness, leprosy, some forms of paralysis—and death—are examples.

(2) The healing was complete.

(3) It was instantaneous.

(4) There were no failures.

I must point out to this authority that the diseases he refers to may well not be the same ones designated by those who wrote the Bible. What was referred to as "leprosy" may have been applied by the authors to a number of similar diseases. As for "no failures," I might suggest that perhaps those who supplied the text failed to mention any.

One common thread emerges from most discussions of what constitutes genuine faith-healing—the expectation of an *instantaneous* cure. Organic ailments like heart conditions, cancer, bacterial infection, and similar problems are excellent choices for the healer to work on, because there is no obvious, external sign of recovery. As mentioned earlier, Oral Roberts has been known to segregate "impossible" cases from the main body of the audience, so that they will not be seen by cameras and skeptics. These are the people who emerge as they went in—still obviously and hopelessly sick. Roberts attempted, early in his televised shows, to provide validation for his healings by showing a notarized document that bore the signature of a local judge, asserting that he had been present at the filming of the show and that "the events and incidents to follow occurred on the spot in a meeting conducted in the great tent cathedral." Nothing was offered concerning the creative editing that improved the films, any follow-ups that were done on those who were said to be healed, or whether there were medical records or reports of any kind to support the diagnoses that were announced.

All the healers persist in claiming that there are countless cases of cures that have occurred at their hands, and they purport to demonstrate them regularly. I have tried to obtain from all possible sources direct, examinable evidence that faith-healing occurs. My standards are simple. I need a case that involves a living person, healed of an otherwise non-self-terminating disease, who recovered from that disease as a result of a faith-healer's actions and can produce before-and-after evidence to establish that fact. I have failed *in any and all cases I have investigated* to obtain a response that satisfies these simple requirements.

It's not as if some of the healers don't offer to provide evidence; they simply fail to fulfill that promise when the time comes.

Oral Roberts Fails Examination

In 1955, when the $1,000 offer for evidence of any cures was being made to Oral Roberts by the Church of Christ, Roberts offered the press two of "the most striking instances of cures" he could muster. Both people believed themselves healed. However, one had never obtained a diagnosis from a physician and the other later underwent orthodox surgery to remove the tumor that had been "healed." A Toronto, Canada, physician looked into 30 of Roberts's healing claims and found *not one* case that could not be attributed to psychological shock or hysteria.

At least one of the "healed" people examined by that physician had died. The following year, Roberts produced on his television program a California woman who testified that she had been healed of cancer. She died 12 hours later. In Oakland, California, one man dropped dead during a Roberts revival, and both a 3-year-old girl and an elderly Indian woman died at the same service. Then, in July 1959, a diabetic woman died after throwing away her insulin at a Detroit crusade. Wanda Beach, a diabetic from Detroit, also threw away her insulin as she watched an Oral Roberts show. She told her family that Roberts had "completely cured" her. That was just before she died. In January 1956, relatives and friends of Mary Vonderscher of Burbank, California, watched her taped appearance on the Oral Roberts television show giving the reverend an enthusiastic testimonial for her healing from spinal cancer. She was enthusiastic, cheerful, and thankful. Three days later, those viewers attended Mary's funeral.

In light of Roberts's claims that he has resurrected several people who died during his services, it seems strange that he allowed these folks to perish. One wonders what claim he will next come up with. The mind boggles.

Allen Spraggett, a Canadian writer who has fallen for even such transparent hoaxes as those of former "psychic" Uri Geller, failed to be deceived by the Roberts healing claims. He spent a harrowing ten days following the Roberts show around and concluded that there was not one cure effected in that time, while hundreds of cures were claimed by the Roberts office. (Because Spraggett considers himself a "psychic researcher," he might have been unable to accept the Roberts claims because he could not find in Roberts's performance any "paradigm" acceptable to parapsychology. The first thing to be sought by these researchers is such a paradigm, and when that is determined, all caution is discarded. As mentioned previously, when Spraggett looked into Kathryn Kuhlman's performance, he accepted her claims because they matched his parapsychological expectations.)

The Reverend Lester Kinsolving, who writes on religious topics for the McNaught Syndicate, looked into the Roberts ministry and its claims in an article titled "The Power of Positive Greed." He examined cases claimed by Kathryn Kuhlman, A. A. Allen, and Christian Science as well. He found no cases of healing in any of these ministries that would withstand examination.

An Epilepsy "Cure" by Peter Popoff

Shortly after the television exposure of evangelist healer Popoff, I appeared on the Sally Jessy Raphael show in St. Louis, with Garry McColman, who was defending the claims of his boss, Popoff. He produced a videotape that Popoff had prepared for him to show. It concerned a small girl, Amanda Bril, who he said had been healed of epilepsy at one of his meetings in Sacramento, California.

When Popoff originally broadcast this videotape as part of one of his regular Sunday programs, he had lambasted skeptics who doubted his healing abilities:

> When we've produced doctors' verified evidence, they're not satisfied. We've had doctors actually come on our program and verify divine healing. And what is their answer? Do they accept this evidence? No! The so-called magician produced another letter that said in rare instances these symptoms would simply subside. In this particular case, it was a case of epilepsy that had miraculously disappeared. And the doctor verified it. . . . And friends, the thing that really hurts is that so many people have begun to side with the magician. Side with the Devil! Why, the Devil must be laughing with joy!

What "letter" the reverend was referring to, I do not know, but the facts of this case and the "evidence" Popoff presented make it quite clear just how he operates. And I think I know who he means when he refers to the "so-called magician."

At a live Popoff appearance in San Francisco, previous to this claim, I'd photographed a very enthusiastic woman who I noticed was going around forcing herself on people, telling everyone that the Popoff miracles were "all real" because her daughter had been healed of epilepsy. She looked to us at first like a hired flack, though it is now evident that she was only an overenthusiastic disciple. She is the mother of that same small girl whose case Popoff offered as his "proof" on that St. Louis TV program.

On his carefully edited videotape, Popoff showed a doctor who said about the little girl:

> She did, however, respond fairly well to medi-
> cation. We would expect the seizures to return
> once the medications had stopped.

Asked if he had seen any further evidence of epilepsy in the girl, he replied: "None at all. None whatsoever." But when Ross Becker, a reporter for Los Angeles TV station KCBS, interviewed the physician, he told Becker that he and his wife were charismatic Christians and thus believed in faith-healing. Such a witness is hardly unbiased. In fact, says Becker, the doctor told him that he is convinced, because of his religious beliefs, that the healing is "a miracle." As a medical person, however, he told Becker that that variety of childhood epilepsy often goes into temporary or permanent remission spontaneously! That part of his medical opinion was not presented on the videotape by the Reverend Popoff. Now, months later, one wonders what has happened to that child, and whether Popoff or the mother has managed a rationalization—if the affliction is once again active. But the mother will not discuss the matter now, nor will the doctor.

In two three-minute telephone conversations with the doctor's wife, David Alexander was unable to get by her to speak with the doctor. Later, the woman told another caller that Alexander had tried, in those calls, to convert her to satanism! If the pursuit of truth and the asking of simple questions amounts to satanism, there is a larger population of satanists in this world than anyone has suspected. Every philosopher, student, scientist, and investigator must belong in that category. And, in fact, that is just what many of the evangelists would have their flocks believe! Asking questions leads to doubt. Doubt leads to loss of faith. Loss of faith leads to loss of paradise. Thus, curiosity is a tool of Satan.

It is well to note that Popoff's original broadcast of that miraculous "healing" had superimposed on the screen the phrase "A True Word of Knowledge" as the preacher was calling out the information relayed to him by his secret electronic "ear." The evidence we developed against this claim was not seen by that TV audience, nor are they likely ever to know of it. How many times can we come up with evidence that proves the case against him? And how many times *must* we do it before someone in authority acts to stop it?

A Nonexistent Tumor "Cured" by Peter Popoff

In his August 17, 1986, TV broadcast, Peter Popoff made a startling healing claim. That is, it would have been startling if it had been true. Briefly, he showed a little girl from Tampa, Florida, who, he said, had been afflicted with severe migraine headaches, the result of an "inoperable, malignant brain-stem tumor" that he said had been confirmed by two CT scans at Tampa General Hospital as well as by doctors at the University of South Florida and at Johns Hopkins University. A CT scan with a "dark mass" was shown to the TV audience. Said Popoff: "There is no radiation, no chemotherapy, no surgery will help."

Miracle time. The girl's grandmother, Popoff said, mailed in a prayer request, and several weeks later the tumor had "disappeared"! That statement, it seemed, was made by the grandmother herself on the Popoff program. What better evidence could we ask for?

The Bare Facts

Dr. Gary P. Posner is a prominent consultant to both the Committee for the Scientific Investigation of Claims of the Paranormal and the Faith-Healing Investigation Project of the Committee for the Scientific Examination of Religion. He resides and practices in St. Petersburg, and both the medical records and the physicians involved in this case were available to him. His research of the matter provided somewhat different facts than those claimed by Popoff and his cohorts.

(1) It was *not* the little girl's grandmother's voice on the Popoff show making the statement about the cure, but that of another (unidentified) woman.

(2) The Popoff broadcast was made without the knowledge or permission of the girl's mother.

(3) The case had been resolved *two years before* Popoff chose to broadcast it. Had the girl actually had such a brain tumor, she would surely have succumbed to it long ago, barring a miracle.

(4) No cure took place. This little girl still suffers from the same severe migraine headaches.

(5) The CT scan was *not* of the "brain-stem" area at all.

(6) The "dark mass" in the CT scan that was used by Popoff was determined by the radiologists to have been simply an artifact (imperfection) of the scanning process, and it did not show up in the second scan, as erroneously reported on Popoff's show. Nor did any of the little girl's doctors suspect a tumor on clinical grounds.

Popoff's TV audience never heard the facts about this case, only the invented miracle that he claimed to have brought about.

A Simple Challenge, Unanswered

Following my first accusations on the CNN broadcast, but before the blow I delivered on the Johnny Carson show, Popoff appealed to his TV viewers to send him healing testimonials to support his divine pretensions. Then he claimed to have received 200,000 replies from satisfied customers. I wrote to him and suggested that he choose at random any *five* of those testimonials and submit them to an independent, neutral medical board for evaluation. He ignored my suggestion. Why? Because, I believe, he knows full well what the results would be. He has attempted to respond to the criticisms and exposures that we have accomplished. He has utterly failed and has proved that he was unprepared for our onslaught. He floundered around, embarrassed and beleaguered, and those who care to know the truth now have it available to them.

The claims made by faith-healers are nothing more than hollow boasts and do not stand up to examination. Prepared culturally to expect miracles, convinced they are helpless without supernatural intervention, and bullied into supporting their gurus far beyond their means, the pathetic victims of the healers have become a disillusioned subculture playing a dangerous game. "The Healing Show," with its cruel lies, vain promises, and glittering trickery, has blinded them to reality and removed them from productive society. They are the dupes of clever, glib, highly organized swindlers who are immune from justice and are confidently aware of that fact.

17
Legal Aspects

In the Introduction, I mentioned a subject that would not occupy much of my attention in this book, because it has been handled well and at length by other writers. That subject is Christian Science. However, at this point I will share with you a thought or two about this religious philosophy that developed during my research.

It would seem that pseudo-medical procedures that bring damage to innocent people would be of interest to both the medical profession and law enforcement authorities. My contacts with the latter group, as mentioned previously, have been mostly futile. As might be expected, some victims of faith-healers have sought remedies through lower courts and some through the Supreme Court. This happened as recently as 1986, when the widow of a Christian Scientist in Plano, Illinois, brought a case against that church. Her husband, suffering from uremic poisoning resulting from prostatitis, was "treated" by a Christian Science practitioner. When the patient got worse and appeared near death, the woman sought to dismiss the practitioner and obtain ˙orthodox medical assistance for her husband. The practitioner forbade it, warning her that if she even spoke to a doctor, the man would die.

Despite the practitioner's earnest prayers, the man did die, miserably and in pain. The widow filed suit to recover damages for the wrongful death of her husband, whose condition usually responds well to surgery and/or medication. In effect, this woman was contending that the First Amendment of the U.S. Constitution does not protect religious faith-healers and their churches from liability in such matters. The Supreme Court refused her suit, arguing that "the issues raised would require an inquiry into whether the tenets of the Christian Science Church are valid, and such an inquiry would violate the First Amendment."

Now, admittedly, I am far from an expert in legal matters. But I recall that some few years back the Rastafarian religion in the United States argued that the religious use of marijuana by its members, a practice long accepted by them and an essential part of their religious beliefs, exempted them from laws against use of the drug. (Personally, I think use of such substances is juvenile and just plain dumb, but I am arguing here a matter of law, not personal preference or prejudice.) The court refused the exemption, pointing out that it is against the law to grow, sell, or use marijuana. This decision certainly questioned whether the tenets of the Rastafarian religion were valid, did it not? And, because the Rastafarians were refused the right to follow this part of their religion by the Supreme Court, it appears that both the inquiry and the refusal violated some First Amendment rights.

I recall a case of far less serious consequence where religious beliefs were pointedly ignored in favor of the public preference. The Doukhobors ("Christians of the Universal Brotherhood") are a Russian religious sect that took root in Canada back at the turn of the century. They got along quite well with their new country-men at first because of their very law-abiding nature and their strict behavior codes. In fact, the prime minister commended the sect, saying that its members had proved exemplary new citizens. Then, in the 1930s, rumors were heard that the Doukhobors were wont to go about naked on occasion and believed that the taking of more than one spouse was quite all right. Again, the law was invoked, and these relatively harmless practices, said to be part of the religious tenets of these Christians, were not respected.

Yet it seems that a process that appears to amount to murder by negligence, supported by the eccentric notions of a Christian sect (admittedly very wealthy and influential), can be carried out by a "practitioner" with no medical training whatsoever. This, and a direct breach of another law—that which prohibits the practice of medicine without proper licenses—can and will be tolerated by the courts. I ask, which is more anti-social, a man with two wives smoking a substance that may be less harmful than tobacco—which certainly has been *proved* to cause illness and death—or a man causing another man to die in agony for lack of proved, established medical procedures?

The occult movement of the '60s spawned a number of kinky religions, brought back some fringe cults, and imported a few foreign ideas, notably from the Far East. A little girl in Long Island, New York, whose parents were members of the Gheez Nation, a sect from Africa that believes in faith-healing, almost died when she was not permitted treatment by orthodox medical physicians. The court intervened, and she survived. But the Church of Christ, Scientist, a sect that attracts some of the biggest of the big-money names, remains immune from such interference.

Many More Cases of Dying Children

In March 1956, a traveling faith-healer named Jack Coe visited Miami, Florida, with his tent show, and preached to 8,000 people. Shortly thereafter, he was taken to court by Ann Clark after he claimed he had healed George, her 3-year-old son, of polio and ordered her to remove his crutches and braces. The boy fell to the floor and two days later underwent emergency treatment. The braces were replaced just in time to prevent serious damage to his limbs. Clark charged Reverend Coe with practicing medicine without a license. He testified in court that he was only practicing his religion. The judge agreed, and he walked away free.

In Barstow, California, in 1973, an 11-year-old diabetic boy died when his parents, Lawrence and Alice Parker, withheld his insulin and decided that prayer and fasting would cure him. Months after his death they continued to believe that he would be resurrected. They were convicted of involuntary manslaughter but placed on probation rather than being sent to prison. Four years later, a judge changed their verdicts to "not guilty." Neither the itinerant faith-healer who had ordered the insulin withheld nor the Assemblies of God Church was charged. Still affiliated with the same church, the parents now believe that their denial of their son's medication and their expectation of his resurrection following his death were "tragic errors." They now blame their errors, not on their church or on themselves, but on "Satan's deception." After this experience, Lawrence Parker decided that

> our error was in thinking that all we had to do was believe hard enough. All of our actions should be based on love. If the thing we are contemplating seems to be in conflict with the principle of love, then that's the wrong thing to do.

Sensible as that statement is, it is in direct contradiction to what faith-healers would have us believe. With them, faith is *everything*, regardless of how illogical it seems. Mr. Parker was denying his faith.

John Barron, county coroner in Ebensburg, Pennsylvania, was satisfied when William Barnhart, 56, and his wife, Linda, were convicted in 1983 of involuntary manslaughter and endangering a child's welfare. Two years previously, their 2-year-old son, Justin, had died of an abdominal tumor while they withheld medical attention because their church, the Faith Tabernacle Congregation, taught that faith, rather than doctors, was their only source of healing. Said Barron:

> Maybe it will put parents on notice they're responsible for their children regardless of their religious beliefs when it comes to the life and death of their children.

But Barnhart felt differently. "This hasn't wavered my faith a bit," he told the press. His faith was partially vindicated when, in August 1985, the prison sentence was changed to probation, with the Barnharts being required to perform public service as a condition of that probation. This is a decision that I find just.

The Church of the First Born in Enid, Oklahoma, prayed for 9-year-old Jason Lockhart to be healed of a ruptured appendix in 1982. When he died from lack of medical help, his parents, Patsy and Dean Lockhart, were tried for manslaughter and acquitted. In Shelbyville, Kentucky, when their second child in 15 months died at birth, the parents were tried for reckless homicide. They were members of the Faith Assembly. In Kosciusko County, Indiana, 26 deaths, including those of several children, were ascribed to the Faith Assembly church, which also forbids medical intervention.

In February 1984, preacher C. D. Long and his wife, members of the Church of God in Summerville, Georgia, were acquitted of involuntary manslaughter after they allowed their 16-year-old son to die of a ruptured appendix because their sect forbids the use of medical help. The judge decided that there was insufficient evidence to convict them. In Charlotte, Michigan, Kenneth Sealy was convicted of child neglect for allowing his 11-day-old daughter to die in accordance with his religious beliefs.

Nationwide, at least 44 states allow parents to refuse medical care for their children on religious grounds. Courts often intervene, but often after it is too late.

A Wise Statement Seldom Heeded

The Supreme Court has not ruled directly on this matter, but in 1944, it came close to doing so. Dealing specifically with a case of a child of Jehovah's Witnesses, the Court held:

> The right to practice religion freely does not include liberty to expose the community or the child to communicable disease or the latter to ill health or death. . . . Parents may be free to become martyrs themselves. But it does not follow that they are free, in identical circumstances, to make martyrs of their children before they have reached the age of full and legal discretion when they can make that choice for themselves.

A Reluctance to Enforce the Law

The *Los Angeles Law Review*, in 1984, looked into a number of faith-healing cases. Reporter Catherine Laughran found that in a large number of manslaughter or criminal neglect cases resulting from failed faith-healing attempts, the convictions had been reversed often on grounds unrelated to the original charge itself. Laughran said:

> This may reflect an unstated judicial policy of sympathy for the plight of parents who are caught between the law of the land and the firm belief that their way of healing is the right one and the one most beneficial to their children's welfare.

I will comment that a large part of that "firm belief" results from exposure to the theatrics of Popoff, Robertson, Grant, and others who use psychological and technical trickery to produce the illusion that they are bringing healing to the afflicted. Uninformed witnesses cannot avoid concluding that healing by faith has been demonstrated to them. That trickery, along with the insistence of the various ministries that they need not or dare not submit appropriate evidence to establish what they preach, and the reluctance of law enforcement authorities to place the welfare of innocent victims above bad interpretations of the U.S. Consti-

tution, has created a dangerous and insidious legal situation that
needs attention from the Supreme Court of this land.

Other Legal Concerns

The field of faith-healing presents all sorts of legal challenges.
For example, California law requires that money solicited for any
specific purpose must be applied to that purpose. But, said Ira
McCorriston, former controller for the Peter Popoff Evangelical
Association, his boss did not do this. Concerning special appeals
Popoff made for one of his harebrained schemes, McCorriston said:

> The people would send their money in for [the
> Russian Bibles project] but the money would
> just go into the daily deposit.

Is there criminal activity involved here? Unless lying, cheating, and swindling are illegal, maybe not. I am not a legal expert.
But Popoff, in two recent services, spoke to his audience about
the terrible doctors who were asking them to put "chemicals" in
their bodies. "Dr. Jesus doesn't *use* any chemicals!" he screamed.
And he told them to come forward and throw their medications up
on the stage. They did. When I examined those substances, I
found—among other medications—nitroglycerin tablets, insulin, and
digitalis compounds. These are substances without which those
people might well die. But Peter Popoff won't be around to answer
for that unfortunate result.

(It is also of interest to note that in the collection of drugs
we recovered in the Houston meeting and two others in California,
there were no "illicit" substances whatsoever: No barbiturates,
tranquilizers, marijuana, or other "dope" that might have been
expected showed up. The crew backstage had lots of opportunity
to remove any such items from the sweepings before it all went
into the trash cans.)

The faith-healers' victims are taught specific "magical" procedures whereby they may ensure continued protection from evil,
and the most effectual of those methods is, as might be expected,
giving financial support to the healer. This is often referred to as
"seed money," and promises are made that the sum donated will
soon return tenfold or even one-hundredfold. Though such a
financial promise might be deemed enforceable by law, the basic
problem remains that the government continues to ignore such
illegalities and will not prosecute the violators. The penalties for

such fraud ($1,000 in some cases) are such that the faith-healers can easily afford to ignore them.

The Internal Revenue Service has shown some fleeting interest in almost every one of the healers. The article of law that applies to the controversial religious exemption upon which there has been so much discussion is section 501(c)(3) of the tax code, which says that a corporation

> organized and operated exclusively for religious and educational purposes with no part of its net earnings inuring to the benefit of any private shareholder or individual [shall be exempt from the payment of taxes].

The "inurement" aspect of that phrase is where the Internal Revenue Service might concentrate some attention. I believe that I have shown, in these pages, that faith-healers have been less than careful in their use of funds sent them for specific purposes. After all, they got Al Capone that way, didn't they?

18
Amen!

We are watching a rough cut of a proposed TV documentary program.

The scene is an outdoor gathering. It is 2:15 on the afternoon of February 23, 1986. At the entrance to the Civic Center Auditorium in San Francisco, California, about 2,000 people are gathering to attend a religious meeting held by the Reverend Peter Popoff, Anointed Minister of God, healer, and evangelist. The meeting has been promoted by newspaper and radio advertisements, and on the weekly Popoff television broadcast. The huge marquee above the entrance proclaims the "Miracle Crusade" that is to take place inside. Several TV news crews are present.

The independent television interviewer who prepared this tape is following his cameraman around the area, microphone in hand, hoping to obtain comments from those who are about to enter for the services inside. The camera approaches, from behind, a tiny boy who is supported by well-worn crutches. He is reading the marquee. The interviewer speaks.

"Excuse me."

The little boy turns, deftly maneuvering himself about on his crutches to face the camera. He is Oriental, neatly dressed and combed, and he appears somewhat startled. The television interviewer speaks again.

"What brings you here today? Why did you come?"

The boy is a bit bewildered. He smiles shyly, and finally he responds.

"I came to see Peter Popoff. We watch him on television."

*Now he smiles broadly, obviously excited that he is "on TV."
It is the kind of smile that gets to you. We now see, in a full-
length shot, how badly twisted his legs are. It is probably polio
that afflicts him.*

"What will Peter Popoff do for you?" asks the interviewer.

*"Peter Popoff can make me well," the child says. "He under-
stands Jesus better than* anyone."

*There is a pause. The interviewer is having a difficult time.
The camera wanders off the subject.*

*"Thank you very much," the interviewer finally says. The
television camera points to the pavement. The screen goes blank.*

* * * *

Following the Peter Popoff spectacle, I saw that little boy outside
the Civic Center again, standing perched on his crutches and
staring down at the pavement. At the service, the highly touted
"healer" had not even come near the kid. As I approached to
speak to him, the cameraman followed me, trailing cables.

The cameras from the TV news shows had recorded the performance inside but were now nowhere to be seen. The boy looked
up as I approached him. His smile was gone, and I saw tears
running down his face. His eyes were red from weeping. I began
to speak, intending to ask him what he now thought of Popoff and
his promises. But I choked up and had to turn away.

The cameraman had only one comment. He said, "I can't do
this." His camera fell to his side, switched off.

I will never forget that terrible moment, as the child realized
that he had just witnessed a cruel, callous hoax. Hundreds of
people at that meeting had believed they would see miracles
performed in the name of Almighty God. Some few had been
touched by the preacher, but none had been healed. Most had
given cash or checks, some in envelopes sent to them by mail
before they attended. One way or another, they were all swindled,
and the perpetrators were protected simply because no one in
state or federal government dares to prosecute them.

Final Thoughts

I cannot end this book without expressing a few strictly personal
thoughts on the subject of faith-healing and religion in general.
Though the reader may feel that I have already expressed too
much of my philosophy, I should like here to make a straight-

forward statement.

I am frequently approached following lectures and asked loudly if I am a Christian and/or whether I believe in God—the assumption being that I understand what the questioner means by both terms. My answer has always been that I have found no compelling reason to adopt such beliefs. Infuriated by such a response, those who cannot handle further discussion usually turn away and leave ringing in the air a declaration that there is just no point in trying to reason with me and that I will be "prayed for."

I have no need of this patronization, nor of such a condescending attitude, and I resent it. I consider such an action to be a feeble defense for a baseless superstition and a retreat from reality.

If I were to offer up a prayer of my own, I would ask a deity to grant my species the ability to adopt a dignified, responsible, and caring exuberance toward living, rather than a quavering, dependent vigil awaiting death. To recognize that nature has neither a preference for our species nor a bias against it takes only a little courage.

I believe that we have evolved to the point where we no longer need gurus to supply us with magical formulas for our lives. We must learn to ignore silly notions invented by opportunists who see us as sheep willing to be sheared—or worse. There is ample evidence in history that we can be led to commit atrocities in the name of God or Satan, or to lay down our lives for some obscure dogma that we have never troubled to question. We cannot surrender to those idiocies and survive as a species.

Albert Einstein saw quite clearly the error of ignoring reality:

> Man tries to make for himself in the fashion that suits him best a simplified and intelligible picture of the world; he then tries to some extent to substitute this cosmos of his for the world of experience, and thus overcome it. This is what the painter, the poet, the speculative philosopher, and the natural scientist do, each in his own fashion. Each makes this cosmos and its construction the pivot of his emotional life, in order to find in this way the peace and security which he cannot find in the narrow whirlpool of personal experience.

I will dare to expand Einstein's statement to include quite ordinary folks along with the painters, poets, philosophers, and scientists who he says require their specially invented universes in order to function emotionally. Often, the need is thrust upon these people by their social background. They grow up nurtured by families who take heaven and hell, demons and angels, and life after death as absolute, unquestioned certainties. The cruel joke is that they can never discover whether there is any truth in these notions, though they never even trouble—or dare—to ask such a question.

Speaking of the origins of religious concepts, Einstein said:

> With primitive man it is above all fear that evokes religious notions—fear of hunger, wild beasts, sickness, death. Since at this stage of existence understanding of causal connections is usually poorly developed, the human mind creates illusory beings more or less analogous to itself on whose wills and actions these fearful happenings depend.

Have we come much further from this primitive state? I think many of us have not. Fear still seems to be the impetus for attendance at evangelical meetings. The message given at these crusades is that God must be constantly invoked, praised, thanked, feared, and propitiated by sacrifice—usually financial. "Getting right with God" is the prime intent, and it costs.

We have been to the moon. Because of our very nature, we will be going to the stars. We cannot get there encumbered with superstitions and a limited vision of our potential. We must put childish things behind us, and belief in faith-healing is one of those things, one of the many incredible myths that most believers are required to accept. It is a view of this world embraced by those impatient for the next one.

Richard Yao, the head of Fundamentalists Anonymous, makes an important point, applicable to faith-healers as well as to the fundamentalists he questions:

> Perhaps the unpardonable sin of fundamentalism is its effort to make people suspicious and afraid of their own minds, their own logic and thinking process. Any thought that contradicts the fundamentalist dogmas is labeled "Satanic" or "demonic." If we cannot depend on our minds to process reality and make choices and

decisions in life, then we are more likely to
depend on fundamentalist preachers like Falwell
or Swaggart. How can a democracy survive if
all of us renounce reason, thinking and logic?

Yao's comments apply very well to those people discussed in this
book.

Fond as they are of quoting scripture, faith-healers should
appreciate a certain appropriate selection from the Good Book in
which they seem to have been anticipated. They appear to be
pious and innocent, but have perpetrated a vicious, callous, and
highly profitable scam on their flocks, bringing grief, economic
loss, and severe health risks to their victims. I ask them to turn
to Matthew 7:15, where it is written:

> Beware of false prophets, men who come to you
> dressed up as sheep while underneath they are
> savage wolves. You will recognize them by the
> fruits they bear.

FINIS

Bibliography

Barrett, Stephen, M.D. *The Health Robbers*. Philadelphia: Stickley, 1980.

Bloch, Marc. *The Royal Touch*. London: Routledge & Kegan Paul, 1973.

Carrel, Alexis. *The Voyage to Lourdes*. New York: Harper and Brothers, 1950.

Frazier, Claude A., M.D. *Faith Healing*. New York: Thomas Nelson, 1973.

Harrell, David, Jr. *Oral Roberts, An American Life*. Bloomington: Indiana University Press, 1985.

Holzer, Hans. *Psychic Healing*. New York: Manor, 1979.

Kurtz, Paul. *The Transcendental Temptation*. Buffalo, N.Y.: Prometheus Books, 1986.

Lastrucci, Carlo. *The Scientific Approach*. Cambridge: Schenkman, 1963.

MacKay, Charles. *Extraordinary Popular Delusions and the Madness of Crowds*. London: Bentley, 1841.

Marnham, Patrick. *Lourdes: A Modern Pilgrimage*. New York: Coward, McCann & Geoghegan, 1981.

Morris, James. *The Preachers*. New York: St. Martin's Press, 1973.

Nolen, William, M.D. *Healing: A Doctor in Search of a Miracle*. New York: Random House, 1974.

Randi, James. *Flim-Flam!* Buffalo, N.Y.: Prometheus Books, 1982.

Rose, Louis. *Faith Healing*. U.K.: Penguin Books, 1971.

Rubin, Stanley. *Medieval English Medicine*. New York: Harper & Row, 1974.

Stearn, Jess. *The Miracle Workers*. New York: Doubleday, 1972.

Straub, Gerard. *Salvation for Sale*. Buffalo, N.Y.: Prometheus Books, 1986.

Taves, Ernest H. *Trouble Enough*. Buffalo, N.Y.: Prometheus Books, 1984.

Warfield, B. *Counterfeit Miracles*. Carlisle, Pa.: Banner of Truth, 1976.

Appendix

This statement outlines the general rules covering my offer concerning psychic, supernatural, or paranormal claims. Since claims will vary greatly in character and scope, specific rules must be formulated for each claimant. However, *claimants* must agree to the rules set forth here before any formal agreement is entered into. A claimant will declare agreement by signing this form before a notary public and returning the form to me at 12000 NW 8th Street, Plantation, FL 33313-1406. The eventual test procedure must be agreed upon by both parties before any testing will take place. I do *not* act as a judge. I do *not* design the protocol independently of the claimant. Claimants *must* identify themselves properly before any discussion takes place. *All correspondence must include a stamped, self-addressed envelope.*

I, James Randi, will pay $10,000 (U.S.) to any person or persons who demonstrate any psychic, supernatural, or paranormal ability of any kind under satisfactory observing conditions. The demonstration must take place under these rules and limitations:

(1) Claimant must state clearly in advance just what powers or abilities will be demonstrated, the limits of the proposed demonstration (so far as time, location, and other variables are concerned), and what will constitute both a positive and a negative result.

(2) Only an actual performance of the stated nature and scope, within the agreed limits, is acceptable.

(3) Claimant agrees that all data (photographic, recorded, written) of any sort gathered as a result of the testing may be used freely by me in any way I choose.

(4) Tests will be designed in such a way that no judging procedure is required. Results will be self-evident to any observer, in accordance with the rules agreed upon by all parties in advance of any formal testing procedure.

(5) I may ask the claimant to perform informally before an appointed representative, if distance and time dictate, for purposes of determining if the claimant is likely to perform as promised in the formal test.

(6) I will not pay for any expenses incurred, such as transportation, accommodation, or other costs.

(7) Entering into this challenge, claimant surrenders any and all rights to legal action against me, as far as this may be done by existing statutes. This applies to injury, accident, or any other damage—physical, emotional, and/or financial or professional—of any kind.

(8) Prior to the commencement of the formal testing procedure, I will give my check for the full amount of the award into the keeping of an independent person chosen by the claimant. **In the event that the claimant is successful under the agreed terms and conditions, that check for $10,000 (U.S.) shall be immediately surrendered to the claimant, in full settlement.**

(9) A copy of this document is available free of charge to any person who sends the required stamped, self-addressed envelope to me requesting it.

(10) This offer is made by me personally and not on behalf of any other person, agency, or organization, although others may become involved in the examination of claims and others may add their reward money to mine in certain circumstances.

(11) This offer is open to any and all persons in any part of the world, regardless of sex, race, educational background, etc., and will continue in effect until the prize is awarded, or until my death. My will states that, upon my death, the award amount will be held in escrow and in charge of the Committee for the Scientific Investigation of Claims of the Paranormal, in Buffalo, New York, which is then empowered to continue the offer for a period of ten years after my demise, after which time the award amount can be used for whatever purpose it desires.

(12) Claimant must agree upon what will constitute a conclusion that he or she does *not* possess the claimed ability or power. This rule *must* be accepted by the claimant without reservation.

Notary Public   Signature

Appendix II

CHRISTIAN MEDICAL FOUNDATION INTERNATIONAL, INC.
7522 NORTH HIMES AVENUE
TAMPA, FLORIDA 33614
TELEPHONE (AREA CODE 813) 932-3688

April 18, 1986

Mr. James Randi
5901 12th Court N.W.
Sunrise, Florida 33313

Dear Mr. Randi,

I have your letter of April 10, 1986 before me. Since I do not know you, I find certain areas of your letter to be rather preplexing. If you identify yourself with "evil men" or as a "noisy person" who is "making static and nonsense" that is your definition. I, certainly not knowing you, do not know your stand or your principles.

With reference to the "lady patient" who suffered from ovarian cancer, this patient appeared on the Christian Broadcasting Network 700 Club on April 2, 1986 so her personal testimony has been on national television and therefore does not need my statements to further verify her cure.

You mention that this "test case" makes me "apparently believe is a strong example of faith healing". I do not like the term faith healing. I believe that is what doctors in general do. I believe in Christian healing and I believe that the patient's case is one of Christian healing.

With reference to your questions which you said would be published verbatim, which statement gives me some pause, because I am not aware of who you are or how you intend to use these statements. Nevertheless, I will answer your questions.

1. Does a similar diminution of tumors ever take place in cases where patients do not pray for divine intervention?

Answer: This question cannot be answered by yes or no. So called spontaneous regression of tumors does occur, but whether or not there has been prayer in the instances is unknown and to the best of my knowledge is not published. In general, in medicine and surgery, the information regarding the use of prayer and the effectiveness of prayer is not a part of medical history nor has it been a part of the ordinary types of medical investigation.

2. Did you ever take a patient for anointing and prayer who did not undergo a similar miraculous change?

Answer: Again, this is a question which cannot be answered by a simple yes or no. It is my belief that something always happens when we pray. In order to determine whether or not a change has occurred in the tumor mass, one would often have to be able to open the person's abdomen or chest in order to determine the accurate answer to this question. This would be a difficult question to answer with reference to chemotherapy or radiation therapy - as well as prayer therapy.

"For with God Nothing Shall Be Impossible" — Luke 1:37

Mr. James Randi   4/18/86   page 2.

Suffice it to say, that something always happens on the level of the spirit, mind and body when the patient is prayed for. Sometimes the effect is primarily on the level of the spirit, sometimes it involves the spirit and the mind and sometimes it affects the spirit, mind and the body. The reason for this variability probably has to do with a belief factor.

3. Did the woman patient receive any orthodox medical treatment from you, and if so, what was that treatment?

Answer: no.

4. May we know who this patient is, etc.

Answer: Because of the doctrine of privilege it is not possible to make this identification. Suffice it to say that the pathlogic slides from her original operation were reviewed by our pathologist here, as well as her operative report and also reports from her oncologist under whom she was receiving chemotherapy at the time when she was originally seen here. This chemotherapy had been given without any obvious beneficial effect.

Very truly yours,

William Standish Reed M.D., M.S.

WSR/rl

Appendix III

①

white dress with flowers ... table 5

A-1
~~Dorothy~~
D. Brownlie — thyroid problem — needs a better job
sal. of loved ones.

Janet Peeler sal. of family

4
  gives
  Mae Ensz — del. from worry
  Ensz   Ruth's emotional healing.
  girlfriend just had stroke on left side
  (Pratty) had to leave at 12:15 P.M.

B. table 2   Kathryne Atchinson   open
  doors that have increase in faith
  Financial breakthrough
C 15 table 3   Betty Conrad
  del. from

Popoff's "crib sheet" from the Inner Circle meeting.

Appendix IV

ORAL ROBERTS

March 28, 1985

Mr. James Randi
51 Lennox Ave
Rumson, NJ 07760

Dear Mr. Randi,

I am honored to pray that you will be healed of every
trace of disease in your liver. And I'm honored that you
would trust me to do it. I'd rather pray for you than eat
when I'm hungry...so never hesitate to let me know your
needs.

Mr. Randi, if I had just one thing to say to you today,
it would be to PLANT A SEED OUT OF YOUR NEED...a seed of
time, money, encouragement, talent, whatever you feel led in
your heart to do. Focus your seed against your need and FOR
A DESIRED RESULT. And when you have done it, EXPECT YOUR
HARVEST (Luke 6:38; II Corinthians 9:10).

Now, I base this on what God Himself did when the devil
had caused mankind to stray away from Him and caused them to
open themselves up to sin and sickness and a lack of all good
things. We're told what it was in John 3:16.

"For God so loved the world, that he gave his only
begotten Son, that whosoever believeth in him should not
perish, but have everlasting life."

God gave us Jesus OUT OF HIS NEED to get lost man back.
He focused ON A DESIRED RESULT -- so that anyone who believes
on Jesus will have eternal life. And He is EXPECTING HIS
HARVEST through the souls of mankind as they make their
choice to serve Him instead of the devil.

So I say again, Mr. Randi, plant a seed out of your
need, knowing this is God's way of doing things...and a sure
way to get results in your life. You WILL REAP A HARVEST
(Galatians 6:7-9). God is a good God.

Your partner always,

Oral Roberts

Oral Roberts suggests the "seed faith" idea.

7697

DATE DUE

NOV 10 '95			

DEMCO 38-297